# What's it worth?

## Awards of General Damages in

### Non-Personal Injury Claims

A Single-Source Digest of Updated Quantum

## Volume 1: Property Claims

Compiled and edited by

## Andrew Goodman LL.B.,FCI.Arb.

Of the Inner Temple, Barrister
Professor of Conflict Management and Dispute
Resolution Studies
Rushmore University

© Andrew Goodman, 2004

ISBN 1 85811 309 1

XPL Publishing

www.xplpublishing.com

A catalogue record for this book is available from
the British Library.

Cover design by Jane Conway

Printed by Lightning Source in the UK and USA.

# Contents

# What's it worth?

## Awards of General Damages in Non-Personal Injury Claims

### A Single-Source Digest of Updated Quantum

### Vol 1 : Property Claims

## Introduction

This work is the first attempt to provide a readily searchable single source digest of all reported awards of general damages since 1985 in non-personal injury claims, or, as appropriate, over a shorter period where there has been Court of Appeal intervention to lay down guidelines for cases where damages are "at large", such as *Thompson & Hsu* v *Commissioner of Police for the Metropolis*[1] in connection with the award of damages in claims against the police. The format lends itself most readily to electronic publishing for ease of search and updating, however for the convenience of an initial digest of cases it is here published in book form. The reported awards are given contemporaneously, have then been updated in line with inflation, and continuing updating may be accessed electronically.

The breadth of the subject matter to be included is huge, but for the purpose of attempting a sensible classification the awards have been grouped into property and property-related claims, which forms the first part of the work, and subsequently volumes will be published relating to contractual claims attracting awards of general damages unrelated to real property, torts involving personal property, economic tort claims leading to an award of general damages or where damages are at large, aggravated and exemplary damages, and awards or compensation provided for by way of statute. Thus it is hoped to provide the reader with a reasonably

---

[1] Times 20th February 1997

comprehensive one stop guide to awards of recent duration in areas as diverse as trespass to property, nuisance, breach of covenant, unlawful eviction, harassment, disrepair and user obligations, professional negligence, breaches of contract for the supply of goods and services including breaches of contracts providing for enjoyment or peace of mind, the loss of use of personal property, employment claims, discrimination and disability, assault, actions against the police, defamation, breach of statutory duty and misfeasance, conversion and interference with goods, malicious falsehood, passing off, conspiracy to injure and inducement to breach of contract. The categories are not closed, and the work, initially in hard copy and afterwards in electronic format is intended to grow and develop, and in that respect the contribution of readers and users will be most welcome.

## Scope

This work is not intended to provide more than the most modest guide to the substantive law on the award of general damages, nor are the citations given by way of digest intended to replace the law reports to which the entries refer, some of which may be reported in more than one publication. They are intended to provide the reader with an idea of the value of that part of his claim for which general damages are recoverable and encourage reading of the substantive reports. It should also be remembered that while the emphasis is here placed on awards of general damages, these may be only one small part of the total value of the claim, and the full law reports may emphasise liability, general principles or some aspect of general procedure, and offer no real discussion as to how the award of general damage is formulated. It should also be remembered with some caution that cases which are reported for quantum only may be so because a Claimant's solicitor has submitted a transcript recording an unusually large award, or a Defendant's solicitor an unusually small one. It is therefore important to consider a range of awards in order to put the facts under consideration into context. In some areas the reader will discover this is easier said than done, since reported awards may be both many and varied for topics such as unlawful eviction, breach of covenant of quiet enjoyment or disrepair claims, and scarce for matters such as derogation from grant or wrongful withholding of consent to assign. This has created something of an imbalance in the book, but it is hoped that having made a start, contributions from readers will help solve this problem.

# Sources

The awards included have been made or assessed by every level of tribunal from the House of Lords to the leasehold valuation tribunal. In cases generating small awards of general damages as the substantive or whole value of the claim, stronger reliance is placed upon the county court, tribunal or first instance decision rather than appellate or Court of Appeal decisions which consider matters of principle and policy. There are also reports in which a small award of general damages is only a fraction of the overall award but is nevertheless a useful guide to the level of award for that part of the claim where similar facts elsewhere may make that level of award amount to the entire claim.

# Law

Over the last decade the House of Lords has considered damages for non-pecuniary loss on three occasions. The leading authority is currently *Farley v Skinner*[2] in which the House revisited its earlier decision in *Ruxley Electronics & Construction Ltd v Forsyth*[3] to consider the approach to damages for deprivation of a contractual benefit, and the principles set out in the Court of Appeal decision in *Watts v Morrow*[4] for consequential damages within the applicable remoteness rules. Their lordships distinguished their own decision on this issue in *Johnson v Gore Wood & Co.*[5] Each of these cases concerned, or in part concerned, whether under the law of obligations the rules governing the recovery of compensation should necessarily distinguish between different kinds of harm. Parts V and VI of the speech of Lord Steyn in *Farley*[6] encapsulate the law relating to the recovery of non-pecuniary damages. Tort law, he says, approaches compensation for physical damage and pure economic loss differently. In the law of contract distinctions are made about the kind of harm which resulted from the breach complained of. The general principle is that compensation is only awarded for financial loss resulting from the breach of contract[7] and does not extend to providing damages for anxiety and

---

[2] [2001] UKHL 49; [2002] PNLR 20
[3] [1996] AC 344
[4] [1991] 1 WLR 1421
[5] [2001] 2 WLR 72
[6] paras [16]-[21]
[7] *Livingstone v Rawyards Coal Co* (1880) 5 App Cas 25 @ 39 per Lord Blackburn

distress consequent upon the breach.[8] The legal policy supporting this proposition was enunciated by Bingham LJ in *Watts v Morrow*: a contract breaker is not *in general* liable for any distress, frustration, anxiety, displeasure, vexation, tension or aggravation which his breach of contract may cause to the innocent party, (as opposed to physical discomfort and inconvenience[9]) a principle founded not so much on considerations of foreseeability as of policy. There are, however, limited exceptions to this rule, one of which is the award of damages for pain, suffering and loss of amenity caused to an individual by a breach of contract.[10]     Others specifically cited by Bingham LJ are for physical inconvenience caused by the breach, and where the very object of the contract is to provide pleasure, relaxation, peace of mind or freedom from molestation. These are the product of the evolutionary developments of case law in the 1970s. In 1971 a Scottish decision of the sheriff court awarded damages for distress and disappointment when a wedding photographer failed to attend the event which he had been contracted to photograph.[11] The celebrated case of *Jarvis v Swan Tours*[12] was the first in which a claimant recovered damages for mental distress following a disagreeable holiday resulting from a travel company's negligent representations. In 1976 the Court of Appeal upheld[13] an award of damages for mental distress and upset against a negligent solicitor who had omitted under his retainer to take any steps to restrain the molestation of his client by a man; and in 1978[14] the Court of Appeal sanctioned an award of damages for disappointment for a spoilt holiday where one of the objects of buying a car, found to be defective under section 14 of the Sale of Goods Act 1893, was to tour France in it.

In *Farley* Lord Steyn found[15] that in the real life of our lower courts non-pecuniary   damages of a modest quantum are regularly awarded on the basis that the defendant's breach of contract deprived the claimant of the very object of the contract, *viz.* pleasure, relaxation, and peace of mind. Such cases arose out of diverse contexts, examples given being the supply of a wedding dress or double glazing, hire purchase transactions, landlord

---

[8]   *Addis v Gramaphone Co Ltd* (1909) AC 488 HL, approved in *Johnson v Gore Wood & Co* (cit. supra)

[9]   see in this regard Beldam L.J. in *Wapshott v Davis Donovan & Co* [1996] PNLR 361 @ 378

[10]   see *McGregor on Damages* 16th edn. Para 96

[11]   *Diesen v Samson* (1971) SLT (Sh Ct) 49

[12]   [1973] QB 233

[13]   *Heywood v Wellers* [1976] QB 446

[14]   *Jackson v Chrysler Acceptances Ltd* [1978] RTR 474

[15]   para 20

and tenant claims, defective works under building contracts, and the inadequate performance of professional services in the engagement of solicitors and estate agents. What has taxed the courts is the precise scope of the exceptional category of cases in which awards of non-pecuniary damages for breach of contract are made. By reason of both *Ruxley* and *Farley* it has been authoritatively established that the courts may make a modest award for a breach of the provision of a pleasurable amenity as part of the object of a contract. For the purposes of this work it should be noted that both Lord Steyn and Lord Scott in *Farley* and Bingham LJ in *Watts v Morrow* concluded that awards in this area should be restrained and modest. Lord Steyn considered it is important that logical and beneficial developments in this corner of the law should not contribute to the creation of a society bent on litigation.

The precise quantum of restrained and modest awards of general damages for non-pecuniary loss is very much a matter of impression for the court in the individual circumstances of each case. The judge must weigh up the seriousness of the loss of amenity or the value of the loss of bargain. However where such heads of damage are recoverable at all the award will be conventional and therefore follow the established pattern of quantum to compensate for the type of harm complained of. This can be demonstrated in the development of common law awards for breaches of covenant of quiet enjoyment, harassment and or unlawful eviction, over the last 15 years or so, and those for housing disrepair.

The principles for the award of general damages are comprehensively discussed in the leading textbooks, namely *McGregor on Damages*, *Chitty on Contract*, and *Clerk & Lindsell on Tort*. In addition specialist textbooks set out the basis of awards of damages in their area, particularly where, as for example in employment law, a statutory framework, which it is beyond the scope of this introduction to address, underpins such awards. The users of this work, which is essentially a digest of quanta, are therefore referred to such texts as *Buckley on Nuisance*, *Charlesworth & Percy on Negligence*, Clayton & Tomlinson on *Civil Actions Against the Police*, *Gatley on Libel and Slander*, *Harvey on Industrial Relations and Employment Law*, *Hill & Redman* or *Woodfall on Landlord and Tenant*, *Jackson & Powell on Professional Negligence*, *Keating on Building Contracts*, Palmer on *Bailment*, Saggerson on *Travel Law and Litigation* and Townshend-Smith on *Discrimination Law* for a discussion of recoverability, not only of general damages but, where appropriate, of aggravated, exemplary and statutory damages.

## Using the work

Each digest entry is the subject of keywords which create an electronic search mechanism which flow from the generic to the specific, e.g. Property – Landlord & Tenant – Unlawful Eviction, or Property – Housing – Breach of Covenant to Repair. Keywords may also be used for cross-referencing. A list of keywords is set out as a separate index. Where the search pattern lists a number of entries these are set out in reverse chronological order. The entry will refer to all of the sources of the case that relate to the quantum reported. Reports may be contained in more than one source. Reports in which an appellate tribunal does not interfere with the quantum below are not referred to; appellate sources that expressly uphold the first instance quantum are.

## Updating

The duty of the court is to assess general damages in the "money of the day", that is at the date of trial not the date of the accrual of the cause of action. The Retail Price Index is used to update the awards, and in this work updating is done automatically. The Index is published in *Kemp & Kemp*, *Current Law*, the *Law Society Gazette*, the Professional Negligence Bar Association's *Facts & Figures: Tables for the Calculation of Damages* and the financial press. The electronic service will prompt users to download an updated calculator with their regular update in the days after the publication of the RPI. To update an award in line with the Index multiply it by the current Index figure and then divide that sum by the Index figure for the month in which the award was originally made.

## Layout

Each digest entry is laid out as follows:

- Case name within *Awards*. To find updated information for this case, using as unique a part of the name as possible in the electronic Search field. The Award Now value will vary according to RPI changes and additional references (e.g. appellate decisions) may have been added.

- Cause of action.

- Tribunal and judge if known.

- Where reported: key reference for further reading.

- Date of award.

- Brief facts of case.

- General damages amount in the original award plus additional categories of award if separated out.

- Award of special damages if any.

- Value of award as at date of search applying RPI.

- Keywords description. This will usually take the form of cause/s of action. To find similar cases type the generic or specific keywords into Quick Search using the electronic database and it will list cases with that reference in.

To use the book, the reader may use either the topic (see Contents or for more detail, the Index), the Table of Statutes or the Table of Cases.

It is hoped that readers will wish to offer constructive criticism in order to develop this service as a substantial time-saving device, particularly when the relevant level of award may be eclipsed by the lawyer's time in searching out information upon it.

Andrew Goodman
1 Serjeants Inn

May 2004.

# Table of Cases

# Table of Statutes

# Unlawful Eviction, Harassment and Peaceful Enjoyment

**Name of Case:**            *Abbott v Bayley*

**Cause/s of Action:**       Breach of covenant for quiet enjoyment –
                             Unlawful eviction

**Tribunal and Judge**:      Court of Appeal

**Where Reported:**          May 1999 LAB 28

**Date of Award:**           January 29, 1999

**Brief Facts of Case:**     B owned a 2-bedroom flat. He granted A an
                             assured tenancy of the second bedroom with
                             shared use of the sitting room, kitchen and
                             bathroom in September 1994. In January 1995 B
                             wrote to A asking him to leave. In February 1995
                             A returned from holiday to find 2 new tenants in
                             the flat one of whom was occupying the second
                             bedroom. A was allowed back into his room and
                             the 3 tenants lived together there for 3 months. A
                             was then subjected to a threatening and abusive
                             telephone conversation from B and B's father
                             threatening to forcibly evict A and his
                             possessions. He vacated on 2 May 1995 as he
                             could not bear the unpleasant conditions.

                             A brought proceedings and was awarded damages
                             under s 27 Housing Act 1988 and for breach of
                             covenant. Appeal dismissed.

**Award:**                   £6,750 statutory damages

                             £2,050 for breach of covenant for quiet enjoyment

**General Damages:**         £2,050

**Value of Award of £2,050 as at April 2004:  £2,330**

*Property – Landlord & Tenant – Breach of covenant for quiet enjoyment*

| | |
|---|---|
| **Name of Case:** | *Abouri and Abouri v Ierodianconcou* |
| **Cause/s of Action:** | Unlawful eviction |
| **Tribunal and Judge:** | Edmonton County Court – Tibber J |
| **Where Reported:** | [1990] CLY 529; December 1990 LAB 13 |
| **Date of Award:** | February 1990 |
| **Brief Facts of Case:** | Ts were joint protected tenants who refused to vacate when given invalid notice. Whilst they were out L changed locks and deposited their belongings outside property. |
| **Award:** | £3,500 compensatory, aggravated and exemplary damages. |
| | (Special damages: £1,154.23 damages for accommodation costs and injury to goods.) |

**Consolidated Damages:** £3,500

**Value of Award of £3,500 as at April 2004: £5,407**

*Property – Landlord & Tenant – Unlawful eviction – Breach of covenant for quiet enjoyment*

---

| | |
|---|---|
| **Name of Case:** | *Adams v Vickers* |
| **Cause/s of Action:** | Breach of covenant for quiet enjoyment – Harassment – Trespass to goods |
| **Tribunal and Judge:** | Manchester County Court – The Circuit Judge |
| **Where Reported:** | June 1994 LAB 11 |
| **Date of Award:** | January 11, 1994 |
| **Brief Facts of Case:** | T occupied bed and breakfast accommodation. L evicted her by locking her out of her room and she had to stay in a hostel for 2 months before finding alternative accommodation. |
| **Award:** | £3,250 general damages for breach of covenant including £1,750 in respect of the harassment in the week prior to being evicted. |

£250 for trespass to goods (interference with mail and going without her toiletries for 3 days after the eviction)

£1,250 aggravated damages

**General Damages:**       £3,250

**Value of Award of £3,250 as at April 2004: £4,271**

*Property – Landlord & Tenant – Breach of covenant for quiet enjoyment – Harassment – Trespass to goods*

| | |
|---|---|
| **Name of Case:** | *Adjei v Achempong* |
| **Cause/s of Action:** | Unlawful eviction |
| **Tribunal and Judge:** | Central London Trial Centre – The Circuit Judge |
| **Where Reported:** | September 1995 LAB 14 |
| **Date of Award:** | November 25, 1994 |
| **Brief Facts of Case:** | T rented a flat from L who was a council tenant. L maintained that there was no tenancy – only a licence as T was his lover. L obtained an injunction and locked T out. T's injunction re-instated her but L failed to comply and there was an application to commit him. The trial judge found for T. |
| **Award:** | £4,000 damages for unlawful eviction. |
| **General Damages:** | £4,000 |

**Value of Award of £4,000 as at April 2004: £5,112**

*Property – Landlord & Tenant – Unlawful eviction*

| | |
|---|---|
| **Name of Case:** | *Ahmed v Bains* |
| **Cause/s of Action:** | Unlawful eviction – Harassment |
| **Tribunal and Judge:** | Brentford County Court – HHJ Marcus-Evans |
| **Where Reported:** | September 2001 LAB 25 |
| **Date of Award:** | June 18, 2001 |
| **Brief Facts of Case:** | T occupied one bedroom (sharing the use of kitchen, bathroom and living room) under an assured shorthold tenancy from May 1997. L began to occupy the living room in September 1997 depriving the tenants of its use. T complained and was threatened with violence. T called the police due to noise and violence on 8 occasions. Ls gave T notice. When it expired L and another assaulted T and removed his keys. Ls disposed of T's property. T stayed with friends until end of December 1997 when he brought proceedings. |
| **Award:** | £13,495 total damages including: |
| | £1,000 for harassment in September |
| | £7,800 general damages for unlawful eviction and homelessness between 14 October 1997 and end December 1997 at £100 per day |
| | £1,500 aggravated damages |
| | £1,500 exemplary damages |
| | Special damages: £1,695 for loss of possessions. |
| **General Damages:** | £7,800 |

**Value of Award of £1,000 for harassment as at April 2004: £1,065**

**Value of Award of general damages for unlawful eviction of £100 per day as at April 2004: £107 per day**

**Value of Award of £1,500 aggravated damages as at April 2004: £1,597**

**Value of Award of £1,500 exemplary damages as at April 2004: £1,597**

*Property – Landlord & Tenant – Harassment – Unlawful eviction*

| | |
|---|---|
| **Name of Case:** | *Aleksi v Bogdanovic* |
| **Cause/s of Action:** | Breach of covenant for quiet enjoyment – Harassment |
| **Tribunal and Judge:** | West London County Court – HHJ Phelan |
| **Where Reported:** | September 1995 LAB 14 |
| **Date of Award:** | February 27, 1995 |
| **Brief Facts of Case:** | T was a licensee. L issued possession proceedings and T counterclaimed for harassment. L had disconnected the gas, electricity and water supplies and had removed furniture. T had been intimidated and hit with a crowbar. |
| **Award:** | £6,000 total damages comprising: |
| | £2,000 general damages |
| | £2,000 aggravated damages |
| | £2,000 exemplary damages |
| **General Damages:** | £2,000 |

**Value of Award of general damages as at April 2004: £2,528**

**Value of Award of aggravated damages as at April 2004: £2,528**

**Value of Award of exemplary damages as at April 2004: £2,528**

*Property – Landlord & Tenant – Breach of covenant for quiet enjoyment – Harassment*

---

| | |
|---|---|
| **Name of Case:** | *Altun & Ulker v Patel* |
| **Cause/s of Action:** | Unlawful eviction |
| **Tribunal and Judge:** | Edmonton County Court – HHJ Tibber |
| **Where Reported:** | March 1996 LAB 14 |
| **Date of Award:** | November 20, 1995 |
| **Brief Facts of Case:** | Ts (joint assured tenants) were evicted 6 months after moving in, owing to delays in payments of their housing benefit. L moved into the flat with his family. Ts resumed occupation 15 days later |

after obtaining an injunction. In the meantime they had had to sleep on friends' floors and sofas and had been denied access to their possessions.

**Award:**     Total of £6,500 damages (from which arrears were deducted):

£2,250 general damages to each T (£150 per night)

£1,000 aggravated damages due to L refusing to readmit them following receipt of a solicitor's letter and removal of the fridge and beds)

**General Damages:**  £3,250

**Value of Award of general damages of £150 per night as at April 2004: £184 per night**

**Value of Award of £1,000 aggravated damages as at April 2004: £1,226**

*Property – Landlord & Tenant – Unlawful eviction*

---

| | |
|---|---|
| **Name of Case:** | *Amusan v Taussig* |
| **Cause/s of Action:** | Unlawful eviction |
| **Tribunal and Judge:** | Westminster County Court – HHJ Harris QC |
| **Where Reported:** | [1987] 9 CL 176; [1987] CLY 2251; December 1987 LAB 13 |
| **Date of Award:** | July 31, 1987 |
| **Brief Facts of Case:** | T (a young female) was given 24 hours' notice to vacate after refusing to have a meal with L. She refused and L and another forced their way into her room. T was punched in the stomach and pushed down the stairs. L disconnected the telephone after which T found alternative accommodation. |
| **Award:** | £1,350 general, aggravated and exemplary damages. |

**Value of Award of £1,350 as at April 2004: £2,463**

*Property – Landlord & Tenant – Unlawful eviction*

**Name of Case:**  *Andreou v Reid*

**Cause/s of Action:**  Unlawful eviction – Breach of covenant for quiet enjoyment – Assault

**Tribunal and Judge:**  Edmonton County Court – HHJ Tibber

**Where Reported:**  [1987] 9 CL 175; September 1987 LAB 14

**Date of Award:**  February 14, 1986

**Brief Facts of Case:**  L unlawfully evicted T twice, putting his possessions in dustbin bags and threatening him with a chisel. L also arranged for T to be attacked whilst he was in temporary accommodation. Two men threatened him with a gun and caused him head injuries requiring stitches after hitting him with iron piping. His chest wall was also bruised.

**Award:**  £3,000 aggravated and exemplary damages for breach of covenant for quiet enjoyment (£2,000 for assault).

**General Damages:**  £3,000

**Value of Award of general and exemplary damages of £1,000 as at April 2004: £1,922**

**Value of Award of general damages for assault of £2,000 as at April 2004: £3,845**

*Property – Landlord & Tenant – Unlawful eviction – Breach of covenant for quiet enjoyment – Assault*

---

**Name of Case:**  *Angelidis & Sellers v Hastereel Ltd*

**Cause/s of Action:**  Breach of covenant for quiet enjoyment – Harassment

**Tribunal and Judge:**  Central London County Court – HHJ Green QC

**Where Reported:**  (1996) H&HI (2) 1:4; May 1997 LAB 20

**Date of Award:**  September 3, 1996

**Brief Facts of Case:**  Ts were the last remaining statutory tenants in a block of 16 flats. In 1991/2 L began refurbishment of the block. Minimal notice was given and the work continued for 11 months. There was no lift service to the flats which were on the 5$^{th}$ and 6$^{th}$ floors for 21 weeks, no entryphone for 22 weeks, no TV aerial for 19 weeks, no refuse collection for 40 weeks, no post or milk deliveries for 18 weeks. Only injunctive relief prevented L from disconnecting the communal heating and hot water system. Throughout the period of works there was noise, no cleaning or lighting of the common parts, work took place at unsociable hours, flooding and malicious damage to Ts' property.

**Award:** £7,000 general damages. Special damages: £5,000.

**General Damages:** £7,000

**Value of Award of £7,000 as at April 2004: £8,452**

*Property – Landlord & Tenant – Breach of covenant for quiet enjoyment – Harassment*

---

| | |
|---|---|
| **Name of Case:** | *Ariwodo v Comfort* |
| **Cause/s of Action:** | Harassment – Assault |
| **Tribunal and Judge:** | Wandsworth County Court – HHJ Sumner |
| **Where Reported:** | March 1992 LAB 15 |
| **Date of Award:** | December 19, 1991 |
| **Brief Facts of Case:** | T was denied access to a shared bathroom and was assaulted by L and his wife. T suffered from a small cut and abrasion to her face and ran to the police station in her nightclothes. |
| **Award:** | £600 general damages |
| | £1,750 aggravated damages |

**Value of Award of £600 general damages as at April 2004: £821**

**Value of Award of £1,750 aggravated damages as at April 2004: £2,395**

*Property – Landlord & Tenant – Harassment – Assault*

| | |
|---|---|
| **Name of Case:** | *Asghar v Ahmed* |
| **Cause/s of Action:** | Unlawful eviction |
| **Tribunal and Judge:** | Court of Appeal – Cumming-Bruce and Griffiths LJJ |
| **Where Reported:** | (1985) 17 HLR 25 |
| **Date of Award:** | May 24, 1984 |
| **Brief Facts of Case:** | P and family were evicted from a property they occupied. An interlocutory order required D to re-admit P but D continued to refuse access for some time. D threw P's possessions out of the property and eventually P vacated. |
| | D was prosecuted under the Protection from Eviction Act 1977 and fined £750. |
| | P sought damages in a civil action and the judge awarded special damages, aggravated and exemplary damages. D appealed. |
| **Award:** | £500 aggravated damages |
| | £1,000 exemplary damages |
| | (Special damages: £1,000.) |
| | (Appeal dismissed.) |

**Value of Award of £500 aggravated damages as at April 2004: £1,044**

**Value of Award of £1,000 exemplary damages as at April 2004: £2,088**

*Property – Landlord & Tenant – Unlawful eviction*

---

| | |
|---|---|
| **Name of Case:** | *Ayari v Jethi* |
| **Cause/s of Action:** | Unlawful eviction – Trespass – Breach of covenant for quiet enjoyment |
| **Tribunal and Judge:** | West London County Court |
| **Where Reported:** | December 1990 LAB 13; March 1991 LAB 16 |
| **Date of Award:** | November 24, 1989 |

**Brief Facts of Case:** T occupied a flat under a Rent Act protected tenancy. One Friday evening L changed the lock and removed T's possessions in dustbin bags. T regained possession of the flat the following Tuesday after obtaining an *ex parte* injunction but failed to recover most of her possessions.

**Award:** £15,733 total damages (it was agreed that the county court's jurisdiction limit be waived) including £1,250 general damages.

Special damages: £11,472 on the basis that L was responsible for the loss of T's belongings.

**General Damages:** £1,250

**Value of Award of £1,250 as at April 2004: £1,959**

*Property – Landlord & Tenant – Unlawful eviction*

---

**Name of Case:** *Bain v Stimpson*

**Cause/s of Action:** Breach of covenant for quiet enjoyment – Unlawful eviction

**Tribunal and Judge:** HHJ Viner QC

**Where Reported:** [1994] CLY 1451; December 1994 LAB 16

**Date of Award:** February 10, 1994

**Brief Facts of Case:** T shared a house with 2 other tenants who complained to L about T's behaviour during a period of illness due to schizophrenia. L unlawfully evicted T by requesting that her parents remove her from the house and depositing T's possessions in her parents' driveway.

**Award:** £1,000 general damages

£3,000 aggravated damages to compensate for hurt pride and injury to T's feelings

£1,000 exemplary damages for L's conduct

£30,500 statutory damages were reduced by one third to £20,334 as T's behaviour had contributed to other tenants leaving the property

Common law damages set off against statutory award.

**General Damages:**     £1,000 out of £15,733.

**Value of Award of general and exemplary damages of £1,000 as at April 2004: £1,307**

**Value of Award of £3,000 aggravated damages as at April 2004: £3,921**

*Property – Landlord & Tenant – Unlawful eviction – Breach of covenant for quiet enjoyment*

| | |
|---|---|
| **Name of Case:** | *Baldwin v Waugh* |
| **Cause/s of Action:** | Unlawful eviction |
| **Tribunal and Judge:** | Weymouth County Court – District Judge Naylor |
| **Where Reported:** | [1993] CLY 1608 |
| **Date of Award:** | October 21, 1993 |
| **Brief Facts of Case:** | T an assured tenant, lived with her 2 teenage children in the property for 18 months. After expiry of a notice to quit – when T was out – L boarded up the house and changed the locks. T had to spend one night living on the streets and 2 months in bed and breakfast establishments before securing other accommodation. |
| **Award:** | £2,500 general and exemplary damages for unlawful eviction of T and her family. |
| | Special damages: £1,270. |
| **General Damages:** | £2,500 |

**Value of Award of general and exemplary damages of £2,500 as at April 2004: £3,274**

*Property - Landlord & Tenant – Unlawful eviction*

**Name of Case:**          *Barros v Yiakoumi*

**Cause/s of Action:**     Unlawful eviction

**Tribunal and Judge:**    Clerkenwell County Court – The Circuit Judge

**Where Reported:**        September 1992 LAB 23

**Date of Award:**         May 8, 1992

**Brief Facts of Case:**   Ts were sub-tenants occupying in breach of a covenant in the head lease. When the mesne tenant surrendered his lease L (the freeholder) changed the lock to the property. An injunction was granted but Ts were out of occupation for 15 days during which time they were forced to sleep in a van.

**Award:**                 £6,500 total damages comprising:

                           £3,000 general damages (£100 per day per T for period when they were out of occupation)

                           £3,500 aggravated and exemplary damages

**General Damages:**       £6,500

**Value of Award of general damages of £100 per day as at April 2004:£133**

**Value of Award of aggravated and exemplary damages of £3,500 as at April 2004: £4,666**

*Property – Landlord & Tenant – Unlawful eviction*

---

**Name of Case:**          *Biga v Martin*

**Cause/s of Action:**     Unlawful eviction

**Tribunal and Judge:**    Ilford County Court – HHJ Platt

**Where Reported:**        June 2001 LAB 25

**Date of Award:**         November 16, 2000

**Brief Facts of Case:**   T occupied premises under an assured shorthold tenancy. L refused to provide documentary evidence in respect of his claim for housing benefit and told him to vacate. Despite a warning from a solicitor as to the consequences L changed the locks and put T's possessions in the corridor. T obtained an injunction allowing him re-entry but L attended with 3 men armed with a sledgehammer. He broke in through the window and assaulted T leaving him very frightened. T stayed for 3 nights in a night shelter and then in bed and breakfast accommodation. He was diagnosed as suffering from post-traumatic stress disorder.

**Award:** £10,000 general damages (including personal injury and aggravated damages)

£2,500 exemplary damages

(Special damages: £900.)

**Value of Award of £2,500 exemplary damages as at April 2004: £2,698**

*Property – Landlord & Tenant – Unlawful eviction*

| | |
|---|---|
| **Name of Case:** | *Blackman and Blackman v Richardson* |
| **Cause/s of Action:** | Breach of covenant quiet enjoyment – Harassment |
| **Tribunal and Judge:** | Lambeth County Court – HHJ Hunter |
| **Where Reported:** | March 1993 LAB 16 |
| **Date of Award:** | November 24, 1992 |
| **Brief Facts of Case:** | L unlawfully sublet his council flat to Ts. Ts returned to find the front door had been kicked in and L had moved in with his family with the intention of exercising his right to buy. L had put some of Ts furniture in a van and left some in the communal parts of the block. The police were called after which Ts were able to resume occupation but they then suffered harassment from L for 5 days. |

**Award:**　　　　　　£3,062 damages including:

£1,000 aggravated damages

£1,500 exemplary damages

(Special damages £62)

**General Damages:**　　£500

**Value of Award of £500 as at April 2004: £665**

**Value of Award of £1,000 aggravated damages as at April 2004: £1,329**

**Value of Award of £1,500 exemplary damages as at April 2004: £1,994**

*Property – Landlord & Tenant - Breach of covenant of quiet enjoyment - Harassment*

---

| | |
|---|---|
| **Name of Case:** | *Breeze v Elden & Hyde* |
| **Cause/s of Action:** | Breach of covenant for quiet enjoyment |
| **Tribunal and Judge:** | Norwich County Court – Mr Deputy Registrar Sheriff |
| **Where Reported:** | [1987] CLY 2120; June 1987 LAB 18 |
| **Date of Award:** | December 3, 1986 |
| **Brief Facts of Case:** | T occupied barber's shop premises since 1979 as a weekly tenant. When L acquired the freehold they served a notice to quit on T. T's solicitors wrote to warn L that the notice was invalid and that he should not attempt to evict T. L was angered and entered the property without consent. The front windows were smashed, door removed and electricity disconnected. T was warned not to trespass and his possessions removed. |
| **Award:** | £500 damages for loss of T's opportunity to claim compensation for disturbance under s37 Landlord and Tenant Act 1954 and for trespass |

£700 exemplary damages in view of L's behaviour

Special damages were also awarded for damage to T's property and loss of earnings.

**General Damages:**          £500

**Value of Award of £500 general damages as at April 2004: £932**

**Value of Award of £700 exemplary damages as at April 2004: £1,305**

*Property – Landlord & Tenant – Breach of covenant for quiet enjoyment*

---

| | |
|---|---|
| **Name of Case:** | *Brook and Arden v Woodcock* |
| **Cause/s of Action:** | Unlawful eviction |
| **Tribunal and Judge:** | Blackpool County Court – HHJ Holt |
| **Where Reported:** | September 1989 LAB 25 |
| **Date of Award:** | August 1, 1989 |
| **Brief Facts of Case:** | After an ongoing dispute between Ts and L regarding disrepair of the property and an application to register a fair rent L and 5 others visited Ts, threatened them with violence, stripped the flat, removed the telephone, bagged up Ts' possessions and changed the locks. |
| **Award:** | £17,000 statutory damages representing the difference between the value of the property with vacant possession (£52,000) and subject to the tenancy (£35,000). |
| **General Damages:** | No separate award. |

*Property – Landlord & Tenant – Unlawful eviction*

| | |
|---|---|
| **Name of Case:** | *Brown v Mansouri* |
| **Cause/s of Action:** | Breach of covenant for quiet enjoyment |
| **Tribunal and Judge:** | Uxbridge County Court – HHJ Marcus Edwards QC |
| **Where Reported:** | [1997] CLY 1244; September 1997 LAB 17 |
| **Date of Award:** | October 3, 1996 |
| **Brief Facts of Case:** | T rented a flat which was in disrepair. A notice was served under s190 of HA 1985. T and his wife agreed to move out of the flat during the daytime and allowed L to store their possessions. L than changed the locks and told them the tenancy ended that day. T and his wife separated and T lived for 7 months in a hostel without his personal effects. |
| **Award:** | £680 general damages in respect of disrepair (25% of rent for 9 months) |
| | £1,500 for inconvenience |
| | £3,000 general damages for breach of covenant for quiet enjoyment (£150 per week for 20 weeks) |
| | £1,500 aggravated damages |
| | £1,500 exemplary damages |
| | (Special damages: £4,000 for replacement value of goods lost.) |
| **General Damages:** | £8,180 |

**Value of Award of £1,500 general damages as at April 2004: £1,811**

**Value of Award of general damages of £150 per week as at April 2004: £181**

**Value of Award of aggravated and exemplary damages of £1,500 as at April 2004: £1,811**

*Property – Landlord & Tenant – Breach of covenant for quiet enjoyment*

| | |
|---|---|
| **Name of Case:** | *Burchett and Strugnell v Vine* |
| **Cause/s of Action:** | Breach of covenant for quiet enjoyment – interference with goods |
| **Tribunal and Judge:** | Southampton County Court – Recorder Boyle |
| **Where Reported:** | [1997] CLY 3284; September 1997 LAB 17 |
| **Date of Award:** | December 12, 1996 |
| **Brief Facts of Case:** | T owed 2 weeks' rent. L changed locks and threw T's possessions in a horsebox damaging some of them and kept the television and microwave against unpaid rent. T and his licensee had to stay with their parents before they were able to secure alternative accommodation. |
| **Award:** | £1,000 general damages for inconvenience and indignity |
| | £50 for detention of goods |
| **General Damages:** | £1050 |

**Value of Award of £1,000 general damages as at April 2004: £1,203**

**Value of Award of £50 general damages as at April 2004: £60**

*Property – Landlord & Tenant – Breach of covenant for quiet enjoyment – Interference with goods*

---

| | |
|---|---|
| **Name of Case:** | *Burke v Berioit* |
| **Cause/s of Action:** | Unlawful eviction – Breach of covenant for quiet enjoyment – Trespass to goods – Assault |
| **Tribunal and Judge:** | Central London County Court – Mr Recorder Hockman QC |
| **Where Reported:** | [1995] CLY 1572; March 1995 LAB 13 |
| **Date of Award:** | September 25, 1994 |
| **Brief Facts of Case:** | L liable for breach of covenant for quiet enjoyment and trespassing his goods and person. |

**Award:**                    £100 per day general damages for T's 2 months of homelessness – total £6,000

£1,500 exemplary damages for threats and violence

£500 damages for trespass to goods

£250 aggravated damages

Total £8,250 exceeded statutory damages assessed at £5,000.

**General Damages:**        £8,250

**Value of Award of general damages, £100 per day as at April 2004: £145**

**Value of Award of £1,500 exemplary damages as at April 2004: £1,921**

**Value of Award of £500 damages for trespass to goods as at April 2004: £640**

**Value of Award of £250 aggravated damages as at April 2004: £320**

*Property – Landlord and Tenant – Unlawful eviction – Breach of covenant for quiet enjoyment and Landlord and Tenant – trespass to goods – assault*

---

**Name of Case:**           *Cadman v Wood*

**Cause/s of Action:**      Unlawful eviction

**Tribunal and Judge:**     Nottingham County Court – HHJ Morrison

**Where Reported:**         [1992] CLY 1796; March 1993 LAB 16

**Date of Award:**          June 18, 1992

**Brief Facts of Case:**    T fell into rent arrears due to delays in the payment of benefits. L and agents disconnected gas and electricity. Ts were threatened with violence by large men and a supposed new tenant came to the flat with a Rottweiler. Ts were so afraid they did not return for one night and when they returned the flat was padlocked and their furniture had been dumped in the yard. They came back to collect it with a van by which time it had been removed.

**Award:**    £4,900 total damages including £3,000 statutory damages. (Special damages: £400.)
£1,500 aggravated damages for injury to feelings

**General Damages:**    £1,500

**Value of Award of £4,900 total damages as at April 2004: £6,532**

**Value of Award of £1,500 aggravated damages as at April 2004: £2,000**

*Property – Landlord & Tenant – Unlawful eviction*

---

**Name of Case:**    *Canlin and Gray v Berkshire Holdings*

**Cause/s of Action:**    Unlawful eviction

**Tribunal and Judge:**    Reading County Court – HHJ Lait

**Where Reported:**    September 1990 LAB 10

**Date of Award:**    April 3, 1990

**Brief Facts of Case:**    Ts were placed in Ls house by the Council in accordance with its obligations to house homeless persons (Housing Act 1985 Part III). Ts failed to co-operate with the Council's enquiries and it refused to accept further responsibility for them. L's employees then disconnected the electricity, removing the gas cooker. Ts moved out and were refused re-admission on the basis that they were only licensees.

**Award:**    £35,000 on the basis of the difference in value of the property with vacant possession (£115,000) and subject to the Ts Rent Act protected tenancy in part of the house (£80,000).

**Statutory Damages:**    £35,000

**Value of Award of £35,000 statutory damages as at April 2004: £51,954**

*Property – Landlord & Tenant – Unlawful eviction*

| | |
|---|---|
| **Name of Case:** | *Chniouer v Nicholaiedes* |
| **Cause/s of Action:** | Breach of covenant for quiet enjoyment – Assault |
| **Tribunal and Judge:** | Wood Green Trial Centre – HHJ Beddard |
| **Where Reported:** | June 1991 LAB 12; September 1991 LAB 18 |
| **Date of Award:** | November 15, 1991 |
| **Brief Facts of Case:** | C was a protected tenant occupying a flat owned by N. N's son broke into the property and broke C's arm when he assaulted him. C and his wife were too frightened to return to the flat despite N's son's arrest and eventual custodial sentence. They had received £2,000 damages and an injunction against N in a previous action. |
| | Following this incident they issued proceedings against N and his son. |
| **Award:** | £32,565 total damages comprising: |
| | £25,000 damages under Housing Act 1988 |
| | £4,000 general damages for breach of covenant for quiet enjoyment |
| | £1,000 exemplary damages |
| | £2,500 damages jointly for assault against N & son |
| | £65 in respect of rent for the period when they were out of occupation of the flat prior to the surrender of the lease |
| **General Damages:** | £4,000 |

**Value of Award of £4,000 general damages as at April 2004: £5,478**

**Value of Award of £1,000 exemplary damages as at April 2004: £1,369**

**Value of Award of £2,500 damages for assault as at April 2004: £3,424**

*Property – Landlord & Tenant – Breach of covenant for quiet enjoyment – Assault*

| | |
|---|---|
| **Name of Case:** | *Choy-Wei v Fastaleh* |
| **Cause/s of Action:** | Breach of covenant for quiet enjoyment |
| **Tribunal and Judge:** | West London County Court – HHJ Harris |
| **Where Reported:** | June 1989 LAB 22 |
| **Date of Award:** | November 25, 1988 |
| **Brief Facts of Case:** | T occupied a room in a house. L changed the front door of the house. T could not resume occupation for 3 days. |
| **Award:** | £500 damages. |
| **General Damages:** | £500 |

**Value of Award of £500 as at April 2004: £844**

*Property – Landlord & Tenant – Breach of covenant for quiet enjoyment*

---

| | |
|---|---|
| **Name of Case:** | *Congdon v Probuild Developments Ltd* |
| **Cause/s of Action:** | Breach of covenant for quiet enjoyment |
| **Tribunal and Judge:** | Wood Green Civil Trial Centre – Assistant Recorder Leech |
| **Where Reported:** | March 1991 LAB 16 |
| **Date of Award:** | January 14, 1991 |
| **Brief Facts of Case:** | T had rented a room for a number of years in a property which was subsequently purchased by L. L wrote to T and then started to gut the property around Ts room, making the bathroom unusable by removing the door and plaster from the walls. T was a shift worker and was unable to sleep during the daytime for 13 weeks before being rehoused. |

**Award:**                    £450 general damages for discomfort and breach of covenant for quiet enjoyment

                              £1,000 aggravated damages

**General Damages:**          £450

**Value of Award of £450 general damages as at April 2004: £642**

**Value of Award of £1,000 aggravated damages as at April 2004: £1,426**

*Property – Landlord & Tenant – Breach of covenant for quiet enjoyment*

---

**Name of Case:**             *Dacouri v Elungu*

**Cause/s of Action:**        Unlawful eviction

**Tribunal and Judge:**       Central London County Court – HHJ Rich QC

**Where Reported:**           December 1997 LAB 14

**Date of Award:**            August 15, 1997

**Brief Facts of Case:**      Notwithstanding the advice of the tenancy relations officer L changed the locks and evicted T (a subtenant) from the flat which L rented from the council. T was readmitted 11 days later.

**Award:**                    £2,350 total damages:

                              £1,000 general damages for the initial eviction

                              £100 for each day of exclusion

                              £250 aggravated damages as L had applied to High Court thereby complicating matters

**General Damages:**          £1,000

**Value of Award of £1,000 general damages as at April 2004: £1,172**

**Value of Award of general damages of £100 per day as at April 2004: £117**

**Value of Award of £250 aggravated damages as at April 2004: £293**

*Property – Landlord & Tenant – Unlawful eviction*

| | |
|---|---|
| **Name of Case:** | *Daniel v Harty* |
| **Cause/s of Action:** | Unlawful eviction – Breach of covenant for quiet enjoyment – Trespass to goods |
| **Tribunal and Judge:** | Edmonton County Court – DJ Morley |
| **Where Reported:** | September 1995 LAB 14 |
| **Date of Award:** | May 26, 1995 |
| **Brief Facts of Case:** | T an assured tenant was evicted by L. He had been threatened and accused of drug-dealing and theft. L's agent had forced entry and his shower had been broken, his furniture and belongings removed. He found that someone had also urinated on his bed linen. He was too frightened to stay at the property. |
| **Award:** | £22,040 total damages including: |
| | £14,000 damages under ss27-28 Housing Act 1988 |
| | £4,675 damages for trespass to goods |
| | £1,500 for breach of covenant for quiet enjoyment over 5 months |
| | £1,250 for aggravated damages for trespass |
| | £280 for disrepair to shower |
| | £250 for return of deposit |
| **General Damages:** | £2,030 |

**Value of Award of £1,500 general damages as at April 2004: £1,862**

**Value of £1,250 aggravated damages as at April 2004: £1,552**

*Property – Landlord & Tenant – Unlawful eviction – Breach of covenant for quiet enjoyment – Trespass to goods*

**Name of Case:**  *Dayalia v Umenegbu*

**Cause/s of Action:**  Unlawful eviction – Breach of covenant for quiet enjoyment

**Tribunal and Judge:**  Wandsworth County Court – HHJ Sumner

**Where Reported:**  December 1990 LAB 13

**Date of Award:**  August 28, 1990

**Brief Facts of Case:**  T agreed to temporarily leave the property for L to carry out works of repair. L failed to complete the works and after 2 years the property was uninhabitable.

**Award:**  £10,000 statutory damages based on the difference in the value of property with vacant possession and subject to the tenancy.

**Statutory Damages:**  £10,000

**Value of Award of £10,000 as at April 2004: £14,496**

*Property – Landlord & Tenant – Unlawful eviction – Breach of covenant for quiet enjoyment*

---

**Name of Case:**  *Deveries v Charlerey*

**Cause/s of Action:**  Unlawful eviction

**Tribunal and Judge:**  Edmonton County Court – HHJ Tibber

**Where Reported:**  June 1995 LAB 20

**Date of Award:**  October 25, 1994

**Brief Facts of Case:**  T occupied a bed-sit. L changed the locks and refused T access for 9 weeks, using the room for storage. L refused to pass on benefit cheques sent to T, and threatened to remove T's possessions.

**Award:**  £800 general damages

£800 aggravated damages

£800 exemplary damages

**General Damages:**    £800

**Value of Award of £800 general, aggravated and exemplary damages as at April 2004: £1,023**

*Property – Landlord & Tenant – Unlawful eviction*

---

| | |
|---|---|
| **Name of Case:** | *Dimoutsikou v Penrose* |
| **Cause/s of Action:** | Unlawful eviction |
| **Tribunal and Judge:** | Leeds County Court – DJ Bellamy |
| **Where Reported:** | October 2000 LAB 24 |
| **Date of Award:** | May 17, 2000 |
| **Brief Facts of Case:** | T occupied a property as an assured shorthold tenant. While she was on holiday L changed the lock. She was contacted by a friend to tell her she had been evicted and she returned to the UK without any accommodation. She had not been in arrears of rent. Her solicitors warned L that the eviction was unlawful but he refused to re-admit her. |
| **Award:** | £4,750 general damages for 38 days of homelessness (£125 per day) rounded up to £5,000 due to alternative accommodation being more expensive and less agreeable |
| | £1,500 aggravated damages |
| | £1,500 exemplary damages |
| | (Special damages: £338.40.) |
| **General Damages:** | £5,000 |

**Value of Award of general damages of £125 per day as at April 2004: £136**

**Value of Award of £1,500 aggravated and exemplary damages as at April 2004: £1,632**

*Property – Landlord & Tenant – Unlawful eviction*

**Name of Case:**          *Ditchfield v Devlin*

**Cause/s of Action:**     Unlawful eviction – Trespass to goods

**Tribunal and Judge:**    Chester County Court – District Judge Newman

**Where Reported:**        [1995] CLY 1849; December 1995 LAB 20

**Date of Award:**         May 22, 1995

**Brief Facts of Case:**   T occupied a flat under a tenancy agreement
                           providing for 6 months notice to quit. L
                           demanded immediate possession, threatening
                           violence with baseball bat, entered unlawfully
                           and left T's belongings on lawn, some of which
                           were stolen. T lived in hostel for the homeless for
                           11 weeks before being rehoused.

**Award:**                 £2,500 general damages to include aggravated
                           damages.

                           (Special damages: £2,414.)

**General Damages:**       £2,500

**Value of Award of £2,500 as at April 2004: £3,103**

*Property – Landlord & Tenant – Unlawful eviction*

*and*

*Property - Landlord & Tenant – Trespass to goods*

---

**Name of Case:**          *Dowden v Southwark LBC*

**Cause/s of Action:**     Unlawful eviction

**Tribunal and Judge:**    Central London County Court – Recorder
                           Simmons

**Where Reported:**        December 1997 LAB 14

**Date of Award:**         November 1, 1996

**Brief Facts of Case:**     T was locked out of her council flat. She was only temporarily absent due to a cockroach infestation but had previously breached the terms of a suspended possession order and so occupied as a tolerated trespasser.

**Award:**     £2,500 for breach of s3 Protection from Eviction Act 1977 but if she had been a tenant she would have received £4,000 for loss of her tenancy.

£1,000 aggravated damages as Homeless Persons Unit staff had laughed at her.

**General Damages:**     £2,500

**Value of Award of £2,500 general damages as at April 2004: £3,017**

**Value of award of £1,000 aggravated damages as at April 2004: £1,207**

*Property – Housing – Unlawful eviction*

---

**Name of Case:**     *Dowkes v Athelston*

**Cause/s of Action:**     Unlawful eviction – Breach of covenant of quiet enjoyment

**Tribunal and Judge:**     HH Judge T. Crowther QC

**Where Reported:**     [1993] CLY 1606; March 1993 LAB 16

**Date of Award:**     November 20, 1993

**Brief Facts of Case:**     T an assured tenant who was 6 months pregnant, had paid a returnable bond on occupation. L entered property to carry out repair work and show round prospective purchasers without notice. T refused to leave when L demanded her to vacate. Gas and electricity supplies were disconnected but reconnected after police attended. T was threatened with violence if rent was not paid prior to due date. T left and on

|  | solicitor's advice did not return but recovered most of her belongings. |
|---|---|
| **Award:** | Total: £14,742.14 comprising: |
|  | £12,200 statutory damages under s28 of Housing Act 1988 |
|  | £1,000 for breach of covenant of quiet enjoyment and trespass (no award for loss of occupation) |
|  | £1,000 exemplary damages (due to L seeking to profit from his actions) |
|  | £192.14 for trespass to goods |
| bond) | £350 for breach of contract (failure to repay |
|  | (Special damages: £192.14 and £350.) |
| **General Damages:** | £1,000 |

**Value of Award of £1,000 as at April 2004: £1,311**

*Property – Landlord & Tenant – Unlawful eviction – Breach of covenant for quiet enjoyment – Trespass to goods*

---

| **Name of Case:** | *Drane v Evangelou* |
|---|---|
| **Cause/s of Action:** | Unlawful eviction – Breach of covenant for quiet enjoyment – Trespass |
| **Tribunal and Judge:** | Court of Appeal – Lord Denning MR, Lawton and Goff LJJ |
| **Where Reported:** | [1978] 1 EGLR 30 |
| **Date of Award:** | November 11, 1977 |
| **Brief Facts of Case:** | E (landlord) gave D (weekly tenant from August 1974) notice to quit when D applied to rent |

officer for a revision of rent. The rent officer fixed a lower rent in October 1975. On 14.10.75 D's access to property was barred, the lock damaged and door bolted. E moved his in-laws into the property and failed to obey injunctions obtained by D. D only gained possession on applying to commit them for contempt. He had been kept out of the property for 10 weeks. County Court Judge awarded exemplary damages in respect of E's behaviour. E appealed.

**Award:**              £1,000 exemplary damages award upheld. (Appeal dismissed.)

**Value of Award of £1,000 exemplary damages as at April 2004: £3,911**

*Property – Landlord & Tenant – Unlawful eviction – Trespass – Breach of covenant for quiet enjoyment*

| | |
|---|---|
| **Name of Case:** | *Dursun v Bellikli* |
| **Cause/s of Action:** | Unlawful eviction |
| **Tribunal and Judge:** | Edmonton County Court – District Judge Silverman |
| **Where Reported:** | December 1994 LAB 16 |
| **Date of Award:** | July 18, 1994 |
| **Brief Facts of Case:** | L changed locks and moved his family into the property. Ts and their family spent 1 night in a hostel and 11 nights in bed and breakfast accommodation. They resumed occupation after obtaining an injunction. |
| **Award:** | £5,880 total comprising: |
| | £2,500 general damages |
| | £1,000 aggravated damages |

£2,000 exemplary damages (as L had ignored warning of tenancy relations officer)

(Special damages: £380.)

**General Damages:**   £2,500

**Value of Award of £2,500 general damages as at April 2004: £3,224**

**Value of Award of £1,000 aggravated damages as at April 2004: £1,290**

**Value of Award of £2,000 exemplary damages as at April 2004: £2,579**

*Property – Landlord & Tenant – Unlawful eviction*

---

| | |
|---|---|
| **Name of Case:** | *Fairweather v Ghafoor* |
| **Cause/s of Action:** | Unlawful eviction – Conversion of goods |
| **Tribunal and Judge:** | CC (Rawtenstall) – District Judge Geddes |
| **Where Reported:** | [2001] CLY 421 |
| **Date of Award:** | September 14, 2000 |
| **Brief Facts of Case:** | G permanently excluded F from property let under assured shorthold tenancy due to rent arrears. F unable to collect possessions (of which some had belonged to her young son who had died). F suffered anxiety and depression for between 18 months and 2 years following eviction. |
| **Award:** | £3,300 statutory damages under ss27-28 of Housing Act 1988; |
| | £300 aggravated damages made for G's conduct in withholding her belongings and at the hearing. |

**Aggravated Damages:**   £300

**Value of Award of £300 as at April 2004: £324**

*Property – Landlord & Tenant – Unlawful eviction – Trespass to goods – Conversion*

| | |
|---|---|
| **Name of Case:** | *Farthing and Hughes v Colisanti* |
| **Cause/s of Action:** | Unlawful eviction |
| **Tribunal and Judge:** | Southampton County Court – District Judge Cooper |
| **Where Reported:** | [1994] CLY 1769; December 1994 LAB 16 |
| **Date of Award:** | June 14, 1994 |
| **Brief Facts of Case:** | Ts became joint assured tenants of a bed-sit in February 1992. L gave them 2 weeks' notice to vacate following delays in housing benefit in April 1992. Ts refused and L removed fuses from circuits for heating and hot water. L visited property with followers, intimidated Ts, put their possessions onto the street and took away their keys. Ts spent several weeks sleeping on floors and 6 months in bed and breakfast before finding other accommodation. |
| **Award:** | £3,000 general damages and £750 aggravated damages to each T set off against £9,000 Housing Act 1988 damages (divided equally between the Ts) |
| | £1,500 exemplary damages |
| | (Statutory damages of £9,000.) |
| **General Damages:** | £3,000 |

**Value of Award of £3,000 general damages as at April 2004: £3,850**

**Value of Award of £1,500 exemplary damages as at April 2004: £1,925**

*Property – Landlord & Tenant – Unlawful eviction*
*Landlord & Tenant – Unlawful eviction*

**Name of Case:**          *Foxall v Akram*

**Cause/s of Action:**     Unlawful eviction

**Tribunal and Judge:**    Birmingham County Court – HHJ Wilson-Mellor

**Where Reported:**        September 1995 LAB 14

**Date of Award:**         July 4, 1995

**Brief Facts of Case:**   T an assured tenant returned home from staying with her mother to find that L had changed the locks. She was 7 months pregnant. She stayed with her mother for a year before obtaining council accommodation.

**Award:**                 £1,000 general damages

                           £1,000 aggravated damages

**General Damages:**       £1,000

**Value of Award of £1,000 as at April 2004: £1,245**

*Property – Landlord & Tenant – Unlawful eviction*

---

**Name of Case:**          *Francis v Brown*

**Cause/s of Action:**     Unlawful eviction

**Tribunal and Judge:**    Court of Appeal – Simon Brown and Peter Gibson LJJ and Sir Iain Glidewell

**Where Reported:**        (1998) 30 HLR 143; September 1997 LAB 17

**Date of Award:**         April 30, 1997

**Brief Facts of Case:**   F was granted a tenancy of a flat by landlord (B's mother). Landlord gave F notice to quit intending to sell the property to B with vacant possession. Landlord and B evicted F. B was convicted of unlawfully depriving F of her occupation under the Protection from Eviction Act 1977 and fined.

F issued proceedings against landlord and B. The judge awarded:

- £1,000 "exemplary" damages against landlord and B
- £40,000 "aggravated" damages against landlord
- £40,000 damages under ss27 & 28 Housing Act 1988 against B (and if this was wrong in law he indicated he would award the statutory damages against landlord and the "aggravated" damages against B)
- special damages against landlord and B.

B appealed on the ground that damages could not be awarded against her as she was not F's landlord. The Court treated the award of aggravated damages as an award for exemplary damages and vice versa and considered whether if statutory damages could not be awarded, an exemplary damages award should be made.

**Award:**    £2,500 total damages against B (reduced from £42,500) comprising £1,000 exemplary damages and the balance for special damages.

(£40,000 statutory damages award and award of exemplary damages against B set aside − as no award of exemplary damages could be made against landlord in addition to statutory damages.)

(Special damages: £1,500.)

**Exemplary Damages:**    £1,000

**Value of Award of £1,000 exemplary damages as at April 2004: £1,188**

*Property − Landlord & Tenant − Unlawful eviction*

**Name of Case:**          *Frankland v Dawkins and Asombang*

**Cause/s of Action:**     Unlawful eviction – Breach of covenant for quiet enjoyment

**Tribunal and Judge:**    West London County Court – Recorder Merriman

**Where Reported:**        March 1998 LAB 13

**Date of Award:**         January 19, 1997

**Brief Facts of Case:**   P was an assured shorthold tenant of a flat in a converted house. His landlord had agreed to sell the house to D1. D1 renovated the flat over a 10-week period. For 10 days P had no gas, no hot water and only 1 cold-water tap. He was threatened by D2 on 2 occasions. The locks were changed and T was evicted.

**Award:**                 £2,000 for breach of covenant for quiet enjoyment

                           £2,750 damages under s27 Housing act 1988

**General Damages:**       £2,000

**Value of Award of £2,000 as at April 2004: £2,405**

*Property – Landlord & Tenant - Unlawful eviction – Breach of covenant for quiet enjoyment*

---

**Name of Case:**          *Friedlander and Whitfield v Painter*

**Cause/s of Action:**     Unlawful eviction – Breach of covenant for quiet enjoyment

**Tribunal and Judge:**    Ilford County Court – HH Judge Birkett-Baker QC

**Where Reported:**        [1994] CLY 1766; June 1994 LAB 12

**Date of Award:**         April 13, 1994

**Brief Facts of Case:** F and W were assured tenants of a flat let by P and fell into arrears. P visited property and frightened one of the tenants by threatening to return to remove her and her partner and retain their belongings. The couple spent 3 weeks with relatives and 6 weeks in a motel before being provided accommodation by local authority.

**Award:** Total of £1,050 general damages, comprising 3 weeks at £75 for each tenant whilst staying with relatives and 6 weeks at £50 for each tenant for their stay in the motel.

**General Damages:** £1,050

**Value of Award of general damages of £75 per week as at April 2004: £97**

**Value of Award of general damages of £50 per week as at April 2004: £64**

*Property - Landlord & Tenant – Unlawful eviction – Breach of covenant for quiet enjoyment*

---

**Name of Case:** *Ghanie v Brade*

**Cause/s of Action:** Unlawful eviction – Breach of covenant for quiet enjoyment – Trespass to goods

**Tribunal and Judge:** Mayor's and City of London County Court – HHJ Byrt QC

**Where Reported:** December 1997 LAB 14

**Date of Award:** September 2, 1997

**Brief Facts of Case:** T was an assured tenant. L's father harassed and intimidated him and then evicted him causing him personal injury. T was unable to recover any of his possessions.

**Award:**                   £5,000 statutory damages

                            £3,000 for breach of covenant for quiet
                            enjoyment

                            £1,000 aggravated damages

                            £750 damages for personal injury

                            £1,500 aggravated damages against L's father

                            £6,500 damages for trespass to goods

**General Damages:**         £3,000

**Value of Award of £3,000 general damages as at April 2004: £3,497**

**Value of Award of £1,000 aggravated damages as at April 2004: £1,167**

**Value of Award of £1,500 aggravated damages as at April 2004: £1,749**

*Property – Landlord & Tenant – Unlawful eviction – Breach of covenant
for quiet enjoyment – Trespass to goods*

---

**Name of Case:**            *Giles v Adley*

**Cause/s of Action:**       Unlawful eviction -Breach of covenant for quiet
                            enjoyment

**Tribunal and Judge:**      Southampton County Court – Assistant Recorder
                            Boothman

**Where Reported:**          March 1987 LAB 21, June 1987 LAB 18, [1987]
                            1 CL 170b

**Date of Award:**           December 1, 1986

**Brief Facts of Case:**     T occupied a bed-sit in a house in multiple
                            occupation under a Rent Act protected tenancy. L
                            entered his room, removed his possessions and

changed the locks. T was forced to sleep rough for a few nights and subsequently found alternative accommodation.

**Award:**          £500 general damages for inconvenience to T (to include discomfort of sleeping rough; having to stay with friends and shock) and £500 exemplary damages.

**General Damages:**          £500

**Value of Awards of £500 as at April 2004: £932**

*Property – Landlord & Tenant – Breach of covenant for quiet enjoyment*

---

**Name of Case:**          *Goodman v Skomorowska*

**Cause/s of Action:**          Unlawful eviction

**Tribunal and Judge:**          Clerkenwell County Court

**Where Reported:**          February 1991 LAB 24; June 1991 LAB 12

**Date of Award:**          October 12, 1991

**Brief Facts of Case:**          G occupied a room in a property owned by S since November 1988. On 31 October 1989 he returned home at 1am and found that his possessions had been bundled into black bags in the greenhouse. The lock to his room had been changed and S would not allow him to re-enter the property even in the presence of the police. G was forced to spend the night on Hampstead Heath.

Later that day an *ex parte* injunction was granted and immediately served on S with which she failed to comply. At the hearing of an application on 2 November to commit her to prison, S undertook to allow G re-entry. G returned and found the room to be uninhabitable due to the fact that S was redecorating. He was unable to resume occupation until 4 November.

**Award:**          On the basis G was out of occupation for 5 days:

£500 aggravated damages

£1,500 exemplary damages

**Value of Award of £500 aggravated damages as at April 2004: £687**

**Value of Award of £1,500 exemplary damages as at April 2004: £2,062**

*Property – Landlord & Tenant – Unlawful eviction*

---

| | |
|---|---|
| **Name of Case:** | *Grey v Barnett* |
| **Cause/s of Action:** | Breach of covenant for quiet enjoyment |
| **Tribunal and Judge:** | Mr Registrar Palmer |
| **Where Reported:** | [1989] CLY 1177; June 1989 LAB 22 |
| **Date of Award:** | June 22, 1988 |
| **Brief Facts of Case:** | Ts 1,2 & 3 were long leaseholders of flats in L's house. T4 occupied ground floor under Rent Act protected tenancy. L arranged to remove roof of house without notice to Ts to build an extra storey. |
| **Award:** | General damages for distress, hardship and inconvenience of building works carried out over a period of 16 months causing intermittent water penetration into flats over 3 month period. |
| | T1 - £800 (due to being confined to one room for 2 weeks and losing part of his holiday) |
| | Ts 2 & 3 - £1,000 each (due to being confined to 1 room for 4 weeks and who had a child aged 1 year) |
| | T4 - £275 |

**Value of Award of £800 general damages as at April 2004: £1,394**

**Value of Award of £1,000 general damages as at April 2004: £1,742**

**Value of Award of £275 general damages as at April 2004: £479**

*Property - Landlord & Tenant – Breach of covenant for quiet enjoyment*

| | |
|---|---|
| **Name of Case:** | *Grillo v Cant and Bassairi Ltd* |
| **Cause/s of Action:** | Unlawful eviction |
| **Tribunal and Judge:** | Central London County Court – HHJ Butter QC |
| **Where Reported:** | March 1998 LAB13 |
| **Date of Award:** | November 17, 1997 |
| **Brief Facts of Case:** | P was an assured tenant of a room. Six months after the start of the tenancy and shortly after D2 had acquired the property D1 evicted P and put her possessions in black dustbin bags in the communal stairway. P spent 2 nights sleeping on the stairway to protect her effects and then slept on a friend's sofa for 2 weeks. She found alternative accommodation but on an assured shorthold tenancy. |
| **Award:** | £6,000 damages for loss of the assured tenancy |
| | £2,000 for the manner of the eviction |
| | £1,000 exemplary damages |
| | (Special damages: £45.) |
| **General Damages:** | £8,000 |

**Value of Award of £8,000 general damages as at April 2004: £9,308**

**Value of Award of £1,000 exemplary damages as at April 2004: £1,164**

*Property – Landlord & Tenant – Unlawful eviction*

**Name of Case:**          *Grocia v Flint, Flint and Doyle*

**Cause/s of Action:**     Unlawful eviction

**Tribunal and Judge:**    Wandsworth County Court – Miss Recorder
                           Baxendale QC

**Where Reported:**        March 1993 LAB 15

**Date of Award:**         December 11, 1992

**Brief Facts of Case:**   T withheld rent due to damage to the bed-sit he
                           occupied. Ls and their agents removed his
                           possessions and re-let the room at a higher rent.
                           Some of his belongings were eventually returned
                           but in a poor state.

**Award:**                 £15,829 total damages

                           £3,329 statutory damages

                           £1,000 aggravated damages against each
                           defendant

                           £1,000 exemplary damages against each
                           defendant

                           (Special damages: £6,529 were awarded.)

**General Damages:**       £4,500

**Value of Award of £4,500 general damages as at April 2004: £6,003**

**Value of Award of £1,000 exemplary damages as at April 2004: £1,334**

**Value of Award of £1,000 aggravated damages as at April 2004: £1,334**

*Property – Landlord & Tenant – Unlawful eviction*

**Name of Case:**       *Harland v Chadda*

**Cause/s of Action:**   Breach of covenant for quiet enjoyment

**Tribunal and Judge:**  Southampton County Court – DJ Edwards

**Where Reported:**      [1997] CLY 3254; December 1997 LAB 14

**Date of Award:**       March 14,1997

**Brief Facts of Case:** T occupied a bed sit under an assured tenancy. He admitted causing nuisance and annoyance to another occupier. T was wrongly accused by L when the bed sit and other parts were damaged following a burglary. L changed the locks and refused to allow T to collect his possessions. T was homeless for a few days before securing alternative accommodation.

**Award:**               £2,200 general damages (including aggravated damages)

                         £200 for lost belongings

**General Damages:**     £2,200

**Value of Award of £2,200 as at April 2004: £2,629**

*Property – Landlord & Tenant – Breach of covenant for quiet enjoyment*

---

**Name of Case:**       *Hasan Hanif v Robinson*

**Cause/s of Action:**   Unlawful eviction

**Tribunal and Judge:**  Court of Appeal

**Where Reported:**      September 1991 LAB 22

**Date of Award:**       June 6, 1992

**Brief Facts of Case:**      L had obtained a possession order whilst T on holiday on the basis that he was a returning owner occupier under Schedule 15 Case 11 of the Rent Act 1977. Before T's application to have the order set aside could be heard L and son evicted T from the flat. T did not resume occupation and issued proceedings. L maintained the eviction was lawful on the basis of the possession order.

The Court found that the eviction was unlawful because execution of an order against a protected tenant was by the issue of a warrant for possession.

**Award:**                    The Court of Appeal upheld the awards made in the county court of:

£26,000 statutory damages under ss27-28 Housing Act 1988

£2,000 for post-viral fatigue syndrome suffered by T

£4,000 rent arrears were set-off against the awards.

(Special damages: £700 for loss of property.)

**Statutory Damages:**      £26,000

**Value of Award of £26,000 as at April 2004: £34,660**

*Property – Landlord & Tenant – Unlawful eviction*

| | |
|---|---|
| **Name of Case:** | *Hazell v Lemus* |
| **Cause/s of Action:** | Unlawful eviction |
| **Tribunal and Judge:** | Bow County Court – District Judge Read |
| **Where Reported:** | September 1992 LAB 23 |
| **Date of Award:** | June 18, 1992 |

**Brief Facts of Case:**    T occupied a bed-sit and notified L that his rent would be delayed due to the processing of his housing benefit claim. L moved T to another bed-sit which was in disrepair. The next day he evicted T keeping all T's possessions. An injunction was granted but it could not be served and T had to move to hostel accommodation.

**Award:**    £10,080 total damages and interest including:

£4,500 general damages

£1,000 aggravated damages

£2,000 exemplary damages

(Special damages: £1,705.)

**General Damages:**    £4,500

**Value of Award of £4,500 general damages as at April 2004: £5,999**

**Value of Award of £2,000 exemplary damages as at April 2004: £2,666**

**Value of Award of £1,000 aggravated damages as at April 2004: £1,333**

*Property – Landlord & Tenant – Unlawful eviction*

**Name of Case:**       *Hodgson v Jacobs*

**Cause/s of Action:**       Breach of covenant for quiet enjoyment

**Tribunal and Judge:**       Edmonton County Court – HHJ Hatton

**Where Reported:**       [1984] 12 CL 88; March 1985 LAB 42

**Date of Award:**       November 12, 1984

**Brief Facts of Case:**       P was 67 years of age and since 1967 had occupied the ground floor flat of a converted 2-storey house. From March 1983 D who had bought the entire premises and moved into the first floor flat, began to continually harass P with the object of obtaining vacant possession. He entered her flat and caused plaster on the ceiling of her bedroom to fall due to excessive banging. P was frightened and slept for a total of 12 months in the living room on a mattress and then a camp bed. She vacated after 15 months.

**Award:**       £2,500 damages for breach of quiet enjoyment (including aggravated and exemplary damages) owing to factors such as P's age, the stress she suffered and the commercial profit made by D as a result of his actions.

**Value of Award of £2,500 as at April 2004: £5,106**

*Property – Landlord & Tenant – Breach of covenant for quiet enjoyment*

---

**Name of Case:**       *Irzoki v Hamed*

**Cause/s of Action:**       Unlawful eviction

**Tribunal and Judge:**       Bloomsbury County Court – HHJ Quarren Evans

**Where Reported:**       December 1991 LAB 19

**Date of Award:**       September 2, 1991

**Brief Facts of Case:** T occupied L's flat since March 1991. Following delays in the rent due to housing benefit problems T returned to find the locks changed and his possessions removed. T obtained two court orders before resuming occupation but was then forced to vacate when the mortgagee obtained a possession order in February 1991. T agreed to leave in August.

**Award:** £5,650 total damages:

General damages of £100 per day that T out of occupation (21 days)

£1,000 aggravated damages

£2,500 exemplary damages

(Special damages: £1,050.)

**General Damages:** £100 per day

**Value of Award of £100 general damages per day as at April 2004: £138**

**Value of Award of £1,000 aggravated damages as at April 2004: £1,380**

**Value of Award of £2,500 exemplary damages as at April 2004: £3,449**

*Property – Landlord & Tenant – Unlawful eviction*

---

**Name of Case:** *Jenkins v Deen*

**Cause/s of Action:** Unlawful eviction

**Tribunal and Judge:** Cardiff County Court – District Judge Hendicott

**Where Reported:** March 1993 LAB 16

**Date of Award:** January 18, 1993

| | |
|---|---|
| **Brief Facts of Case:** | L evicted T notwithstanding a warning from the local housing advice centre. L had threatened T and pushed him across the room. T obtained an injunction but due to problems of service was out of occupation for 13 days during which time he had to sleep on his parents' sofa. |
| **Award:** | £1,500 general damages |
| | £1,000 exemplary damages |
| | £1,000 aggravated damages |
| | (Special damages: £200.) |
| **General Damages:** | £1,500 |

**Value of Award of £1,500 general damages as at April 2004: £2,020**

**Value of Awards of aggravated and exemplary damages of £1,000 as at April 2004: £1,347**

*Property – Landlord & Tenant – Unlawful eviction*

---

| | |
|---|---|
| **Name of Case:** | *JS Bloor (Measham) Ltd v Calcott* |
| **Cause/s of Action:** | Trespass |
| **Tribunal and Judge:** | Chancery Division – Hart J |
| **Where Reported:** | [2002] 09 EG 222 |
| **Date of Award:** | November 23, 2001 |
| **Brief Facts of Case:** | B purchased 38 acres of agricultural land with planning permission from W for £2.5 million on 1 July 1997.On 28 July1997 B entered the land to start development and learnt of an agricultural tenancy of the land granted to C by W in 1993. The tenancy was protected by the Agricultural Holdings Act 1986 and had been intended for the period 1 November 1992 to 31 November 1993 but owing to C's delay in signing the agreement less than 12 months of the term remained by June 1993.C commenced proceedings against B in August claiming damages for trespass (including aggravated damages) and an injunction |

restraining entry and requiring the removal of B's equipment and an interlocutory injunction to restrain B from continuing to work on the land. B's counterclaim was for the rescission of the 1993 agreement. C recovered £1,200 damages from B for trespass (not including aggravated damages) in the county court but the judge found that C was not entitled to equitable relief due to its deceit in avoiding signing the 1993 agreement and encouraging W to act to its detriment and not take steps to end the tenancy. C's claim for an injunction and B's counterclaim were dismissed.

B served a notice to quit terminating C's tenancy on June 2000 and in October 1997 commenced proceedings seeking a declaration that it was entitled to occupy the land and continue development on the basis that a proprietary estoppel had arisen due to C's behaviour. C counterclaimed for damages for breach of covenant for quiet enjoyment and trespass arguing that a 1986 Act tenancy could not be defeated by proprietary estoppel.

Held: claim allowed. B entitled to possession between October 1997 and June 2000. The equitable remedy of proprietary estoppel was not barred by county court order. Nothing in 1986 Act prevented B from asserting claim either positively (by claiming the right to use the land) or negatively (in denying C's damages for such use). In trespass claimant elects to recover damages representing either loss to him or value of benefit to defendant.

**Award:**     If so entitled to damages C would have been entitled to the tenancy rental value between October 1997 and June 2000.

*Property – Agricultural tenancy –Trespass*

**Name of Case:** *Kaur v Gill*

**Cause/s of Action:** Breach of covenant for quiet enjoyment – Unlawful eviction

**Tribunal and Judge:** Court of Appeal

**Where Reported:** *The Times* 15 June 1995, CA; September 1995 LAB 14

**Date of Award:** 1995

**Brief Facts of Case:** L appealed against HHJ Orme's award of £500 for breach of covenant for quiet enjoyment and £15,000 for unlawful eviction under ss27-28 Housing Act 1988. L relying on *Mason v Nwokerie* (1993) *The Times* 19 October, maintained that the common law damages should have been set off against the statutory award.

**Award:** £15,500 damages award upheld.

(Appeal dismissed. *Mason v Nwokerie* distinguished as in this case general damages were awarded for breaches of covenant and not loss of right to occupy.)

**General Damages:** £15,500

**Value of Award of £15,500 as at April 2004: £19,240**

*Property – Landlord & Tenant – Breach of covenant for quiet enjoyment – Unlawful eviction*

| | |
|---|---|
| **Name of Case:** | *King v Jackson* |
| **Cause/s of Action:** | Unlawful eviction – Breach of covenant for quiet enjoyment |
| **Tribunal and Judge:** | Court of Appeal – Morritt and Pill LJJ |
| **Where Reported:** | September 1997 LAB 17; (1998) 30 HLR 541; [1998] 1 EGLR 30 |
| **Date of Award:** | July 16, 1997 |

**Brief Facts of Case:**

In March 1994 L let flat to T on an assured shorthold tenancy for 6 months. In April T orally gave L 4 weeks' notice to quit expiring on May 12 1994. L advertised and showed a prospective tenant around with T's consent on May 1. On May 5 L asked T in writing to leave as she was in rent arrears. On May 6 whilst T was out L entered flat and changed the locks.

Judge awarded statutory damages of £11,000 under ss27-28 of Housing Act 1988 but directed that if he was incorrect damages of £1,500 for breach of covenant for quiet enjoyment should be awarded. L appealed.

Court of Appeal held that L had acted in reliance on the agreement with T that she would leave on May 12. T was estopped from resiling from the agreement.

**Award:**

£1,500 damages for breach of quiet enjoyment to be substituted for £11,000 statutory damages to reflect that at the time of her eviction T's right to occupy was limited to a further 6 days. Award of statutory damages was manifestly wrong.

**General Damages:** £1,500

**Value of Award of £1,500 as at April 2004: £1,767**

*Property – Landlord & Tenant – Unlawful eviction – Breach of covenant for quiet enjoyment*

**Name of Case:**          *King Jackson and Dodd v Isleham Marina*

**Cause/s of Action:**     Breach of covenant of quiet enjoyment –
                           Harassment

**Tribunal and Judge:**    Cambridge County Court – District Judge Kirby

**Where Reported:**        [1996] CLY 3734; March 1997 LAB 14

**Date of Award:**         October 8, 1996

**Brief Facts of Case:**   Ts were long lessees of 3 holiday chalets on
                           development owned by L. There had been a long-
                           running dispute over service charges. Other
                           lessees had obtained undertakings as part of court
                           proceedings to stop L from harassing them. L's
                           workmen arranged to saw lengths out of the
                           sewage pipes to Ts properties which left them
                           uninhabitable for one week.

**Award:**                 £500 aggravated damages to each T.
                           (DJ Kirby made the award on the basis that L
                           told Ts what had been done immediately. If L
                           had not told Ts about the pipes the damages
                           would have been higher.)

**Value of Award of £500 aggravated damages as at April 2004: £604**

*Property – Landlord & Tenant – Harassment*

---

**Name of Case:**          *Kinsella v Bi and Rashid*

**Cause/s of Action:**     Unlawful eviction – trespass to goods

**Tribunal and Judge:**    Birmingham County Court – HHJ Harris

**Where Reported:**        September 1994 LAB 13

**Date of Award:**         April 13, 1994

**Brief Facts of Case:** L changed lock to T's home following delays in the payment of T's housing benefit. T was unable to resume occupation. Only some of his possessions were returned following the grant of an injunction.

**Award:** £12,850 total damages comprising:

£11,000 statutory damages (representing the difference between the value of the house tenanted and with vacant possession)

£450 for loss of use of personal effects

£500 for distress

(Special damages: £900.)

**General Damages:** £950

**Value of Award of £500 general damages for distress as at April 2004: £644**

*Property – Landlord & Tenant – Unlawful eviction – Trespass to goods*

**Name of Case:** *Kirkham v Mason*

**Cause/s of Action:** Breach of covenant for quiet enjoyment

**Tribunal and Judge:** Bow County Court – HHJ Butter QC

**Where Reported:** September 1993 LAB 17

**Date of Award:** July 13, 1993

**Brief Facts of Case:** T an assured tenant was evicted after building society had obtained a possession order against L owing to L's mortgage arrears.

**Award:** £2,500 general damages for loss of assured tenancy.

(Special damages: £800 occupation expenses and removal expenses.)

**General Damages:**     £2,500

**Value of Award of £2,500 as at April 2004: £3,300**

*Property – Landlord & Tenant – Breach of covenant for quiet enjoyment*

---

| | |
|---|---|
| **Name of Case:** | *Kuik and Baker v Cook* |
| **Cause/s of Action:** | Unlawful eviction |
| **Tribunal and Judge:** | Bournemouth County Court – HH Judge Foley QC |
| **Where Reported:** | March 1995 LAB 13; [1994] CLY 1768 |
| **Date of Award:** | November 4, 1994 |
| **Brief Facts of Case:** | When two out of four joint tenants vacated the property the remaining Ts fell into arrears. L threatened physically to evict them and their belongings unless the rent was paid and so the Ts vacated. |
| **Award:** | To each T: £500 general damages and £250 aggravated damages. |
| **General Damages:** | £500 |

**Value of Award of £500 general damages as at April 2004: £639**

**Value of Award of £250 aggravated damages as at April 2004: £320**

*Property – Landlord & Tenant – Unlawful eviction*

---

**Name of Case:**   *Lally v Whiteley*

**Cause/s of Action:**   Breach of covenant to repair – breach of covenant for quiet enjoyment

**Tribunal and Judge:**   Liverpool County Court – HHJ Downey

**Where Reported:**   [1995] CLY 1852

**Date of Award:**   December 21, 1994

**Brief Facts of Case:**   T (who lived alone) was required to vacate a 4-bedroom property for 8 weeks whilst L carried out works of repair. Local authority placed him in a 1-bedroom flat which was cramped due to storage of T's furniture.

**Award:**   £500 general damages for the inconvenience of having to live in flat for 8 weeks.

**General Damages:**   £500

**Value of Award of £500 as at April 2004: £636**

*Property – Landlord & Tenant – Breach of covenant to repair – Breach of covenant for quiet enjoyment*

---

**Name of Case:**   *Lane v Baig*

**Cause/s of Action:**   Breach of covenant for quiet enjoyment

**Tribunal and Judge:**   Cardiff County Court – Deputy District Judge Williams

**Where Reported:**   [1994] CLY 1449; December 1994 LAB 16

**Date of Award:**   March 3, 1994

**Brief Facts of Case:**   T, his wife and 2 children occupied a flat let by L who after 12 months started to demand entry to the property, was abusive to T's wife and threatened violence to T's family and damage to his property. L entered the flat on occasions without consent of T or his wife. T was intimidated, vacated the property with his family and found alternative accommodation.

**Award:**　　　　　£750 damages for breach of covenant for quiet enjoyment due to T experiencing L's threat against his sister first-hand and being frightened by it and his being aware of the effect of L's conduct towards his wife and family, causing them to move.

**General Damages:**　　£750

**Value of Award of £750 as at April 2004: £977**

*Property – Landlord & Tenant – Breach of covenant for quiet enjoyment*

---

**Name of Case:**　　　*Lawson v Hartley-Brown*

**Cause/s of Action:**　Breach of covenant for quiet enjoyment – Trespass - derogation from grant

**Tribunal and Judge:**　Court of Appeal – Hirst and Aldous LJJ and Forbes J

**Where Reported:**　　(1996) 71 P&CR 242

**Date of Award:**　　November 8, 1995

**Brief Facts of Case:**　T was tenant of retail premises which L was to redevelop by adding 2 additional floors. T sought possession of roof and air space over unit by bringing proceedings in the County Court which were consolidated with proceedings in the High Court. In 1998 L served notice to terminate the tenancy under s25 Landlord and Tenant Act 1954. T applied for the grant of a new tenancy. This was subsequently withdrawn and T vacated in 1992. L brought proceedings for arrears of rent which were consolidated with the other proceedings.

T appealed against County Court Judge's award of £20 nominal damages for trespass by L of flat roof which had been demised to T.

**Award:** £8,100 damages for trespass (equivalent to 1 ½ years rent) based on the bargain that may have been struck by a willing lessor and lessee taking into account the advantage to L, the disturbance and potential loss of profit to T.(Appeal allowed in part.)

**General Damages:** £8,100

**Value of Award of £8,100 as at April 2004: £10,041**

*Property – Breach of Covenant for Quiet Enjoyment – Derogation from Grant – Trespass*

---

| | |
|---|---|
| **Name of Case:** | *Levi v Gordon* |
| **Cause/s of Action:** | Breach of covenant of quiet enjoyment |
| **Tribunal and Judge:** | Bloomsbury County Court – HHJ Martin QC |
| **Where Reported:** | December 1991 LAB 19; for facts see *Hampstead & Highgate Express* 2 August 1991 |
| **Date of Award:** | July 29, 1991 |
| **Brief Facts of Case:** | Long lessee suffered from freeholder's behaviour over a period of 6 years. She had trapped his hand in a door and punched him in the face. She pulled down estate agents' boards when he was trying to sell his flat. |
| **General Damages:** | £18,000 |
| **Award:** | £18,000 damages. |

**Value of Award of £18,000 as at April 2004: £24,982**

*Property – Landlord & Tenant – Breach of covenant of quiet enjoyment*

---

**Name of Case:**            *Loasby v Quadhri*

**Cause/s of Action:**        Unlawful eviction

**Tribunal and Judge:**       Reading County Court

**Where Reported:**           March 1990 LAB 16

**Date of Award:**            December 15, 1989

**Brief Facts of Case:**      Ts were forced to move from bed-sit to other smaller accommodation and then evicted from that accommodation also.

**Award:**                    Assessed on the difference between the vacant possession and tenanted values of the 2 properties:

£4,500 damages for the first eviction

£4,000 damages for the second eviction

**General Damages:**          £8,500

**Value of Awards of £8,500 at April 2004: £13,287**

*Property – Landlord & Tenant – Unlawful eviction*

---

**Name of Case:**            *Lord and Haslewood-Ogram v Jessop*

**Cause/s of Action:**        Unlawful eviction – Breach of covenant for quiet enjoyment

**Tribunal and Judge:**       Court of Appeal

**Where Reported:**           August 1999 LAB 28

**Date of Award:**            April 21, 1999

**Brief Facts of Case:**      L and H occupied bed-sits with shared use of toilet and bathroom. L fell into arrears due to reduction in benefit entitlement. J threatened her with eviction, telephoning her daily, entered her home without consent was aggressive and threatened violence. J changed the locks and refused to issue her with a key. L suffered from stress and her health was affected. She attempted suicide. H complained about the lack of heating and whilst she was out J changed the locks and deposited her belongings outside leaving her in the clothes she was still wearing.

**Award:**

For L £5,716.99 including:

£1,000 damages for breach of covenant of quiet enjoyment prior to eviction

£2,000 damages for unlawful eviction

£2,000 aggravated damages

For H £4,948.95 including:

£1,000 damages for breach of covenant of quiet enjoyment prior to eviction

£2,000 damages for unlawful eviction

£1,000 aggravated damages

(Special damages: for L: £420; for H: £430.)

**General Damages for L: £5,000**

**General Damages for H: £4,000**

**Value of Award of £5,000 as at April 2004: £5,620**

**Value of Award of £4,000 as at April 2004: £4,496**

*Property – Landlord & Tenant – Unlawful eviction – Breach of covenant for quiet enjoyment*

| | |
|---|---|
| **Name of Case:** | *Malik v Majid* |
| **Cause/s of Action:** | Breach of covenant for quiet enjoyment – Harassment |
| **Tribunal and Judge:** | Central London County Court – HHJ Greenwood |
| **Where Reported:** | November 1999 LAB 29 |
| **Date of Award:** | August 4, 1999 |
| **Brief Facts of Case:** | T was aged 77 and suffered from ill-health. He occupied two ground floor rooms under a 1-year assured shorthold fixed term tenancy. His daughter and family rented the upper floor. When she moved out L moved four young people in and told them that T would move out if they made his life difficult. One of them, encouraged by L's agent broke into his room and removed his personal effects. T was rehoused 17 months later. He was suffering from distress. |
| **Award:** | £4,750 damages for breach of covenant and trespass including an exemplary award. |
| **General Damages:** | £4,750 |

**Value of Award of £4,750 as at April 2004: £5,330**

*Property – Landlord & Tenant – Breach of covenant for quiet enjoyment – Harassment*

---

| | |
|---|---|
| **Name of Case:** | *Mangan v Kincaide* |
| **Cause/s of Action:** | Unlawful eviction |
| **Tribunal and Judge:** | Birmingham County Court – HHJ Bray |
| **Where Reported:** | September 1993 LAB 17 |
| **Date of Award:** | March 12, 1993 |

**Brief Facts of Case:**     T had rented a room since 1987. Resident L refused to give T a key to her room after her bag was stolen. L was annoyed when T went to CAB for advice and grabbed her neck and pushed her down stairs before kicking her and pushing her down more stairs. She was in pain for 4 weeks.

**Award:**     £4,948 total damages:

£350 general damages

£1,000 aggravated damages

£1,000 exemplary damages

£2,548 statutory damages on basis that if L were to sell T would become a Rent Act protected tenant. The difference between the rent she was paying and the rent that could be charged by a new landlord was £7 per week. The award was based on £7 per week over 7 years.

**General Damages:**     £350

**Value of Award of £350 as at April 2004: £467**

**Value of Award of £1,000 aggravated damages as at April 2004: £1,333**

**Value of Award of £1,000 exemplary damages as at April 2004: £1,333**

*Property – Landlord & Tenant – Unlawful eviction*

**Name of Case:**          *Mason v Nwcorrie*

**Cause/s of Action:**     Unlawful eviction

**Tribunal and Judge:**    Court of Appeal – Dillon LJ and Hollis J

**Where Reported:**        December 1992 LAB 20; [1993] EGCS 161;
                           (1993) *The Times* 19 October; December 1993
                           LAB 12

**Date of Award:**         October 11, 1993

**Brief Facts of Case:**   T shared house with resident L under a restricted
                           contract. L served notice to quit on T and after 14
                           days denied T access and bundled T's
                           possessions in dustbin bags. T was forced to
                           spend six months without permanent
                           accommodation either sleeping rough or staying
                           with friends. T had a history of mental and
                           emotional illness.

                           L appealed against the award of HHJ Goldstein
                           (sitting at Bow County Court) of £6,000 damages
                           including:

                           £500 general damages

                           £1,000 exemplary damages

                           £4,500 statutory damages

                           Damages were assessed on the diminished value
                           of the property with a tenant who could lawfully
                           be removed from the property within 6 months.

**Award:**                 Total damages reduced to £4,500.

                           (The common law award should have been set
                           off against the statutory award.)

**General Damages:**       £4,500

**Value of Award of £4,500 as at April 2004: £5,893**

**Value of Award of £1,000 exemplary damages as at April 2004: £1,310**

*Property – Landlord & Tenant – Unlawful eviction*

**Name of Case:**          *McCaffrey v Ekango*

**Cause/s of Action:**     Unlawful eviction

**Tribunal and Judge:**    Willesden County Court – District Judge Morris

**Where Reported:**        March 1992 LAB 15

**Date of Award:**         January 13, 1992

**Brief Facts of Case:**   T fell into arrears with his rent for the bed-sit room he occupied due to delays with his housing benefit payments. Notwithstanding warnings from the council's tenancy relations officer, L unlawfully evicted him. T had to stay with friends for 2 months before finding alternative accommodation.

(Special damages: £240.)

**Award:**                 £7,160 total damages:

£3,920 general damages

£1,000 aggravated damages

£2,000 exemplary damages

**General Damages:**       £3,920

**Value of Award of £3,920 as at April 2004: £5,368**

**Value of Award of £1,000 aggravated damages as at April 2004: £1,369**

**Value of Award of £2,000 exemplary damages as at April 2004: £2,739**

*Property – Landlord & Tenant – Unlawful eviction*

| | |
|---|---|
| **Name of Case:** | *McCormack v Namjou* |
| **Cause/s of Action:** | Unlawful eviction |
| **Tribunal and Judge:** | Bloomsbury County Court – HH Judge Edwards |
| **Where Reported:** | [1990] CLY 1725; December 1990 LAB 13 |
| **Date of Award:** | December 21, 1989 |
| **Brief Facts of Case:** | T occupied flat with son holding over as statutory tenant paying rent. L told T he wanted him to vacate. Despite written warning to L by council official against unlawful eviction of T, locks were changed and T's son was assaulted in the process. T and son allowed back into flat following grant of an injunction, having incurred hotel, food and clothing expenses |
| **Award:** | £1,260 general damages (7 days @ £180 per day); |
| | £1,500 aggravated damages to reflect severity of the case without excuse including assault on T's son) |
| | £2,000 exemplary damages for deliberate attempt to flout the law |
| | Total: £4,760 |
| **General Damages:** | £1,260 |

**Value of Award of £1,260 as at April 2004: £1,970**

**Value of Award of £180 per day as at April 2004: £281**

**Value of Award of £1,500 aggravated damages as at April 2004: £2,345**

**Value of Award of £2,000 exemplary damages as at April 2004: £3,126**

*Property – Landlord & Tenant – Unlawful eviction*

**Name of Case:**      *McLaren v Walker*

**Cause/s of Action:**      Unlawful eviction

**Tribunal and Judge:**      Bloomsbury County Court – HHJ Dobry QC

**Where Reported:**      September 1989 LAB 25

**Date of Award:**      May 18, 1989

**Brief Facts of Case:**      Student T was evicted by L just 6 days after tenancy started when L changed the locks. T was forced to sleep on a friend's sofa for 3 nights, missed 2 days of the university term looking for alternative accommodation and then spent 3 weeks commuting daily from Warrington, where her parents lived to London before securing other accommodation.

**Award:**      £560 general damages.

**General Damages:**      £560

**Value of Award of £560 as at April 2004: £904**

*Property – Landlord & Tenant – Unlawful eviction*

---

**Name of Case:**      *McLaughlin v Leith*

**Cause/s of Action:**      Unlawful eviction

**Tribunal and Judge:**      Bow County Court – HHJ Butter QC

**Where Reported:**      September 1993 LAB 17

**Date of Award:**      June 23, 1993

**Brief Facts of Case:**      T occupied one room in a house in multiple occupation. Following delays in the payment of T's housing benefit, L removed the door to her room and threw food and drink over her possessions (some of which he removed and damaged) and her bed. T had to stay with relatives before being rehoused.

**Award:**      £3,750 general damages.

(No statutory, aggravated or exemplary damages were pleaded.)

(Special damages: £250.)

**General Damages:**      £3,750

**Value of Award of £3,750 as at April 2004: £4,939**

*Property – Landlord & Tenant – Unlawful eviction*

---

**Name of Case:**      *McMillan v Singh*

**Cause/s of Action:**      Unlawful eviction –Breach of covenant for quiet enjoyment

**Tribunal and Judge:**      Court of Appeal – Sir John Arnold and Lincoln J

**Where Reported:**      (1985) 17 HLR 120

**Date of Award:**      February 17, 1984

**Brief Facts of Case:**      From 1979 P was tenant of a bed-sitting room owned by D. In April 1983 D threw P's possessions out of the room while he was out. When he returned he found his belongings gone but he stayed there overnight. The next day D threw out the remainder of P's belongings and threatened P with physical violence if he re-entered.

P issued proceedings and an order was made to re-instate him. D had taken advantage of P's absence by letting out the property for an increased rent. The judge declined to award exemplary damages as P had been in arrears of rent.

P appealed.

The Court of Appeal held there was no defence to the common law claim for damages that P had fallen into rent arrears.

**Award:**          £250 aggravated damages, £250 exemplary damages. (Appeal allowed.)

**Value of Award of £250 as at April 2004: £533**

*Property – Landlord & Tenant – Unlawful eviction – Breach of covenant for quiet enjoyment*

---

| | |
|---|---|
| **Name of Case:** | *Mehta v Royal Bank of Scotland* |
| **Cause/s of Action:** | Unlawful eviction |
| **Tribunal and Judge:** | High Court – Mr R Southwell QC (sitting as a deputy High Court Judge) |
| **Where Reported:** | (1999) 78 P & CR D11; (2000) 32 HLR 45 |
| **Date of Award:** | January 14, 1999 |
| **Brief Facts of Case:** | A hotel was in financial difficulties and a receiver was appointed by the mortgagee, RBS. M took up occupation of a hotel room under an oral agreement with the hotel manager which was approved by the receiver and mortgagee. He had exclusive occupation of the room "on a long term basis" and paid a monthly rent. The hotel cleaned his room and changed the bed. After 6 months M was unlawfully evicted to enable the sale of the hotel with vacant possession – RBS was to take the proceeds of sale. |
| **Award:** | £45,000 damages under ss27-28 Housing Act 1988 against former landlord based on amount of discount a purchaser would have required with M in occupation. |

In respect of awards which would not be recoverable in addition to statutory damages the High Court granted:

£10,000 general damages including element for mental distress

£10,000 aggravated damages

£7,500 exemplary damages

(£45,000 statutory damages)

**General Damages:**      £10,000

**Value of Award of £10,000 as at April 2004: £11,365**

**Value of Award of £7,500 exemplary damages as at April 2004: £8,524**

*Property – Landlord & Tenant – Unlawful eviction*

---

| | |
|---|---|
| **Name of Case:** | *Melossi v Simon* |
| **Cause/s of Action:** | Unlawful eviction |
| **Tribunal and Judge:** | Central London County Court – Recorder Bailey |
| **Where Reported:** | June 1998 LAB 14 |
| **Date of Award:** | December 3, 1997 |
| **Brief Facts of Case:** | T was an American student who had paid 6 months rent in advance to the letting agents. She was not aware that the premises were unlawfully let by a council tenant. When the council found out L deposited her possessions in dustbin bags and on her return demanded that she vacate and was intimidating. |
| **Award:** | £3,000 general damages |
| | £1,000 aggravated damages |

£500 exemplary damages (as L's motive was to make a profit from his security of tenure)

(Special damages: £4,975 – the balance of the rent paid in advance.)

**General Damages:** £3,000

**Value of Award of £3,000 as at April 2004: £3,482**

**Value of Award of £500 exemplary damages as at April 2004: £580**

**Value of Award of £1,000 aggravated damages as at April 2004: £1,161**

*Property – Landlord & Tenant – Unlawful eviction*

| | |
|---|---|
| **Name of Case:** | *Melville v Bruton* |
| **Cause/s of Action:** | Unlawful eviction – Trespass to goods |
| **Tribunal and Judge:** | Court of Appeal – Stuart-Smith, Hutchinson and Buckley LJJ |
| **Where Reported:** | [1996] EGCS 57; (1996) *Times* 29 March; June 1996 LAB 13; (1997) 29 HLR 319 |
| **Date of Award:** | March 21, 1996 |
| **Brief Facts of Case:** | In January 1993 M granted 6 month secure shorthold tenancy of part of property. Two others were already in occupation of the remainder. The property was subject to a covenant restricting use other than as a private dwelling in single occupation. After 5 weeks M was excluded from the property and her belongings removed. |
| | Judge awarded £15,000 damages under ss.27,28 Housing Act 1988 being the difference between the value of the landlord's interest in the property immediately before and after M's eviction and £2,379 damages for conversion of her |

possessions. B appealed against award of statutory damages.

**Award:**          Statutory damages set aside. Common law damages of £500 awarded for inconvenience, discomfort and distress.

In assessing value of the property the existence of the 2 other occupiers had been disregarded. (Appeal allowed in part.)

**General Damages:**     £500

**Value of Award of £500 as at April 2004: £613**

*Property – Landlord & Tenant – Unlawful eviction – Trespass*

*and*

*Trespass to goods – conversion*

---

**Name of Case:**          *Miller and Wartnaby v Clarke*

**Cause/s of Action:**      Breach of covenant for quiet enjoyment - assault

**Tribunal and Judge:**     Lambeth County Court – HHJ James

**Where Reported:**        June 1994 LAB 11

**Date of Award:**          February 16, 1994

**Brief Facts of Case:**    Ts occupied a flat over a shop. Building works were carried out to the shop over a week during which time the gas supply to the flat was disconnected.

When Ts brought this to the tenancy relation officer's attention L was abusive and threatened to evict Ts. He cut the wires to the electricity meter and assaulted one of the Ts. Electricity was restored within 3 weeks of an injunction being obtained.

**Award:** £1,226 total damages (including interest) comprising:

£400 to each T general damages for breach of covenant for quiet enjoyment

£200 for assault

(Special damages: £226.)

**General Damages:** £600

**Value of Award of £400 as at April 2004: £523**

**Value of Award of £200 as at April 2004: £261**

*Property – Landlord & Tenant – Breach of covenant for quiet enjoyment - Assault*

---

**Name of Case:** *Millington v Duffy*

**Cause/s of Action:** Unlawful eviction – Breach of covenant for quiet enjoyment

**Tribunal and Judge:** Court of Appeal – Sir John Arnold and Sheldon J

**Where Reported:** (1985) 17 HLR 232

**Date of Award:** June 7, 1984

**Brief Facts of Case:** M was tenant of a single room in a house for 15 years. He was told to leave and the landlord D removed his belongings. He then re-let the room at a higher rent. M stayed with a friend and then slept rough until he was found accommodation by the local authority.

M issued proceedings and was awarded £119.50 for loss of his belongings and £150 general damages for distress and inconvenience. M appealed against the award for general damages.

(He had abandoned his claim for aggravated or exemplary damages.)

The Court of Appeal substituted a higher figure as £150 award was so low as to be plainly wrong and held that if the claim for exemplary damages had been maintained the award would have been higher still.

(Special damages: £119.50.)

**Award:** £500 general damages.

**General Damages:** £500

**Value of Award of £500 as at April 2004: £1,041**

*Property – Unlawful eviction – Breach of covenant for quiet enjoyment*

---

**Name of Case:** *Mira v Aylmer Square Investments Ltd*

**Cause/s of Action:** Breach of covenant for quiet enjoyment

**Tribunal and Judge:** Court of Appeal – Dillon, Stuart-Smith, Ralph Gibson LJJ

**Where Reported:** (1989) 21 HLR 284; (1990) 22 HLR 182

**Date of Award:** January 31, 1990

**Brief Facts of Case:** A owned 3 blocks of flats and started works in 1985 to construct penthouses in the roofs. The tenants suffered substantial interference by way of dust, noise, dirt, damp, cracks and holes in bedroom ceiling. They brought actions against A and alleged loss of rental income in two representative cases.

M had acquired a 125-year lease of a flat on the assurance that the work would be completed within 6 months and damages rectified. They went abroad but were unable to let out their flat due to the interference.

Dr B was an assignee of a lease. In February 1985 he let out his flat for 6 months with an option to renew but the sub-tenants complained about the interference and he reduced the rent from April 1985. They then left in September 1985.

A appealed against the Judge's finding that:

1) M would have been able to let the flat at £210 per week from November 9 1985 to June 19 1986. He awarded damages on that basis in addition to general damages.

2) Dr B could not recover the voluntary reduction in rent (£50 per week) but after the first 6 months he was entitled to recover £50 per week until the sub-tenants moved out and thereafter £250 per week until judgment.

*Property – Landlord & Tenant – Breach of covenant of quiet enjoyment*

| | |
|---|---|
| **Name of Case:** | *Molyneux-Child v Coe* |
| **Cause/s of Action:** | Breach of covenant for quiet enjoyment |
| **Tribunal and Judge:** | Guildford County Court – District Judge Stephen Gold |
| **Where Reported:** | [1996] CLY 3722; March 1997 LAB 14 |
| **Date of Award:** | September 13, 1996 |
| **Brief Facts of Case:** | T was in arrears of rent by £400. L faxed T at work demanding £4,807 and that she leave the property within the next 4 days. L was aware that he was not entitled to immediate possession and that the amount was not due. T was embarrassed at work by receiving the faxes. |

**Award:** £750 general damages for breach of covenant for quiet enjoyment.

**General Damages:** £750

**Value of Award of £750 as at April 2004: £906**

*Property – Landlord & Tenant – Breach of covenant for quiet enjoyment*

---

**Name of Case:** *Morris v Synard*

**Cause/s of Action:** Unlawful eviction – Breach of covenant for quiet enjoyment

**Tribunal and Judge:** Cheltenham County Court – District Judge Greenslade

**Where Reported:** [1993] 11 CL 195; [1993] CLY 1399; March 1994 LAB 13

**Date of Award:** July 16, 1993

**Brief Facts of Case:** T occupied a bed-sit and was arrested on suspicion of breaking into an electricity meter in the room and stealing its contents. He was later released and no further action was taken. T returned to discover that he had been locked out of the room. He slept on a relative's sofa for 2 weeks and then obtained an injunction and resumed occupation.

**Award:** £1,000 general damages

£1,000 exemplary damages

**General Damages:** £1,000

**Value of Award of £1,000 as at April 2004: £1,320**

*Property – Landlord & Tenant – Unlawful eviction – Breach of covenant for quiet enjoyment*

---

| | |
|---|---|
| **Name of Case:** | *Murphy and Tenty v Al Doori* |
| **Cause/s of Action:** | Unlawful eviction – Breach of covenant for quiet enjoyment |
| **Tribunal and Judge:** | Newport (Gwent) County Court – District Judge Rachel Evans |
| **Where Reported:** | [1994] CLY 1767; December 1994 LAB 16 |
| **Date of Award:** | July 24, 1994 |
| **Brief Facts of Case:** | L putting pressure on Ts to leave flat 2 weeks after a notice to quit was served. L attended flat – assaulted T1 by slapping him around the face and later forced entry and threw Ts belongings onto street. Ts left when their remaining possessions had been removed by L. An injunction enabled them to return to the flat which they vacated after a month. |
| **Award:** | Total: £4,463.70 to each T including: |
| | £2,000 general damages to include aggravated damages |
| | £2,000 exemplary damages |
| | (Special damages £463.70.) |
| **General Damages:** | £2,000 |

**Value of Award of £2,000 as at April 2004: £2,579**

*Property – Landlord & Tenant – Unlawful eviction – Breach of covenant for quiet enjoyment*

---

| | |
|---|---|
| **Name of Case:** | *Murray v Aslam* |
| **Cause/s of Action:** | Unlawful eviction |
| **Tribunal and Judge:** | Court of Appeal – Sir Thomas Bingham MR, Simon Brown LJ, Sir Ralph Gibson |

**Where Reported:**          [1994] EGCS 160 CA; December 1994 LAB 16

**Date of Award:**           October 18, 1994

**Brief Facts of Case:**     L excluded T from the property by changing the locks and removing her possessions to the street. She was allowed back in a few hours later but decided to vacate some weeks later.

The county court judge awarded statutory damages of £34,560 and special damages. L applied to have the judgment set aside which was refused and L appealed.

**Award:**                   Statutory damages award set aside. (Court held it was questionable whether the case fell within s27 of Housing Act 1988.)

(Special damages award of £5,703 allowed to stand.)

*Property – Landlord & Tenant – Unlawful eviction*

---

**Name of Case:**            *Nawaz v Shafak*

**Cause/s of Action:**       Unlawful eviction

**Tribunal and Judge:**      Birmingham County Court – HHJ Gosling

**Where Reported:**          September 1989 LAB 25

**Date of Award:**           July 6, 1989

**Brief Facts of Case:**     Whilst T was visiting his wife in hospital (an expectant mother) L removed T's possessions. T returned home to find his belongings in the street together with L and members of his family. Too frightened to apply for an injunction T, his wife, their new-born baby and 2 other sons spent 6 months in a hostel.

**Award:**                £5,000 total damages comprising special damages and:
£4,000 exemplary damages

£850 general damages for distress and inconvenience

(Special damages: £150 for costs of removal.)

**General Damages:**      £850

**Value of Award of £850 as at April 2004: £1,367**

**Value of Award of £4000 exemplary damages as at April 2004: £6,431**

*Property – Landlord & Tenant – Unlawful eviction*

---

**Name of Case:**         *Nwokorie v Mason*

**Cause/s of Action:**    Unlawful eviction

**Tribunal and Judge:**   Court of Appeal – Dillon LJ and Hollis J

**Where Reported:**       (1994) 26 HLR 60

**Date of Award:**        October 11, 1993

**Brief Facts of Case:**  T occupied bed sitting room under a 6 month agreement from 9.11.1988 in a house where L was resident. Cooking, washing and WC facilities were shared. In 1989 L gave T 14 days notice to leave and then unlawfully evicted him.

Judge held T was entitled to 28 days notice to quit and a court order. L appealed against Judge's award of:

£500 general damages

£1,000 exemplary damages

£4,500 damages under ss27-28 of Housing Act 1988

The Court of Appeal held:

(i) general damages should be set off against statutory damages

(ii) the award for exemplary damages should be an aggravated damages award and set off against statutory damages (as there was no financial motive for L to evict T).

**Award:** £6,000 total reduced to £4,500.

**General Damages:** £500

**Value of Award of £500 as at April 2004: £655**

**Value of Award of £1000 aggravated damages as at April 2004: £1,310**

*Property – Landlord & Tenant – Unlawful eviction*

---

**Name of Case:** *Ogunlolu v Bird*

**Cause/s of Action:** Unlawful eviction

**Tribunal and Judge:** Edmonton County Court – District Judge Silverman

**Where Reported:** June 1993 LAB 13

**Date of Award:** January 25, 1993

**Brief Facts of Case:** T was an assured tenant. L moved her possessions into the garden and changed the lock. T obtained an injunction but did not regain access. She was forced to stay in temporary local authority accommodation for 1 night and then spent 3 nights on a relative's sofa. Thereafter she spent 6 months in dirty premises and then in a room where she shared kitchen and bathroom facilities with 9 men.

**Award:** £4,500 general damages. (No claim for statutory damages under ss27-28 of the Housing Act 1988 was made. Aggravated and exemplary damages were not pleaded.)

(Special damages: £852.69.)

**General Damages:** £4,500

**Value of Award of £4,500 as at April 2004: £6,060**

*Property – Landlord & Tenant – Unlawful eviction*

---

**Name of Case:** *O'Reilly v Webb*

**Cause/s of Action:** Unlawful eviction

**Tribunal and Judge:** Birmingham County Court – HHJ Alan Taylor

**Where Reported:** December 1992 LAB 19

**Date of Award:** September 16, 1992

**Brief Facts of Case:** L thought T had quit the property owing 3 months' rent. L changed the locks and T could not resume occupation for 3 days until an injunction was ordered.

**Award:** £600 general damages of £200 per night

£1,000 exemplary damages

**General Damages:** £600

**Value of Awards of £600 as at April 2004: £799**

**Value of Award of £200 per night as at April 2004: £266**

**Value of Award of £1,000 exemplary damages as at April 2004: £1,332**

*Property – Landlord & Tenant – Unlawful eviction*

**Name of Case:**          *Ozeerkhan v Charitou*

**Cause/s of Action:**     Breach of covenant for quiet enjoyment

**Tribunal and Judge:**    Watford County Court – HHJ Goldstone

**Where Reported:**        September 1991 LAB 18

**Date of Award:**         May 2, 1991

**Brief Facts of Case:**   T was a protected tenant of a flat which was subsequently purchased by L. T returned home to find L in occupation. T issued possession proceedings and evicted L 7 months later. Despite there being a possession order in place L again moved in and prevented her occupation for 4 days and nights. T and her 15-month-old son had to spend one night in a car and 3 nights with friends. Upon her re-entry L threatened her and broke the glass in her door. T was unable to recover some of her possessions.

**Award:**                 £1,895 total damages including:

                           £500 general damages

                           £1,000 exemplary and aggravated damages

                           (Special damages: £395.)

**General Damages:**       **£500**

**Value of Award of £500 as at April 2004: £696**

**Value of Award of £1,000 exemplary and aggravated damages as at April 2004: £1,391**

*Property – Landlord & Tenant – Breach of covenant for quiet enjoyment*

| | |
|---|---|
| **Name of Case:** | *Ozer Properties Ltd v Ghaydi* |
| **Cause/s of Action:** | Unlawful eviction – Breach of covenant for quiet enjoyment |
| **Tribunal and Judge:** | Court of Appeal – Sir John Donaldson MR and Stocker LJ |
| **Where Reported:** | (1988) 20 HLR 232 |
| **Date of Award:** | September 29,1987 |
| **Brief Facts of Case:** | O was owner of a residential property which was previously owned by a company which had employed S to manage the property, but in 1981 he was dismissed and managing agents were appointed. In March 1984 however S showed G a room in the property took a deposit and 1 weeks' rent from her and then disappeared. |

The company then contracted to sell it to a purchaser who was to collect rents pending completion. In June 1984 G returned to find the locks had been changed. She obtained an injunction for re-entry. Damages were assessed for breach of quiet enjoyment. The property was not sold to the purchaser but to O who obtained a possession order against G.

G appealed on the basis that that the judgment in default created a case of *res judicata* on the issue of whether she was a tenant under the Rent Acts.

Held: G was always a trespasser but nonetheless entitled to common law damages as if a tenant.

| | |
|---|---|
| **Award:** | £525 general damages. (Appeal dismissed.) |
| **General Damages:** | £525 |

**Value of Award of £525 as at April 2004: £952**

*Property – Landlord & Tenant – Unlawful eviction – Breach of covenant for quiet enjoyment*

**Name of Case:**        *Patel v Southwark LBC*

**Cause/s of Action:**    Unlawful eviction

**Tribunal and Judge:**    Lambeth County Court – District Judge Jacey

**Where Reported:**    September 1992 LAB 23

**Date of Award:**    June 4, 1992

**Brief Facts of Case:**    T owed Council 13 months' rent due to a dispute. He returned to the property to find the locks changed and a note for him to contact a housing officer. The officer was abusive on the telephone and he was informed that the issue of rent arrears was one of the reasons for the eviction.

T was forced to spend 3 nights on his parents' sofa before he was able to resume occupation.

**Award:**    £2,486 total damages including:

£600 general damages

£1,500 exemplary and aggravated damages

**General Damages:**    £600

**Value of Award of £600 as at April 2004: £800**

**Value of Award of £1,500 exemplary and aggravated damages as at April 2004: £2,000**

*Property – Housing – Unlawful eviction – Harassment*

---

**Name of Case:**    *Pearce v Quadhri*

**Cause/s of Action:**    Unlawful eviction

**Tribunal and Judge:**    Reading County Court

**Where Reported:**    March 1990 LAB 16

**Date of Award:**        December 15, 1989

**Brief Facts of Case:**  An 18-year-old T was evicted from a bed-sit.

**Award:**                £5,500 damages assessed on the difference between the vacant possession and tenanted value of the property.

**Statutory Damages:**    £5,500

**Value of Award of £5,500 as at April 2004: £8,597**

*Property – Landlord & Tenant – Unlawful eviction*

---

**Name of Case:**         *Perez v Quereshi*

**Cause/s of Action:**    Breach of covenant for quiet enjoyment

**Tribunal and Judge:**   Bloomsbury County Court – Assistant Recorder Mulcahy

**Where Reported:**       June 1987 LAB 18

**Date of Award:**        September 4, 1986

**Brief Facts of Case:**  Since 1972 Ts had occupied a flat as Rent Act protected tenants. While Ts were on holiday L damaged their possessions and removed the door to the flat and they were unable to resume occupation.

**Award:**                Limited to £5,000 due to the Court's jurisdiction but comprising:

£2,500 general damages (including loss of their protected tenancy and the higher rent they paid for alternative accommodation);

£2,000 exemplary damages

(Special damages: £1,500.)

**General Damages:**     £2,500

**Value of Award of £2,500 as at April 2004: £4,723**

**Value of Award of £2,000 exemplary damages as at April 2004: £3,778**

*Property – Landlord & Tenant – Breach of covenant for quiet enjoyment*

---

| | |
|---|---|
| **Name of Case:** | *Pillai v Amendra* |
| **Cause/s of Action:** | Unlawful eviction – Trespass to goods |
| **Tribunal and Judge:** | Central London County Court – HHJ Green QC |
| **Where Reported:** | October 2000 LAB 24 |
| **Date of Award:** | July 27, 2000 |
| **Brief Facts of Case:** | T occupied a 1-bedroom flat as a weekly assured tenant. He refused to leave to allow L to avoid a benefit fraud investigation in respect of a previous tenant. L locked out T when he returned from holiday and deposited his belongings in the garden. His windscreen was smashed and he was left a threatening note. The police secured his re-entry and he was then locked out again and his effects thrown out again. L failed to comply with an injunction and T was too frightened to return. He stayed with a friend for 6 months and lost his job because of the amount of time he had to take off. |
| **Award:** | £36,000 total damages including: |
| | £6,000 general damages |
| | £10,000 aggravated and exemplary damages for trespass to land |
| | £3,000 aggravated damages for trespass to goods |

(Special damages: £17,000 for loss of goods and other expenditure.)

**General Damages:**     £6,000

**Value of Award of £6,000 as at April 2004: £6,535**

**Value of Award of £3,000 aggravated damages as at April 2004: £3,267**

**Value of Award of £10,000 aggravated and exemplary damages as at April 2004: £10,892**

*Property – Landlord & Tenant – Unlawful eviction – Trespass to goods*

---

| | |
|---|---|
| **Name of Case:** | *Pursey v Acrochoice Investments Ltd* |
| **Cause/s of Action:** | Breach of covenant of quiet enjoyment |
| **Tribunal and Judge:** | Willesden County Court – HHJ Krikler |
| **Where Reported:** | December 1988 LAB 18 |
| **Date of Award:** | October 11, 1988 |
| **Brief Facts of Case:** | A acquired a property of which P had been a tenant for 41 years. A threatened to remove the roof, whereby P moved to other temporary accommodation (where his health deteriorated) and A then contracted to sell the property. |
| **Award:** | General damages of £4,500 (£500 for each month P was in alternative accommodation). |

**General Damages:**     £4,500

**Value of Award of £4,500 as at April 2004: £7,632**

*Property – Landlord & Tenant – Breach of covenant of quiet enjoyment*

| | |
|---|---|
| **Name of Case:** | *Raeburn v Coppolaro* |
| **Cause/s of Action:** | Breach of covenant for quiet enjoyment – Unlawful eviction |
| **Tribunal and Judge:** | Cambridge County Court – The Circuit Judge |
| **Where Reported:** | December 1995 LAB 20 |
| **Date of Award:** | June 22, 1995 |
| **Brief Facts of Case:** | L entered T's room without consent, shouted at T and removed the door lock. L's agent attacked T. L threatened T who vacated. L and his agent were convicted under Protection from Eviction Act 1977. |
| **Award:** | Against L total: £32,000 damages; against L's agent: £4,500 damages comprising: |

£4,000 general damages

£1,000 aggravated damages

£2,000 exemplary damages

to be apportioned equally between L and his agent.

£30,000 damages under ss27-28 of the Housing Act 1988 against L.

(General and aggravated damages against L were deducted by set-off from the total.)

**General Damages:**   £4,000

**Value of Award of £4,000 as at April 2004: £4,959**

**Value of Award of £1,000 aggravated damages as at April 2004: £1,240**

**Value of Award of £2,000 exemplary damages as at April 2004: £2,479**

*Property – Landlord & Tenant – Breach of covenant for quiet enjoyment – Unlawful eviction*

| | |
|---|---|
| **Name of Case:** | *Rahman v Erdogan* |
| **Cause/s of Action:** | Breach of covenant for quiet enjoyment – Trespass –Trespass to goods |
| **Tribunal and Judge:** | Edmonton County Court/ Central London Civil trial Centre – HHJ Previte QC |
| **Where Reported:** | June 1998 LAB 14 |
| **Date of Award:** | February 11, 1998 |
| **Brief Facts of Case:** | L issued possession proceedings against T and her husband alleging arrears of rent under an assured shorthold tenancy. The proceedings were adjourned and within 1 month L evicted T while she was out and put her possessions in black bin bags. She was unable to gain access for 1 ½ hours and only able to retrieve her possessions for about 8 hours. |
| **Award:** | £750 for breach of covenant and trespass |
| | £250 for trespass to goods |
| | £2,000 aggravated damages |
| | £1,000 exemplary damages |
| | (Special damages: £340.) |
| **General Damages:** | £1,000 |

**Value of Award of £1,000 as at April 2004: £1,158**

**Value of Award of £2,000 aggravated damages as at April 2004: £2,317**

**Value of Award of £1,000 exemplary damages as at April 2004: £1,158**

**Value of Award of £250 as at April 2004: £290**

*Property – Landlord & Tenant – Breach of covenant for quiet enjoyment – Trespass – Trespass to goods*

**Name of Case:** *Ramdath v Daley & Daley*

**Cause/s of Action:** Unlawful eviction –Breach of covenant for quiet enjoyment

**Tribunal and Judge:** Willesden County Court – Mr Recorder Bridges-Adams.

Court of Appeal – Nourse and Steyn LJJ

**Where Reported:** [1992] CLY 1795; June 1992 LAB 12; (1993) *Times* 21 January; March 1993 LAB 15; (1993) 25 HLR 273

**Date of Award:** January 18, 1993

**Brief Facts of Case:** D1 was lessee of a flat which he sub-let. In 1982 P moved in as licensee of sub-tenant. In 1988 sub-tenant died and D1 accepted P as new sub-tenant. In June 1991 D2 (D1's son) started to manage the premises on behalf of D1. P refused to pay the increase in rent demanded by D2 in July. In August the locks were changed, a key withheld, P's belongings were put in the corridor and D2 threatened P. D1 had been warned against evicting P without issuing proceedings. P was unable to resume occupation for 5 weeks and returned to find his possessions missing.

Ds appealed against Judge's award:

- Against D1  Total - £2,830
    £2,000 general damages
    £510 special damages
    £1,000 exemplary damages

- Against D2  Total - £6,397
    £1,250 general damages
    (including aggravated damages)
    £2,647 special damages
    £2,500 exemplary damages

The Court of Appeal held D2 should not have exemplary damages awarded against him as he did not have sufficient interest in the matter to fall within the criteria in *Rookes v Barnard* [1964] AC 1129 per Lord Devlin at p. 1221

**Award:** Against D1 total of £2,830 upheld and against D2 total reduced from £6,397 to £3,897.

(Special damages: £510 against D1 and £2,647 against D2.)

**General Damages:** £2,000 and £1,250

**Value of Awards of £2,000 and £1,250 as at April 2004: £2,693 and £1,683**

**Value of Award of £1,000 exemplary damages as at April 2004: £1,347**

*Property – Landlord & Tenant – Unlawful eviction – Breach of covenant for quiet enjoyment*

---

**Name of Case:** *Ramsay v Lewis*

**Cause/s of Action:** Unlawful eviction

**Tribunal and Judge:** Braintree County Court – HHJ Brandt

**Where Reported:** September 1993 LAB 16

**Date of Award:** 10 May 1991

**Brief Facts of Case:** T had a protected shorthold tenancy of a property. L served notice which fell short of the required 3 months' notice period under the Rent Act 1977. While T was out L changed the locks and removed Ts clothes and possessions.

**Award:** £6,000 damages taking into account the effect of failing to obtain immediate vacant possession on a notional purchaser.

**Statutory Damages under ss.27-28 of Housing Act 1988:** £6,000

**Value of Award as at April 2004: £8,346**

*Property – Landlord & Tenant – Unlawful eviction*

---

**Name of Case:**          *Rathod v Vijeyakumar*

**Cause/s of Action:**     Breach of covenant for quiet enjoyment

**Tribunal and Judge:**    Willesden County Court – HHJ Sich

**Where Reported:**        [1989] CLY 1176; [1989] 6 CL 136; September
                           1989 LAB 25

**Date of Award:**         November 23, 1988

**Brief Facts of Case:**   L putting pressure on T and family to leave
                           statutory tenancy. L entered premises with
                           followers against T's wishes and refused to go
                           until police were called to attend.

**Award:**                 £500 for general damages to include award of
                           aggravated damages for invasion of privacy and
                           feelings of threatened security.

**General Damages:**       £500

**Value of Award of £500 as at April 2004: £874**

*Property – Landlord & Tenant – Breach of covenant for quiet enjoyment*

---

**Name of Case:**          *Regalgrand Ltd v Dickerson and Wade*

**Cause/s of Action:**     Unlawful eviction

**Tribunal and Judge:**    Court of Appeal – Aldous and Ward LJJ

**Where Reported:**        [1996] EGCS 182; March 1997 LAB 14; (1997)
                           74 P & CR 312

**Date of Award:**         November 12, 1996

**Brief Facts of Case:**   In July 1990 Ts were granted a monthly assured
                           shorthold tenancy of a flat owned by L. From
                           December 1990 Ts stopped paying rent due to
                           damp, lack of heating and hot water and resolved
                           to leave in February 1991. L entered flat in

February and thought the flat had been abandoned. Ts were sued for arrears of rent and counterclaimed damages under ss27-28 of Housing Act 1988 for unlawful deprivation of their residential occupation.

Judge awarded agreed sum of £12,000 but reduced the award under s27(7)(a) of Housing Act to £1,500 for conduct of Ts in withholding rent without prior notice/justification and in view of their intention to move out by end of February. Ts appealed.

**Award:**                    Reduced award of £1,500 upheld. (Appeal dismissed.)

**General Damages:**      £1,500

**Value of Award of £1,500 as at April 2004: £1,810**

*Property – Landlord & Tenant – Unlawful eviction*

| | |
|---|---|
| **Name of Case:** | *Reid v Sinclair* |
| **Cause/s of Action:** | Unlawful eviction |
| **Tribunal and Judge:** | Bow County Court – District Judge Mahoney |
| **Where Reported:** | September 1993 LAB 17 |
| **Date of Award:** | May 13, 1993 |
| **Brief Facts of Case:** | T was an assured shorthold tenant. L changed the locks to the property and removed T's possessions. L failed to comply with two injunctions. T was only able to resume occupation after 19 days when the head landlord granted him a new assured tenancy. L tried to punch him on his return. T had been forced to stay in bed and breakfast accommodation and with his friends. |

**Award:**              £2,850 general damages (19 days @ £150 per day)

                        £2,000 aggravated damages for disregard of court orders and attempted assault

                        £2,000 exemplary damages

                        (Special damages: £3,425 for missing possessions.)

**General damages:**    £2,850

**Value of Award of £2,850 as at April 2004: £3,751**

**Value of Award of £150 per day as at April 2004: £197**

**Value of Award of £2,000 as at April 2004: £2,632**

*Property – Landlord & Tenant – Unlawful eviction*

---

**Name of Case:**       *Richardson v Holowkiewicz*

**Cause/s of Action:**  Unlawful eviction

**Tribunal and Judge:** York County Court – DJ Hill

**Where Reported:**     [1997] JHL D27; March 1998 LAB 13

**Date of Award:**      1997

**Brief Facts of Case:** L served notice to quit on T. T's solicitor told him T would not be able to leave until the date specified in the notice but whilst she and her 3 children were on holiday L changed the locks. T had to spend the night on her ex-husband's sofa. She resumed occupation the next day.

**Award:**              £250 general damages for the night on the sofa

                        £1,750 exemplary damages as the L had knowingly acted unlawfully.

                        (Special damages: £575 to include damaged food in freezer.)

**General Damages:** £250

**Value of Award of £250 as at April 2004: £291**

**Value of Award of £1,750 exemplary damages as at April 2004: £2,037**

*Property – Landlord & Tenant – Unlawful eviction*

---

| | |
|---|---|
| **Name of Case:** | *Rowlands v Liverpool CC* |
| **Cause/s of Action:** | Breach of covenant for quiet enjoyment |
| **Tribunal and Judge:** | Liverpool County Court – HHJ Mackay |
| **Where Reported:** | March 1994 LAB 11; [1994] CLY 1447 |
| **Date of Award:** | January 13, 1994 |
| **Brief Facts of Case:** | To escape harassment from her ex-boyfriend T (a tenant for 12 months) temporarily went to stay with her relatives. After her ex-boyfriend broke in the Council secured the property and treated it as abandoned. T returned to find that within 3 weeks the Council had removed her possessions and re-let the flat. |
| **Award:** | £500 damages for loss of tenancy to include disappointment and loss of amenity. (R would have been entitled to a higher award if she had not refused the Council's offer to re-house her in alternative comparable property.) |
| | (Special damages: £1,000 - loss of contents of flat.) |

**General Damages:** £500

**Value of Award of £500 as at April 2004: £657**

*Property – Housing – Breach of covenant for quiet enjoyment*

---

**Name of Case:**          *Rush v Hussain*

**Cause/s of Action:**     Breach of covenant of quiet enjoyment

**Tribunal and Judge:**    Westminster County Court – District Judge
                           Tilbury

**Where Reported:**        September 1992 LAB 23

**Date of Award:**         July 13, 1992

**Brief Facts of Case:**   T had lived in the house since 1945 and became a
                           tenant in 1980. L acquired the head lease in 1991.
                           L wanted to buy the freehold reversion and when
                           the freeholder refused he obtained keys from T
                           by deception and whilst T was staying in hospital
                           moved his father into one of the rooms intending
                           to claim rights under the Leasehold Reform Act
                           1967 at a later date. Other elements of the
                           harassment included a minor assault on T.

**Award:**                 £3,500 total damages including:

                           £1,500 general and aggravated damages

                           £1,750 exemplary damages

                           (Special damages: £300.)

**General Damages:**       £1,500

**Value of Award of £3,500 as at April 2004: £4,683**

**Value of Award of £1,500 as at April 2004: £2,007**

**Value of Award of £1,750 exemplary damages as at April 2004: £2,341**

*Property – Landlord & Tenant – Breach of covenant of quiet enjoyment*

**Name of Case:** *Saleem v Teji*

**Cause/s of Action:** Unlawful eviction

**Tribunal and Judge:** Central London County Court – HHJ Sir Frank White

**Where Reported:** March 1998 LAB 13

**Date of Award:** November 29, 1997

**Brief Facts of Case:** L had agreed to sell his maisonette with vacant possession. He served notice on T the assured shorthold tenant who occupied with her husband and 2 young children. T intimated that she would leave but failed to do so. L changed the locks and deposited T's possessions outside the property. L's family helped T to move her effects to a storage space temporarily. The family had to spend 5 months in bed and breakfast accommodation.

**Award:** £4,000 general and aggravated damages

£1,000 exemplary damages

**General Damages:** £4,000

**Value of Award of £4,000 as at April 2004: £4,654**

**Value of Award of £1,000 exemplary damages as at April 2004: £1,164**

*Property – Landlord & Tenant – Unlawful eviction*

---

**Name of Case:** *Sampson v Floyd*

**Cause/s of Action:** Breach of covenant for quiet enjoyment

**Tribunal and Judge:** Court of Appeal

**Where Reported:** [1989] EGCS 22; [1989] 2 EGLR 49; June 1989 LAB 21

**Date of Award:**      February 15, 1989

**Brief Facts of Case:**      T leased a chalet and restaurant on a Devon holiday complex owned by L. L refused to pay for a meal at T's restaurant and a fight broke out leading Ts frightened wife to hide under a caravan. T vacated and removed his belongings with the aid of a police escort. T brought proceedings in the High Court claiming £10,000 for damages for loss of his lease, conveyancing costs and distress. L appealed on basis that there had been no physical eviction.

**Award:**      The Court upheld the award of £10,000 damages.

**General Damages:**      £10,000

**Value of Award of £10,000 as at April 2004: £16,610**

*Property – Landlord & Tenant – Breach of covenant for quiet enjoyment*

---

**Name of Case:**      *Sam-Yorke v Ali Jawad*

**Cause/s of Action:**      Harassment– Breach of covenant for quiet enjoyment– Assault

**Tribunal and Judge:**      Wandsworth County Court – HHJ Winstanley

**Where Reported:**      March 2003 LAB 30

**Date of Award:**      November 21, 2002

**Brief Facts of Case:**      L was involved in three incidents. Firstly he said to T (an assured tenant) "I want to find you gone", then grabbed a key from T's wife who was alone with their young child and refused to leave until police arrived and finally slapped T in the face and kicked him in the waist causing bruising to the head, groin and shoulder.

Held: the last incident was a trespass to the person and also a breach of covenant for quiet enjoyment.

**Award:** £900 in respect of all 3 incidents.

**General Damages:** £900

**Value of Award of £900 as at April 2004: £938**

*Property – Landlord & Tenant – Harassment – Breach of covenant for quiet enjoyment – Assault*

---

**Name of Case:** *Shafer v Yagambrun*

**Cause/s of Action:** Breach of covenant for quiet enjoyment

**Tribunal and Judge:** Cardiff County Court – Mr Recorder Whiteman

**Where Reported:** [1994] CLY 1450; December 1994 LAB 16

**Date of Award:** October 4, 1994

**Brief Facts of Case:** T had an assured tenancy and was studying for her A-levels. L fell into mortgage arrears and agreed to hand the keys back to the building society. He left a note for T to advise her to leave before the house was repossessed the next day. T vacated and stayed overnight with her father and then with friends for 8 days before finding another assured shorthold tenancy. She maintained that the reason for her mediocre exam grades was that her studying had been disrupted – the eviction had taken place only 1 month before her exams.

**Award:** £3,000 general damages for nights of discomfort, disrupted studies and the reduced security of tenure of the new accommodation.

**General Damages:**      £3,000

**Value of Award of £3,000 as at April 2004: £3,837**

*Property – Landlord & Tenant – Breach of covenant for quiet enjoyment*

| | |
|---|---|
| **Name of Case:** | *Sharma v Kirwan and Coppock* |
| **Cause/s of Action:** | Unlawful eviction – Assault |
| **Tribunal and Judge:** | Central London County Court – HHJ Quentin Edwards QC |
| **Where Reported:** | [1995] CLY 1850; June 1995 LAB 20 |
| **Date of Award:** | February 9, 1995 |
| **Brief Facts of Case:** | Ts were separate assured tenants of 2 rooms in a house and were threatened and harassed by L or his followers prior to return date for possession proceedings. L slapped and threatened Ts with violence, moved in men who disturbed Ts and damaged their property. Judge allowed Ts to remain until determination but they were forced to flee when 5 men visited property. Ts stayed with friends before finding accommodation. One T was unable to recover possessions. |
| **Award:** | For T1: |

Damages for 2 assaults: £400 for slap, £600 for being chased and grabbed;

£750 general damages for wrongful eviction;

£1,500 exemplary damages;

£2,650 statutory damages under ss27 & 28 Housing Act 1988

For T2:

£850 damages for assault;

£750 general damages for wrongful eviction;

£1,500 exemplary damages;

£2,650 statutory damages under ss27 & 28 Housing Act 1988;

(Special damages: £2,302.44.)

**General Damages:**        £750

**Value of Award of £750 as at April 2004: £948**

**Value of Awards of £400, £600 and £850 respectively as at April 2004: £506, £758 and £1,075**

**Value of Award of £1,500 exemplary damages as at April 2004:  £1,896**

*Property – Landlord & Tenant – Unlawful eviction – Assault*

| | |
|---|---|
| **Name of Case:** | *Silva v Coelho* |
| **Cause/s of Action:** | Unlawful eviction – Breach of covenant for quiet enjoyment – Trespass to goods |
| **Tribunal and Judge:** | Wandsworth County Court – DJ Gittens |
| **Where Reported:** | March 1998 LAB 13 |
| **Date of Award:** | January 5, 1998 |
| **Brief Facts of Case:** | T was an assured tenant of a bed-sit. L gave T 20 days' notice to quit. Later in the month he put T's possessions in the street, front garden and common hallway. The door was removed from its hinges. T was allowed re-entry when the police were called but his belongings and the door were not replaced. L was advised about the Protection from Eviction Act 1977 by a tenancy relations officer but proceeded to remove the remaining possessions from the room. T and his |

family vacated and had to spend 1 month in bed and breakfast accommodation and 6 months in a temporary flat before being rehoused.

**Award:**          £6,264.88 total damages (taking into account compensation order in criminal proceedings):

£3,500 general damages for breach of covenant for quiet enjoyment and trespass to goods

£1,500 aggravated damages

£1,500 exemplary damages

(Special damages: £514.88.)

**General Damages:**          £3,500

**Value of Award of £3,500 as at April 2004: £4.075**

**Value of Award of £1,500 exemplary/aggravated damages as at April 2004: £1,746**

*Property – Landlord & Tenant – Unlawful eviction – Breach of covenant for quiet enjoyment – Trespass to goods*

---

**Name of Case:**          *Stalker v Karim*

**Cause/s of Action:**          Breach of covenant for quiet enjoyment

**Tribunal and Judge:**          Peterborough County Court – The District Judge

**Where Reported:**          June 1994 LAB 12

**Date of Award:**          February 2, 1994

**Brief Facts of Case:**          T (a man in his 40s) was evicted by L's mortgagee. He was forced to spend 12 weeks in hostels with his two sons (who shared a bed) and 9 months in temporary local authority accommodation and was then rehoused.

**Award:**              £3,000 general damages.

**General Damages:**    £3,000

**Value of Award of £3,000 as at April 2004: £3,920**

*Property – Landlord & Tenant – Breach of covenant for quiet enjoyment*

---

| | |
|---|---|
| **Name of Case:** | *Stephenson v Southwark LBC* |
| **Cause/s of Action:** | Unlawful Eviction – Breach of covenant for quiet enjoyment – Trespass |
| **Tribunal and Judge:** | Edmonton County Court sitting at Willesden County Court – HHJ Latham |
| **Where Reported:** | March 2003 LAB 29 |
| **Date of Award:** | October 24, 2002 |
| **Brief Facts of Case:** | S was son of a council tenant claiming to be entitled to succeed to the council tenancy. Whilst S was on holiday in August 2001 the Council forced entry to carry out gas maintenance, putting grilles over the windows and doors and refusing S entry despite the Council being subsequently provided with proof of identity from S's solicitors. Between February and August 2002 the property was squatted. S stayed with friends (sleeping in their living rooms) for 6 months and at his girlfriend's parents' house and for 6 months in a room at his mother's property.<br><br>Held: S entitled to succeed to the tenancy. |
| **Award:** | £5,300 general damages for breach of covenant for quiet enjoyment and trespass (covering period of 1 year following the date on which he gave evidence of his identity).<br><br>(Special damages: £7,500 for loss of chattels in respect of which the Council was bailee and had |

failed to prove that it had taken reasonable steps to preserve his belongings.)

**General Damages:**     £5,300

**Value of Award of £5,300 as at April 2004: £5,532**

*Property – Housing – Unlawful Eviction – Breach of covenant for quiet enjoyment – Trespass*

---

**Name of Case:**          *Stewart v Dawson*

**Cause/s of Action:**     Unlawful eviction

**Tribunal and Judge:**    Salford County Court – HHJ Elizabeth Steel

**Where Reported:**        September 1994 LAB 13

**Date of Award:**         April 15, 1994

**Brief Facts of Case:**   T withheld rent following advice from a housing centre on the basis that L might not return his deposit. L removed door, put T's possessions into dustbin bags and sent them by taxi to his girlfriend's home. L had been warned in writing about harassment on 2 previous occasions.

**Award:**                 £500 general damages

                           £2,500 aggravated damages

                           (No exemplary damages were awarded as L had pleaded guilty to a Protection from Eviction Act 1977 offence.)

                           (Special damages of £66 for damaged items.)

**General Damages:**       £500

**Value of Award of £500 as at April 2004: £644**

**Value of award of £2,500 aggravated damages as at April 2004: £3,219**

*Property – Landlord & Tenant – Unlawful eviction*

---

**Name of Case:**            *Sullman v Little, Little & Little*

**Cause/s of Action:**       Trespass to goods –Unlawful eviction

**Tribunal and Judge:**      Canterbury County Court – HH Judge Peppitt QC

**Where Reported:**          [1993] CLY 1604; March 1994 LAB 13

**Date of Award:**           July 23, 1993

**Brief Facts of Case:**     S occupied an annexe owned by L under an oral agreement with L's wife. S was evicted and his possessions removed. S had breached the agreement by keeping cats on the premises and refusing to leave on a date previously agreed between the parties.

**Award:**                   Statutory damages of £3,000 (reduced by four-fifths under s 27(7)(a) of Housing Act 1988 in respect of S's conduct); £250 for trespass to goods. No award of aggravated damages.

**General Damages:**         £250

**Value of Award of £250 as at April 2004: £330**

*Property - Landlord & Tenant – Unlawful eviction – Trespass to goods*

---

**Name of Case:**            *Sutherland v Wall and Wall*

**Cause/s of Action:**       Breach of covenant for quiet enjoyment - loss of protected tenancy

**Tribunal and Judge:**      Dartford County Court – District Judge Weedon

**Where Reported:**          [1994] CLY 1448; June 1994 LAB 12

**Date of Award:**           May 3, 1994

**Brief Facts of Case:**     T (aged 75) protected tenant of flat – Ls took a mortgage on the property prior to start of tenancy and then defaulted. Lenders repossessed flat and T moved into sheltered accommodation provided by local authority at a similar rent

**Award:**              £2,500 general damages for loss of Rent Act protected tenancy

(Special damages: £309.65 plus £50 interest for expenses incurred as a result of eviction.)

**General Damages:**    £2,500

**Value of Award of £2,500 as at April 2004: £3,208**

*Property – Landlord & Tenant – Breach of covenant for quiet enjoyment - Loss of protected tenancy*

---

**Name of Case:**         *Syed v Dzudzor*

**Cause/s of Action:**    Unlawful eviction

**Tribunal and Judge:**   Wandsworth County Court – The Circuit Judge

**Where Reported:**       September 1994 LAB 13

**Date of Award:**        June 14, 1994

**Brief Facts of Case:**  T was in rent arrears due to a delay in the payment of his housing benefit. L removed T's possessions from the bed-sit and put them into black sacks. T had to sleep rough on a park bench for 2 months before he found other accommodation.

**Award:**                £11,995 total damages comprising:

£3,500 general damages (£250 per day)

£1,500 damages for mental shock

£5,000 aggravated damages

(Special damages: £1,500.)

**General Damages:**      £3,500

**Value of Award of £3,500 as at April 2004: £4,491**

**Value of Award of £250 per day as at April 2004: £321**

**Value of Award of £5,000 aggravated damages as at April 2004: £6,417**

*Property – Landlord & Tenant – Unlawful eviction*

---

| | |
|---|---|
| **Name of Case:** | *Taylor v Clayton* |
| **Cause/s of Action:** | Breach of covenant of quiet enjoyment – Harassment |
| **Tribunal and Judge:** | Worthing County Court – HH Judge Kenny |
| **Where Reported:** | [1990] CLY 1530; June 1990 LAB 12 |
| **Date of Award:** | February 16, 1990 |
| **Brief Facts of Case:** | T was tenant of the ground floor of a house. L asked him to leave and then removed 2 fuses for T's electrical supply causing food to be damaged in fridge. L had also entered T's bedroom early in the morning and pulled out the television aerial on 3 occasions. |
| **Award:** | £846 general aggravated and exemplary damages. |
| | (Claim limited to £1,000.) |
| | (Special damages: £154.) |
| **General Damages:** | £846 |

**Value of Award of £846 as at April 2004: £1,307**

*Property - Landlord & Tenant – Breach of covenant for quiet enjoyment – Harassment*

---

**Name of Case:** *Tvrtkovic v Tomas*

**Cause/s of Action:** Unlawful eviction

**Tribunal and Judge:** Brentford County Court – HHJ Oppenheimer

**Where Reported:** August 1999 LAB 19

**Date of Award:** May 10, 1999

**Brief Facts of Case:** T rented double room in a house under an assured tenancy with shared use of living room, bathroom and kitchen from February 1996. In May 1996 L demanded a rent increase backdated to the start of the tenancy. T paid for some of it then L visited the property, demanded cash and told her to leave. She was frightened and left, giving him the keys. She shared a bed with a friend for 1 night and then spent 3 nights in a hotel. She then stayed with a family rent free. She had to sit law exams the day after the eviction and for a few days thereafter. She did not recover her possessions.

**Award:** £250 per night general damages for the 4 nights before T found alternative accommodation

£1,250 aggravated damages

£1,250 exemplary damages

(Special damages: £4,198.25.)

**General Damages:** £250

**Value of Award of £250 as at April 2004: £280**

**Value of Award of £1,250 aggravated and exemplary damages as at April 2004: £1,402**

*Property – Housing – Unlawful eviction*

**Name of Case:**          *Uckuzular (Nilhan) v Sandford-Hill (Jayne)*

**Cause/s of Action:**     Unlawful eviction

**Tribunal and Judge:**    West London County Court – District Judge
                           Haselgrove

**Where Reported:**        [1994] CLY 1770; March 1995 LAB 12

**Date of Award:**         October 25, 1994

**Brief Facts of Case:**   T occupied property under assured shorthold
                           from January 1993. Unable to gain access one
                           night as L and another were in occupation of the
                           property and that locks had been changed. She
                           had to spend the night at a friend's property but
                           managed to gain re-entry at 5pm the following
                           day after seeking legal advice. She had been so
                           distressed that she had attended hospital but was
                           not prescribed with medication.

                           (Special damages: £9.)

**Award:**                 £100 general damages

                           £650 aggravated damages

**General Damages:**       £100

**Value of Award of £100 as at April 2004: £128**

**Value of Award of £650 aggravated damages as at April 2004: £831**

*Property – Landlord & Tenant – Unlawful eviction – Breach of covenant
for quiet enjoyment*

**Name of Case:**      *Vass v Pank*

**Cause/s of Action:**      Unlawful eviction – Breach of covenant to repair

**Tribunal and Judge:**      Court of Appeal – Pill LJ, Sir Anthony Evans.

**Where Reported:**      July 2001 LAB 25

**Date of Award:**      November 14, 2000

**Brief Facts of Case:**      T brought proceedings for disrepair and unlawful eviction. L counterclaimed for unpaid rent. The district judge awarded damages. T applied for permission to appeal.

**Award:**      £500 damages. Application dismissed.

**General Damages:**      £500

**Value of Award of £500 as at April 2004: £540**

*Property – Landlord & Tenant – Unlawful eviction – Breach of covenant to repair*

---

**Name of Case:**      *Veerly, Duffell and Bird v Grant*

**Cause/s of Action:**      Harassment - Breach of covenant for quiet enjoyment

**Tribunal and Judge:**      Great Yarmouth County Court – HHJ Hyam

**Where Reported:**      June 1990 LAB 12

**Date of Award:**      January 18, 1990

**Brief Facts of Case:**      One T refused to pay an electricity bill to recover amount of overpaid rent. L disconnected the electricity supply to all 3 Ts occupying separate flats. L was committed to prison for contempt when he failed to comply with an *ex parte* injunction. He was released after giving an undertaking to restore electricity to the property but disconnected it again the next day.

**Award:**          Total damages for inconvenience to all 3 Ts: £2,050

General damages assessed at rate of £50 per day per T (11 days of disconnection in total)

In addition aggravated damages of £100 awarded additionally to 2 Ts and £200 to the third pregnant T.

**General damages:**     £2,050

**Value of Award of £2,050 as at April 2004: £3,187**

**Value of Award of £50 per day as at April 2004: £78**

**Value of Award of £100 aggravated damages as at April 2004: £155**

**Value of Award of £200 aggravated damages as at April 2004: £311**

*Property – Landlord & Tenant – Harassment*

---

**Name of Case:**        *Wandsworth London Borough Council v Osei-Bonsu*

**Cause/s of Action:**    Unlawful eviction

**Tribunal and Judge:**   Court of Appeal – Simon Brown, Pill & Thorpe LJJ

**Where Reported:**       (1998) *Times* 4 November CA; [1999] 1 EGLR 26; March 1997 LAB 12; December 1998 LAB 27

**Date of Award:**        October 22, 1998

**Brief Facts of Case:**  T and his wife were jointly granted a secure tenancy of council house. Wife left property after allegations of violence by T. Ouster injunction granted against T who refused to surrender tenancy by T. Wife gave and Council accepted a notice to quit of less than 28 days. Council recovered possession of property without a court order. Injunction subsequently discharged but Council refused T re-admission.

On appeal by T Court of Appeal made declaration that T remained a joint tenant as tenancy had not been validly determined. Council caused wife to serve a second valid notice to quit. T sought damages for wrongful eviction.

County Court judge awarded T statutory damages of £30,000 plus common law damages of £282.94 for additional accommodation expenses and declared T entitled to reinstatement into possession. Council appealed.

**Award:** Statutory damages award reduced to £10,000 as respondent's behaviour made it appropriate to mitigate damages substantially pursuant to s.27(7)(a) of Housing Act 1988. (Appeal allowed in part. Declaration that T's tenancy continued was discharged.)

**Value of Award of £10,000 as at April 2004: £11,289**

*Property – Housing – Unlawful eviction*

| | |
|---|---|
| **Name of Case:** | *Weston v Maloney* |
| **Cause/s of Action:** | Unlawful eviction |
| **Tribunal and Judge:** | Blackpool County Court – Mr Recorder Tattersall |
| **Where Reported:** | August 1991 LAB 4; September 1991 LAB 18; December 1991 LAB 19 |
| **Date of Award:** | June 24, 1991 |
| **Brief Facts of Case:** | Ts suffered after doors were smashed, children victimised and services disconnected. |

**Award:**                    £34,000 damages under s28 Housing Act 1988.

(Special damages were awarded.)

**Value of Award of £34,000 as at April 2004: £47,083**

*Property – Landlord & Tenant – Unlawful eviction*

---

**Name of Case:**           *White v Lambeth LBC*

**Cause/s of Action:**      Breach of covenant for quiet enjoyment – Trespass

**Tribunal and Judge:**     Lambeth County Court – Recorder Rylance

**Where Reported:**         June 1995 LAB 20

**Date of Award:**          March 6, 1995

**Brief Facts of Case:**    An absolute possession order had been obtained against T (a secure tenant) but was subsequently set aside. The Council, in the mistaken belief that the order was still in force and that T had abandoned the flat, instructed contractors to force entry to carry out works. T returned to the flat to find that most of his belongings had been removed and the flat was like a building site. T was without accommodation for 15 weeks before he was able to gain access to another flat that had been offered by the Council.

**Award:**                   £18,000 statutory damages under ss27-28 Housing Act 1988

£1,500 damages for interference with goods

£8,000 damages for trespass to land and breach of covenant for quiet enjoyment

£2,000 aggravated damages

(Award limited to £19,500 total damages.)

**General Damages:**          £9,500

**Value of Award of £9,500 as at April 2004: £11,960**

**Value of Award of £8,000 as at April 2004: £10,072**

**Value of Award of £1,500 as at April 2004: £1,888**

**Value of Award of £2,000 aggravated damages as at April 2004: £2,518**

*Property – Housing – Breach of covenant for quiet enjoyment –
interference with goods*

---

**Name of Case:**          *Youziel v Andrews*

**Cause/s of Action:**     Harassment – Unlawful eviction – Assault –
                           Breach of covenant for quiet enjoyment

**Tribunal and Judge:**    Lambeth County Court – DJ Jacey

**Where Reported:**        LAB March 2003 30

**Date of Award:**         January 23, 2003

**Brief Facts of Case:**   P was assured shorthold tenant of a flat. Initially
                           R was his landlord but he subsequently
                           transferred his interest to a third party without
                           giving notice of the transfer under s 3 Landlord
                           and Tenant Act 1985. R continued to manage the
                           property.

                           P (an asylum-seeker) was in rent arrears due to
                           his ineligibility for housing benefits. R harassed
                           P on 10 occasions over a period of 6 weeks by
                           threatening him (including shouting that he
                           "would pay with his life"), telephoning, entering
                           without permission. R and his 2 friends also
                           assaulted P by slapping, kicking and throwing
                           him to the ground in respect of which R was
                           prosecuted. P sustained a knee injury found to be
                           within the upper end of the scale of the moderate
                           category (assessed at £7,750 to £14,000) by the

JSB guidelines for general damages for personal injury). P suffered anxiety and stress causing him to lose 12lbs in weight. He left the property 6 months later.

**Award:** £20,000 total damages comprising:

13,000 for personal injury

£4,300 aggravated damages for the assault

£2,700 damages for breach of covenant for quiet enjoyment in respect of other incidents

£200 interest

**General Damages:** £2,700

**Value of Award of £2,700 as at April 2004: £2,810**

**Value of Award of £4,000 aggravated damages as at April 2004: £4,164**

*Property – Landlord & Tenant – Harassment – Unlawful eviction – Assault – Breach of covenant for quiet enjoyment*

## Disrepair Claims

| | |
|---|---|
| **Name of Case:** | *Abdullah and others v South Tyneside BC* |
| **Cause/s of Action:** | Breach of covenant to repair |
| **Tribunal and Judge:** | South Shields County Court – HHJ Paling |
| **Where Reported:** | September 1987 LAB 12 |
| **Date of Award:** | July 22, 1987 |
| **Brief Facts of Case:** | Ts occupied council flats suffering from condensation dampness. |
| **Award:** | £1,200 general damages for 4 years' condensation and roof leaks (£300 per annum). |
| | Others were awarded £350 for 2 years' condensation (£175 per annum) and £150 for 1 years' condensation. |
| **General Damages:** | £1,200 |

**Value of Award of General Damages of £300 per annum as at April 2004: £547 per annum**

*Property – Housing – Breach of covenant to repair*

---

| | |
|---|---|
| **Name of Case:** | *Adam v Melhuish and Kensey* |
| **Cause/s of Action:** | Breach of covenant to repair |
| **Tribunal and Judge:** | Guildford County Court – HHJ Michael Cook |
| **Where Reported:** | August 1994 LAB 17 |
| **Date of Award:** | 1994 |
| **Brief Facts of Case:** | T occupied an old property which had been declared 'unfit' by the local authority. It was subject to penetrating dampness, extensive mould growth and rotten floorboards. The walls and plaster were saturated with damp. |
| **Award:** | £2,080 per year general damages (£40 per week from 1 January 1990 to the date of the hearing and per week thereafter until repair was completed). |

Special damages: £1,360 for furnishings ruined by damp and mould.

**General Damages:**    £2,080

**Value of Award of General Damages at £40 per week  at April 2004: £51 per week**

*Property – Landlord & Tenant – Breach of covenant to repair*

| | |
|---|---|
| **Name of Case:** | *Ahmad v Cirant* |
| **Cause/s of Action:** | Breach of covenant of repair under s11 Landlord and Tenant Act 1985 – Breach of duty under s4 Defective Premises Act 1972 |
| **Tribunal and Judge:** | Bristol County Court – Assistant Recorder Rutherford |
| **Where Reported:** | March 1992 LAB 13 |
| **Date of Award:** | January 17, 1992 |
| **Brief Facts of Case:** | L sought possession for arrears of rent. T lodged a defence and counterclaim for damages. T had withheld rent after L refused to carry out works of repair contained in a 9-page schedule of works. |
| **Award:** | General damages of £18 per week for 6 years |
| | Total: £5,616 to be set off against unpaid rent. |
| | Ts recovered balance of £2,700. |
| | (Special damages: £500.) |

**General Damages:**    £5,616

**Value of Award of General Damages  of £18 per week as at April 2004: £25 per week**

*Property – Landlord & Tenant – Breach of covenant to repair – Breach of statutory duty*

| | |
|---|---|
| **Name of Case:** | *Alexander v Lambeth LBC* |
| **Cause/s of Action:** | Breach of covenant to repair |
| **Tribunal and Judge:** | Lambeth CC – District Judge Simpson |
| **Where Reported:** | [2000] CLY 3931; [2000] 2 CL 386; July 2001 LAB 26 |
| **Date of Award:** | December 14, 1999 |
| **Brief Facts of Case:** | A was a tenant of a council flat which required remedial work from the start of the tenancy in April 1996. L told A that its remedial work would not interfere with the improvements A wished to make. A spent £12,000 on the property. L then offered to re-house A as L could not afford to complete the works. A refused but moved in with a friend when conditions became intolerable. |
| **Award:** | Total £21,670 including: |
| | £9,375 general damages for 3 years and 9 months @ £2,500 per annum. |
| | Special damages: £12,295 for additional weekly rent of £60 for period in temporary accommodation. |
| **General Damages:** | £9,375 |

**Value of Award of General Damages of £2,500 per annum as at April 2004: £2,775**

*Property – Housing – Breach of covenant to repair*

---

| | |
|---|---|
| **Name of Case:** | *Ali v Birmingham CC* |
| **Cause/s of Action:** | Breach of covenant to repair |
| **Tribunal and Judge:** | Birmingham County Court – HHJ Alton |
| **Where Reported:** | June 1995 LAB 22 |
| **Date of Award:** | December 9, 1994 |
| **Brief Facts of Case:** | Ts lived a Victorian terrace house which suffered from disrepair since before March 1987.There was penetrating damp through the walls and rising damp through the floors. |

Thereafter conditions worsened and in April 1992 the family were offered temporary accommodation whilst works were carried out. Ts were unable to resume occupation until January 1993 although works were outstanding and not completed until November 1994.

**Award:** £15,750 general damages for discomfort and inconvenience (based on £2,000 per annum).

(A claim for damages for diminution in value had not been pursued.)

(Special damages: agreed at £750.)

**General Damages:** £15,750

**Value of Award of General damages of £2,000 per annum as at April 2004: £2,544**

*Property – Housing – Breach of covenant to repair*

| | |
|---|---|
| **Name of Case:** | *Alienus v Tower Hamlets LBC* |
| **Cause/s of Action:** | Breach of covenant to repair |
| **Tribunal and Judge:** | Central London County Court – Mr Recorder Haines |
| **Where Reported:** | [1998] CLY 2987; May 1998 LAB 23 |
| **Date of Award:** | September 25, 1997 |
| **Brief Facts of Case:** | T's flat was affected by excessive mould growth and condensation dampness between 1986 and 1993 because of a defect in its construction. Expert evidence was that half of the condensation was through the ceiling. T sought damages for injury to health and his son personal injury damages for asthma, due to the damp conditions. |

**Award:**               £18,135 total award reduced by 50% on finding that half the dampness was due to breach of repairing obligation.

For T: £1,250 per year for discomfort

50 % of rent for diminution in value for each of 3 years within personal injury limitation period

For T's child: £11,000 for personal injury over 7 years

Special damages: £885 for T's child.

**General Damages:**     £18,135

**Value of Award of General Damages of £1,250 per annum as at April 2004: £1,457**

*Property – Housing – Breach of covenant to repair*

---

**Name of Case:**        *Archer and Archer v Leighton and Marsh*

**Cause/s of Action:**   Breach of covenant to repair

**Tribunal and Judge:**  Manchester County Court – Mr Registrar Delroy

**Where Reported:**      December 1990 LAB 17; (1990) 7 CL 192; [1990] CLY 1709

**Date of Award:**       July 10, 1990

**Brief Facts of Case:** Property affected by dampness.

**Award:**               £300 awarded to each T for the effects of dampness and smells which led them to become "edgy, argumentative and depressed".

**General Damages:**     £300

**Value of Award as at April 2004: £439**

*Property – Landlord & Tenant – Breach of covenant to repair*

| | |
|---|---|
| **Name of Case:** | *Arnold v Greenwich LBC* |
| **Cause/s of Action:** | Breach of covenant to repair |
| **Tribunal and Judge:** | Woolwich County Court – HHJ Gibson |
| **Where Reported:** | [1998] CLY 3618; May 1998 LAB 21 |
| **Date of Award:** | October 9, 1997 |
| **Brief Facts of Case:** | T occupied a council flat under an agreement whereby L covenanted to 'maintain the dwelling in good condition and repair'. T complained of condensation causing damp and mould, smells from refuse storage area below and noise nuisance from others using the rubbish chute which woke him from sleep. |
| **Award:** | £8,750 general damages for discomfort and inconvenience over an almost 6-year period. |
| **General Damages:** | £8,750 |

**Value of Award as at April 2004: £10,187**

*Property – Housing – Breach of covenant to repair*

---

| | |
|---|---|
| **Name of Case:** | *Ashford v Adams* |
| **Cause/s of Action:** | Breach of covenant to repair |
| **Tribunal and Judge:** | Weymouth County Court – HHJ Jack |
| **Where Reported:** | [1993] CLY 1370; September 1993 LAB 16 |
| **Date of Award:** | October 23, 1992 |
| **Brief Facts of Case:** | T was a disabled protected tenant occupying a ground floor flat at £15 rent per week. Six months into the tenancy L persuaded T to vacate the bedroom whilst he carried out repairs. These were not completed making the bedroom uninhabitable. T was unable to use the bedroom for more than 5 years. |
| **Award:** | Total damages: £4,311 |
| | Loss of bedroom @ £4.50 per week for 5 years 8 months based on a flat rental of £15 per week - £1,323 general damages |

Diminution in value caused by disrepair in living room @£4 per week for 4 years 11 months

£1,206 general damages for hardship over 5 years

Aggravated damages for trespass @ £2 per week for retention of bedroom - £458

£300 for other minor disrepairs

**General Damages:**    £4,311

**Value of Award of £4,311 as at April 2004: £5722**

*Property – Landlord & Tenant – Breach of covenant to repair*

---

| | |
|---|---|
| **Name of Case:** | *Banton v Lambeth LBC* |
| **Cause/s of Action:** | Breach of covenant to repair |
| **Tribunal and Judge:** | Lambeth County Court – HHJ Cox |
| **Where Reported:** | December 1995 LAB 22 |
| **Date of Award:** | November 3, 1995 |
| **Brief Facts of Case:** | T (of a 2-bedroom flat) first noticed damp in hallway from leaking central heating pipe above in March 1986. Repairs were ineffective and over a period of 7 years the damp spread causing wet walls in the hall, bathroom and lounge and a musty smell throughout the whole flat. The hot water and central heating could not be used for two winters. Work was completed in October 1993. |
| **Award:** | £12,000 general damages. |
| | Special damages: £2,425 for redecoration, furnishings and carpets. |

**General Damages:**    £12,000

**Value of Award of General Damages as at April 2004: £14,876**

*Property – Housing – Breach of covenant to repair*

| Name of Case: | *Barrett v Lounova (1982) Ltd* |
|---|---|
| Cause/s of Action: | Breach of express covenant to repair and under s3(2) Rent Act 1977; breach of duty under s4 Defective Premises Act 1972 |
| Tribunal and Judge: | Shoreditch County Court – Recorder D Keane QC |
| Where Reported: | June 1988 LAB 20 |
| Date of Award: | December 10, 1987 |
| Brief Facts of Case: | T occupied property under a tenancy granted in 1941 whereby T covenanted to effect inside repairs. The property suffered from disrepair to the structure about which the agreement was silent. |
| Award: | £1,250 for 2 years' disrepair under either head of contract or tort. |
| | No special damages |
| General Damages: | £1,250 |

**Value of Award of £625 per annum as at April 2004: £2,247**

*Property – Landlord and tenant – Breach of covenant to repair*

| Name of Case: | *Barrett v Thayer Holdings Ltd* |
|---|---|
| Cause/s of Action: | Breach of covenant to repair |
| Tribunal and Judge: | Central London County Court – HHJ White |
| Where Reported: | December 1992 LAB 23 |
| Date of Award: | October 23, 1992 |
| Brief Facts of Case: | T occupied a maisonette as an assured shorthold tenant form November 1989 to December 1990 at a rent of £201 per week. The property was affected by disrepair. There was a failure of the hot water and heating system and a defective washing machine over a period of 8 months; a water leak for 2 weeks causing flooding; a faulty shower door and soil pipe blockage resulting in back surge and rat infestation for 3 months. |

**Award:**            £5,444 general damages (assessed at between £40 and £140 per week depending on the severity of the disrepair throughout the period).

**General Damages:**    £5,444

**Value of Award of £40 per week as at April 2004: £53**

**Value of Award of £140 per week as at April 2004: £186**

*Property – Landlord & Tenant – Breach of covenant to repair*

---

**Name of Case:**       *Battersea Freehold and Leasehold Property Co Ltd v Norman;*

                        *Inworth Property Co Ltd v Presslee*

**Cause/s of Action:**  Breach of covenant to repair

**Tribunal and Judge:** Lambeth County Court – HHJ MacNair

**Where Reported:**     October 1990 LAB 24

**Date of Award:**      August 3, 1990

**Brief Facts of Case:** Ps were two property companies in the same property group owning neighbouring properties occupied by Ts. Ps acquired the properties in 1982 and failed to carry out repairs/maintenance despite complaints from Ts and environmental health officers' involvement. They offered alternative accommodation which was refused as Ts had strong community ties and had lived in the properties for a very long time. Ps sought possession on the basis of the offer of alternative accommodation and Ts counterclaimed for disrepair.

**Award:**              £5,000 damages to each T (and mandatory injunctions to carry out repairs).

**General Damages:**    £5,000

**Value of Award as at April 2004: £7,248**

*Property – Landlord & Tenant – Breach of covenant to repair*

| **Name of Case:** | *Bell v Mazehead Ltd* |
|---|---|
| **Cause/s of Action:** | Breach of covenant to repair |
| **Tribunal and Judge:** | Shoreditch County Court – Recorder Rayner James |
| **Where Reported:** | March 1996 LAB 14 |
| **Date of Award:** | May 18, 1995 |
| **Brief Facts of Case:** | T occupied a 3-storey maisonette. The property was affected by water penetration through the roof and dampness throughout her tenancy (1990-1995). |
| **Award:** | £16,735 total damages comprising: |
| | £10,250 damages for diminution in value (50 % of the rent for the first year rising to 5% per year over the 5-year period) |
| | £1,000 per year for discomfort and inconvenience |
| **General Damages:** | £16,735 |

**Value of Award of £1,000 per annum as at April 2004: £1,241**

*Property – Landlord & Tenant – Breach of covenant to repair*

---

| **Name of Case:** | *Berry v Avrisons Co Ltd* |
|---|---|
| **Cause/s of Action:** | Breach of covenant to repair |
| **Tribunal and Judge:** | Wandsworth County Court – HHJ Hunter |
| **Where Reported:** | March 1991 LAB 15 |
| **Date of Award:** | September 17, 1990 |
| **Brief Facts of Case:** | T was a single man occupying property suffering from dampness, disrepair and an interrupted hot water supply over a period of 4 years. |
| **Award:** | £5,000 general damages. |
| **General Damages:** | £5,000 |

**Value of Award as at April 2004: £7,181**

*Property – Landlord & Tenant – Breach of covenant to repair*

**Name of Case:** *Bird v Hackney LBC*

**Cause/s of Action:** Breach of covenant to repair – Nuisance by noise

**Tribunal and Judge:** Central London County Court – Recorder Lawson QC

**Where Reported:** July 2001 LAB 25

**Date of Award:** June 15, 2000

**Brief Facts of Case:** T was granted a secure tenancy of a flat in a tower block which was destined for demolition. The remainder of the estate was being redeveloped and the block was in the middle of a building site. There was serious disrepair. The windows and balcony doors were ill-fitting leaving the flat cold in winter and allowing in dust and noise. The heating system frequently broke down and between December 1996 and February 1997 there was no heating. There were holes in the floor of the flat and a gap under the front door. The neighbouring tower block was covered by plastic sheeting which made a noise when windy and prevented T's family from sleeping.

The judge found L liable for breach of repair under s11 of Landlord and Tenant Act 1985 until remedial work took place in January 1998 and in nuisance for the noise.

**Award:** £2,500 general damages for December 1996 to November 1997 to include the problems of heating and noise

£1,800 damages per annum for the remaining period between commencement and repair (£2,500 per child for respiratory problems)

(Special damages: £780 for extra heating costs – £5 per week for 6 months of the year for 6 years.)

**General Damages:** £2,500 and £1,800 per annum

**Value of Award of £2,500 as at April 2004: £2,713**

**Value of Award of £1,800 per annum as at April 2004: £1,954**

*Property – Housing – Breach of covenant to repair – Nuisance by noise*

---

| | |
|---|---|
| **Name of Case:** | *Brent London Borough Council v Carmel (sued as Murphy)* |
| **Cause/s of Action:** | Breach of covenant for repair |
| **Tribunal and Judge:** | Court of Appeal – Leggatt, Roch and Aldous LJJ |
| **Where Reported:** | August 1994 LAB 17; June 1995 LAB 22; [1995] CLY 1575; (1996) 28 HLR 203 |
| **Date of Award:** | March 10, 1995 |
| **Brief Facts of Case:** | D was a secure tenant of a council maisonette where she lived with two young children. The council had covenanted to provide adequate heating. The property suffered from damp caused by water penetration through the roof, walls and window frames which made two out of three bedrooms uninhabitable in winter. Despite D's complaints the Council did not remedy the defects and D started to withhold rent. The Council brought possession proceedings for arrears of rent. D pleaded a defence and set-off for breach of the repairing covenant. |
| | The Council's claim for possession was withdrawn during the trial. The Council omitted to plead any limitation defence to counterclaim. HH Judge Cooke awarded D damages over entire period of occupation. The Council sought leave to appeal against *inter alia* the quantum of damages. |
| **Award:** | (Upheld on appeal) £14,000 general for discomfort and inconvenience: |
| | £1,000 per annum from 1981 to 1986 |
| | £1,500 per annum from August 1987 to August 1993 |

Damages for loss of value of premises assessed at 30% of rent for 1986-87 and 50% between 1988 and 1993.

(Application for leave to appeal dismissed.)

Special damages of £20,000 plus interest were awarded.

**General Damages:** £14,000

**Value of Award of £1,000 per annum as at April 2004: £1,259**

**Value of Award of £1,500 per annum as at April 2004: £1,888**

*Property – Housing – Breach of covenant to repair*

---

| | |
|---|---|
| **Name of Case:** | *Broadwater Court Management Co Ltd v Jackson-Mann* |
| **Cause/s of Action:** | Breach of covenant to repair |
| **Tribunal and Judge:** | Court of Appeal |
| **Where Reported:** | [1997] EGCS 145, CA; March 1998 LAB 12 |
| **Date of Award:** | 1997 |
| **Brief Facts of Case:** | T was a long lessee under a lease whereby she covenanted to pay service charges to L's management company which had acquired the freehold. T claimed that the charges took into account administrative matters not mentioned in the lease and part of the charges were not reasonably incurred for works which were not of a reasonable standard. She alleged that L had failed to comply with the requirements of s20 of L&TA 1985 in respect of estimates and consultation. |
| | At first instance the recorder gave judgment for L but awarded T damages on T's counterclaim for breach of a repairing covenant in respect of a verandah and conservatory. T appealed. |

| | |
|---|---|
| **Award:** | £775 damages award for loss of amenity value (31 months @ £25 per month) was not interfered with. |
| **General Damages:** | £775 |

**Value of Award of £25 per month as at April 2004: £29**

*Property – Landlord & Tenant – Breach of covenant to repair*

---

| | |
|---|---|
| **Name of Case:** | *Brydon v Islington LBC* |
| **Cause/s of Action:** | Breach of covenant to repair |
| **Tribunal and Judge:** | CC (Clerkenwell) – HH Judge Gibson |
| **Where Reported:** | [1997] CLY 1754; May 1997 LAB 18 |
| **Date of Award:** | February 27, 1997 |
| **Brief Facts of Case:** | Leak from bath penetrating pantry and causing damage reported by T to L. Following inspection (when tiling was smashed and bath panel not replaced), L blamed defect on installation of a toilet carried out by T. T's wife suffered from multiple sclerosis and T was her registered carer. |
| **Award:** | £2,250 damages (£750 per annum) and interest of £236 taking into account the inconvenience to B of the works whilst being carried out over 3 years |
| | £1,508 diminution in value. Special damages: £15 for cost of new shelves. |
| **General Damages:** | £2,250 |

**Value of Award of £750 per annum as at April 2004: £899**

*Property – Housing – Breach of covenant to repair*

---

| | |
|---|---|
| **Name of Case:** | *Bygraves v Southwark LBC* |
| **Cause/s of Action:** | Breach of covenant to repair |
| **Tribunal and Judge:** | Lambeth County Court – Recorder Dohmann QC |
| **Where Reported:** | December 1990 LAB 16 |
| **Date of Award:** | September 20, 1990 |
| **Brief Facts of Case:** | T accepted L's payment into court of £3,500 for her claim for general and special damages but |

pursued an action on behalf of her son who had been born and raised in her damp flat and had developed severe asthma.

**Award:**        £12,000 total damages:

£4,000 for 4 years' health pain and suffering

£5,000 for disruption to his schooling and possible psychological consequences up to age of 18 years

£3,000 for 3 ½ years of inconvenience, distress and discomfort (c£850 per annum)

**General Damages:**        £3,000

**Value of Award of £850 per annum as at April 2004: £1,221**

*Property – Housing – Breach of covenant to repair*

---

**Name of Case:**        *Cahill v Binchy*

**Cause/s of Action:**        Breach of covenant to repair

**Tribunal and Judge:**        Clerkenwell County Court – Mr Recorder Hayward

**Where Reported:**        [1994] CLY 1455; December 1994 LAB 18

**Date of Award:**        July 7, 1994

**Brief Facts of Case:**        Ts were tenants of a ground floor flat. Property suffered rainwater damage from the upper storeys, roof, exterior of building and other common parts which were almost in a state of disrepair. T1 who had a young child worried about effect of incoming rainwater on the electrical circuit.

**Award:**        Damages for distress and inconvenience together with diminution in value of property – property's condition had deteriorated over 7 ½ years:

T2 (who occupied the property for first 2 years) awarded total of £1,000 representing £500 per annum for first 2 years;

T1 awarded total of £7,875 (£500 per annum for first 2 years and £1,250 per annum for remaining 5½ years).

**General Damages:**     £8,875

**Value of Awards of £500 per annum, £1,000 per annum and £1,250 per annum as at April 2004: £645, £1,290 and £1,612 per annum**

*Property – Landlord & Tenant – Breach of covenant to repair*

---

| | |
|---|---|
| **Name of Case:** | *Callaghan v Greenwich LBC* |
| **Cause/s of Action:** | Breach of covenant to repair. |
| **Tribunal and Judge:** | Woolwich County Court – HHJ Cox |
| **Where Reported:** | May 1997 LAB 18 |
| **Date of Award:** | April 20, 1996 |
| **Brief Facts of Case:** | T occupied a one-bedroom council flat. The flat was affected by dampness for 5 years. There was penetrating dampness in the kitchen and a leak in the soil vent pipe in the flat above caused dampness in adjoining rooms and smells. |
| **Award:** | £1,500 damages per year for 5 years. |
| **General Damages:** | £7,500 |

**Value of Award of £1,500 per annum as at April 2004: £1,825**

*Property – Housing – Breach of covenant to repair*

---

**Name of Case:**      *Camden LBC v Witten and Witten*

**Cause/s of Action:**   Breach of covenant to repair

**Tribunal and Judge:**   Central London County Court

**Where Reported:**     September 1993 LAB 15

**Date of Award:**      June 18, 1993

**Brief Facts of Case:**   Council brought possession proceedings and 2 joint Ts separately counterclaimed for disrepair. The male T had contracted asthma as a result in part of the dampness caused by the disrepair.

**Award:**            £36,565.60 total damages:

£17,500 personal injury

1,500 aggravated damages

£1,000 per year for inconvenience and discomfort for each year of disrepair; (balance – compensatory damages for 3 children)

(Special damages were awarded.)

**General Damages:**    £1,000 per annum

**Value of Award of £1,000 per annum as at April 2004: £1,317**

**Value of Award of £1,500 aggravated damages as at April 2004: £1,976**

*Property – Housing – Breach of covenant to repair*

| | |
|---|---|
| **Name of Case:** | *Chiodi v DeMarney* |
| **Cause/s of Action:** | Breach of covenant to repair |
| **Tribunal and Judge:** | Court of Appeal – Ralph Gibson & Butler Sloss LJJ |
| **Where Reported:** | December 1988 LAB 20; (1988) 41 EG 80; [1988] 2 EGLR 64; (1988) 28 HLR 6 |
| **Date of Award:** | June 7, 1988 |

**Brief Facts of Case:**

T occupied a one bedroom top floor flat registered with a fair rent. Despite T starting to complain of disrepair in 1980 no repairs were carried out between 1980-1983. T was then re-housed by the Council temporarily while the Council undertook structural repairs in default of repair notices served on L. In 1985 L brought possession proceedings. T counterclaimed for damages for disrepair. The property suffered from a broken water heater (T had had no hot water for 5 years), damp, broken windows, cracks in walls holes in the roof and dangerous cables and wiring.

L appealed against county court award for general damages on the basis that it was too high and failed to take into account the low registered rent.

**Award:**

The Court declined to interfere with the award of £5,460 damages for general inconvenience and distress @ £30 per week for 3 ½ years.

(Special damages: £4,657 for furniture, decorations and clothing affected by damp and £1,500 for injury to T's health comprising exacerbated colds, influenza and arthritis.)

**General Damages:**     £5,460

**Value of Award of £30 per week as at April 2004: £52**

*Property – Landlord & Tenant – Breach of covenant to repair*

**Name of Case:**          *Clarke v Brent LBC*

**Cause/s of Action:**     Breach of covenant to repair

**Tribunal and Judge:**    Wood Green Trial Centre – HHJ Gee

**Where Reported:**        August 1994 LAB 17

**Date of Award:**         January 13, 1994

**Brief Facts of Case:**   T and her 3 children occupied a council flat which was subject to severe condensation, dampness and mould growth. The conditions had been aggravated by disrepair. The installation of replacement windows which had reduced ventilation and the insertion of an air brick had further worsened the conditions. There was a defective heating system, a defective extractor fan and wood rot.

**Award:**                 Total of £18,630 over period of 9 years including:

£7,475 for diminution in value

£3,000 for inconvenience

£3,000 for ill-health

(Special damages: £2,250 for damage to goods.)

**General Damages:**       £3,000

**Value of Award of £3,000 as at April 2004: £3,943**

*Property – Housing – Breach of covenant to repair*

---

**Name of Case:**          *Coldbeck v Mohamed*

**Cause/s of Action:**     Breach of covenant to repair

**Tribunal and Judge:**    Nottingham County Court – HH Judge Macduff QC

| | |
|---|---|
| **Where Reported:** | [1999] CLY 1399; August 1999 LAB 27 |
| **Date of Award:** | January 13, 1999 |
| **Brief Facts of Case:** | C was a joint tenant of property owned by M and another between January and November 1998. Complaints were made of disrepair at the start of the tenancy including damp, defective electrics, gas heaters and windows and lack of hot water for part of tenancy. |
| **Award:** | £2,500 general damages for 9-month period (taking into account deterioration to clothing, bedding and soft furnishing). |
| **General Damages:** | £2,500 |

**Value of Award of £2,500 as at April 2004: £2,841**

*Property – Landlord & Tenant – Breach of covenant to repair*

---

| | |
|---|---|
| **Name of Case:** | *Conroy and others v Hire Token Ltd* |
| **Cause/s of Action:** | Breach of covenant to repair –Breach of duty of care under s4 Defective Premises Act 1972 |
| **Tribunal and Judge:** | Manchester County Court – HHJ Holman |
| **Where Reported:** | February 2002 LAB 22 |
| **Date of Award:** | May 29, 2001 |
| **Brief Facts of Case:** | T occupied under an assured shorthold tenancy but vacated after 6 months due to L's failure to carry out repair to premises which were affected by dampness and mould growth. T claimed damages for personal injury for breach of duty of care under s4 Defective Premises Act 1972 in respect of her daughter aged 4 and son aged 3 for coughs and colds over a 6-month period. |

**Award:**                    £650 damages for each child.

**General Damages:**          £650

**Value of Award of £650 as at April 2004: £693**

*Property – Landlord & Tenant – Breach of covenant to repair – Breach of statutory duty*

---

**Name of Case:**             *Cook v Horford Investment Ltd and Mohammed Taj*

**Cause/s of Action:**        Breach of covenant to repair

**Tribunal and Judge:**       West London County Court – HHJ Phelan

**Where Reported:**           September 1993 LAB 16

**Date of Award:**            November 2, 1992

**Brief Facts of Case:**      Ts occupied flat in serious disrepair with water penetration through the roof and defective windows. Ls had failed to comply with statutory notices.

                              Damages assessed in lieu of specific performance due to difficulty of enforcing an order.

**Award:**                    Interim award of £11,500 for remedial works.

                              £13,200 total damages for disrepair:

                              £1,958 (diminution in value of 50 % of rent)

                              £5,250 (£1,500 per year) damages for inconvenience and discomfort

                              £3,000 exemplary damages

                              (Special damages: £ 2,095.)

**General Damages:**          £5,250

**Value of Award of £1,500 per annum general damages as at April 2004: £1,994**

**Value of Award of £3,000 exemplary damages as at April 2004: £3,988**

*Property – Landlord & Tenant – Breach of covenant to repair – Specific Performance*

| | |
|---|---|
| **Name of Case:** | *Crewe Services & Investment Corporation v Silk* |
| **Cause/s of Action:** | Breach of tenant's covenant to repair |
| **Tribunal and Judge:** | Court of Appeal – Lord Woolf MR, Millett and Walker LJJ |
| **Where Reported:** | [1998] 2 EGLR 1 |
| **Date of Award:** | December 2, 1997 |
| **Brief Facts of Case:** | T (appellant) held annual tenancy of agricultural holding. T had covenanted to destroy weeds, cultivate one field, maintain hedges and gates and repair buildings and fixtures. County Court Judge found T to be in breach of his covenant to repair. Damages were assessed at £15,940. T appealed. |
| **Award:** | Damages discounted to £3,000 in respect of allowable repair costs. (Appeal allowed – Judge wrong to treat undiscounted costs of repair as measure of damage to the reversion.) |
| **General Damages:** | £3,000 |

**Value of Award of £3,000 as at April 2004: £3,482**

*Property – Landlord & Tenant – Tenant's covenant to repair*

| | |
|---|---|
| **Name of Case:** | *Dadd v Christian Action (Enfield) Housing Association* |
| **Cause/s of Action:** | Breach of covenant to repair – Nuisance by infestation |
| **Tribunal and Judge:** | Central London County Court – DJ Langley |

**Where Reported:**          December 1994 LAB 18

**Date of Award:**          September 28, 1994

**Brief Facts of Case:**          T was a single parent occupying a 2-bedroom flat in a converted house with her 2 children aged 2 and 4 years between November 1990 and May 1993. The house was infested with rats throughout the tenancy. The rats did not enter the flat but could be heard at night. When treated with poison the rotting carcasses attracted flies and the rats returned a few weeks later. There was dampness in the kitchen and the heating and hot water supply was defective.

**Award:**          £7,476 total damages including:

£3,250 general damages (£1,300 per year)

£790 per year damages for diminution in value (40% of rent)

(Special damages: £1,950.)

**General Damages:**          £3,250

**Value of Award of £1,300 per annum as at April 2004: £1,665**

*Property – Housing – Breach of covenant to repair – Nuisance – Infestation by rats*

---

**Name of Case:**          *Das v Crown Estate Commissioners*

**Cause/s of Action:**          Breach of covenant to repair

**Tribunal and Judge:**          Bloomsbury County Court – HHJ Evans

**Where Reported:**          September 1990 LAB 8

**Date of Award:**          July 2, 1990

**Brief Facts of Case:**          T issued proceedings on the basis of disrepair of the structure and exterior of his flat and the common parts of a house in multiple occupation.

Offers of alternative accommodation were made by L and finally accepted by T.

**Award:** £2,225 general damages for inconvenience to T over a period of 5 years (£445 per annum).

**General Damages:** £2,225

**Value of Award of £445 per annum as at April 2004: £652 per annum**

*Property – Landlord & Tenant – Breach of covenant to repair*

---

**Name of Case:** *Davies v Peterson*

**Cause/s of Action:** Breach of covenant to repair

**Tribunal and Judge:** Court of Appeal – Kerr LJ

**Where Reported:** December 1988 LAB 20

**Date of Award:** October 12, 1988

**Brief Facts of Case:** T appealed against the county court award of £250 damages for inconvenience, distress and anxiety for a disrepair counterclaim.

The Court found that the property had been in disrepair over a period of more than 12 months.

**Award:** The Court substituted £1,000 as the general damages award.

(Special damages were awarded by the county court and not appealed against.)

**General Damages:** £1,000

**Value of Award of £1,000 as at April 2004: £1,696**

*Property – Landlord & Tenant – Breach of covenant to repair*

---

**Name of Case:** *De La Rosa v Liverpool CC*

**Cause/s of Action:** Breach of covenant to repair

**Tribunal and Judge:** Liverpool County Court – HHJ Steele

**Where Reported:** August 1999 LAB 26; July 2001 LAB 27

**Date of Award:** July 1, 1999

**Brief Facts of Case:** T occupied a 3-bedroom council house with her 3 children. There was a leaking roof and gutters, ill-fitting windows and dampness in all rooms except one bedroom and kitchen. Black fungus was growing on some of the walls.

**Award:** £10,250 total:

£2,250 per year general damages for 4 ½ years

The award was subsequently reduced to £5,000 on L's application to set aside the award on the basis of fresh evidence indicating that T had misled the court as to her circumstances.

(Special damages: £1,500 for re-decoration.)

**General Damages:** £10,250

**Value of £2,250 per annum general damages as at April 2004: £2,531**

*Property – Housing – Breach of covenant to repair*

---

**Name of Case:** *Dean v Ainsley*

**Cause/s of Action:** Breach of covenant to repair

**Tribunal and Judge:** Court of Appeal – Kerr, Glidewell LJJ and Sir George Waller

**Where Reported:** December 1987 LAB 16, [1987] 137 NLJ 830, *The Times* 5 August 1987

**Date of Award:** July 14, 1987

**Brief Facts of Case:** Vendor covenanted with purchaser to carry out repairs to ensure cellar was free from water penetration but failed to carry out the works.
Purchaser brought proceedings for breach of contract and was awarded £5 nominal damages at first instance. Purchaser appealed.

**Award:**                    Court of Appeal set aside nominal award and substituted £7,500 damages.

**General Damages:**          £7,500

**Value of £7,500 as at April 2004: £13,681**

*Property – Vendor/purchaser – Breach of covenant to repair*

---

**Name of Case:**             *Derby and Woodward v Southwark LBC*

**Cause/s of Action:**        Breach of covenant to repair

**Tribunal and Judge:**       Lambeth County Court – HHJ Cox

**Where Reported:**           [1998] H&HI (3) 4.4; August 1999 LAB 26

**Date of Award:**            1998

**Brief Facts of Case:**      Ps rented a 1-bedroom council flat from October 1994. They reported cracked sanitary ware, stained and cracked ceiling plaster and defective bathroom handles. By winter 1994 there was damp in the kitchen and bathroom. Not all the remedial work could be completed as the male T suffered from agoraphobia and claustrophobia and works could not be carried out with him in occupation. Ts were rehoused in September 1997.

**Award:**                    £3,300 general damages.

                              (Special damages: £615.)

**General Damages:**          £3,300

**Value of £3,300 as at April 2004: £3,725**

*Property – Housing – Breach of covenant to repair*

---

**Name of Case:**   *Dorrington v Greenwich LBC*

**Cause/s of Action:**   Breach of covenant to repair

**Tribunal and Judge:**   Woolwich County Court – HHJ Gibson

**Where Reported:**   August 1999 LAB 26

**Date of Award:**   June 22, 1999

**Brief Facts of Case:**   From 1988 T occupied a property affected by dampness and the smell of damp and mould growth but could only establish disrepair from October 1993.

From May 1991 to October 1993 (1st period) T's home was affected by dampness and mould growth.

Between October 1993 and January 1995 (2nd period) the mould growth worsened and dampness spread.

The cause was a defective hot-water pipe under the bathroom floor.

**Award:**   £3,250 total general damages:

£1,875 for the 1st period (£750 per year);

£1,375 for the 2nd period (£1,250 per year reduced by 10% due to T's failure to adequately heat the premises).

(Special damages: £150.)

**General Damages:**   £3,250

**Value of Award of £1,250 per annum as at April 2004: £1,402**

**Value of Award of £750 per annum as at April 2004: £841**

*Property – Housing – Breach of covenant to repair*

**Name of Case:**          *Downie v London Borough of Lambeth*

**Cause/s of Action:**     Breach of covenant to repair

**Tribunal and Judge:**    Wandsworth County Court – HHJ White

**Where Reported:**        July 1986 LAB 95

**Date of Award:**         June 3, 1986

**Brief Facts of Case:**   T and his wife had occupied their council house
                           since 1966. Following environmental health
                           officers' inspections two notices were served on
                           the Council specifying repair works in October
                           1981 and April 1982. The Council failed to carry
                           out any repairs but offered alternative
                           accommodation in April 1983 which T was
                           unable to accept due to his ill-health.

                           In November 1983 the house was found to be
                           unfit for habitation due to a lack of maintenance
                           over a substantial period. The problems suffered
                           included damp, a leaking soil pipe, inadequate
                           ventilation and waste disposal facilities and an
                           unsuitable kitchen.

**Award:**                 £4,000 general damages for Ts discomfort over 4
                           year period on the basis that the property had
                           been unfit since November 1981.

                           (Special damages: £451.)

**General Damages:**       £4,000

**Value of Award of £1,000 per annum as at April 2004: £1,899**

*Property – Housing – Breach of covenant to repair*

**Name of Case:**          *Essapen v Jouaneau*

**Cause/s of Action:**      Breach of covenant to repair

**Tribunal and Judge:**     Bow County Court – HHJ Goldstein

**Where Reported:**        June 1995 LAB 22

**Date of Award:**         March 1, 1995

**Brief Facts of Case:**    L brought possession proceedings and T counterclaimed for disrepair. Property suffered from dampness, intermittent heating, defective electrical installations, a leaking roof and windows that could not be opened.

**Award:**                 Total: £10,740 including:

                           £9,240 for loss of value (monthly rent reduced from £400 to £120 for 33 months)

                           £1,000 generally for inconvenience and distress

                           £500 for interference with the hot water supply

**General damages:**       £1,500

**Value of Award of £1,500 as at April 2004: £1,888**

*Property – Landlord & Tenant – Breach of covenant to repair*

---

**Name of Case:**          *Evans v Midland Area Improvement Housing Association*

**Cause/s of Action:**      Breach of covenant to repair

**Tribunal and Judge:**     QBD Birmingham District Registry

**Where Reported:**        December 1991 LAB 22

**Date of Award:**         1991

**Brief Facts of Case:**    T occupied property suffering from bad disrepair over a period of 10 years. Evidence from consultant rheumatologist that damp and cold led to deterioration in T's health.

**Award:**    £10,000 damages.

**General Damages:**    £10,000

**Value of Award of £1,000 per annum as at April 2004: £1,385**

*Property – Housing – Breach of covenant to repair*

---

**Name of Case:**    *Fallon v McKeown*

**Cause/s of Action:**    Breach of covenant to repair

**Tribunal and Judge:**    Lambeth County Court

**Where Reported:**    December 1991 LAB 22; *The Guardian* 10 May 1991

**Date of Award:**    1990

**Brief Facts of Case:**    T and children occupied top-floor flat suffering from damp and mould growth. One child suffered severe bronchitis and the youngest child died of acute pneumonitis.

**Award:**    £7,600 damages.

**General Damages:**    £7,600

**Value of Award of £7,600 as at April 2004: £10,856**

*Property – Landlord & Tenant – Breach of covenant to repair*

**Name of Case:**      *Felix v Karachristos and Jachini*

**Cause/s of Action:**      Breach of covenant to repair

**Tribunal and Judge:**      Bloomsbury County Court – HHJ Dobry

**Where Reported:**      August 1987 LAB 17

**Date of Award:**      March 4, 1987

**Brief Facts of Case:**      Ds moved into 1-bedroom flat in September 1982 under purported licence agreements. Ds complained of disrepair from the outset including rotten window frames, damp bathroom walls and ceiling, defective wiring and rainwater penetrating the outside hallway. In April 1985 the hallway ceiling collapsed and between January to April 1985 a broken drain led to a sewage smell reaching the Ts' second floor flat.

L issued possession proceedings on the basis of non-payment of licence fees and termination of the licences in 1985. Ds counterclaimed for damages for Ls breach of covenant.

**Award:**      £5,000 for inconvenience and general suffering over a period of 4 ¼ years.

**General Damages:**      £5,000

**Value of £5,000 as at April 2004: £9,230**

*Property – Landlord & Tenant – Breach of covenant to repair*

---

**Name of Case:**      *Finch v Manchester CC*

**Cause/s of Action:**      Breach of covenant to repair

**Tribunal and Judge:**      QBD Manchester District Registry – Rose J

**Where Reported:**      December 1986 LAB 167, June 1987 LAB 21

| | |
|---|---|
| **Date of Award:** | October 10, 1986 |
| **Brief Facts of Case:** | T and his family consisting of his wife and three children occupied a property suffering from disrepair over a period of 3 to 4 years leading to the death of one child from bronchio-pneumonia. |
| **Award:** | £13,000 total damages. |
| | General damages apportioned as follows: |
| | £3,000 to T |
| | £2,000 to T's wife |
| | £3,000 to the 3 surviving children |
| **General Damages:** | £8,000 |

**Value of Award of £8,000 as at April 2004: £15,082**

*Property – Housing – Breach of covenant to repair*

---

| | |
|---|---|
| **Name of Case:** | *Foster v Donaghey* |
| **Cause/s of Action:** | Breach of covenant to repair |
| **Tribunal and Judge:** | Huddersfield County Court – District Judge Harrison |
| **Where Reported:** | [1994] CLY 1454; August 1994 LAB 17 |
| **Date of Award:** | April 12, 1994 |
| **Brief Facts of Case:** | T took up occupation of a house let by L in reliance on L's promise that extensive works of renovation were due to be carried out. Defects included only one working tap in the house situated in the living room, missing lavatory cistern, penetrating and rising damp, draughts, dangerous fumes from gas fire and trailing electrical wires. Eight-and-a-half months later no |

works had been done and T was re-housed by local authority.

(Special damages: £190.)

**Award:**                £2,000 general damages.

**General Damages:**      £2,000

**Value of Award of £2,000 as at April 2004: £2,576**

*Property – Landlord & Tenant – Breach of covenant to repair*

---

**Name of Case:**         *Fraser v Hopewood Properties*

**Cause/s of Action:**    Breach of covenant to repair

**Tribunal and Judge:**   West London County Court – HHJ Parker

**Where Reported:**       [1986] CLY 1843; June 1986 LAB 81

**Date of Award:**        October 29, 1985

**Brief Facts of Case:**  T occupied a top floor flat which suffered from damp penetration and roof leaks over a period of 3 ½ years.

**Award:**                £2,000 general damages

                          (Special damages: £2,250 for redecoration £200 for soft furnishings.)

**General Damages:**      £2,000

**Value of Award of £2,000 as at   April 2004: £3,887**

*Property – Landlord & Tenant – Breach of covenant to repair*

---

**Name of Case:**           *Gates v London Borough of Southwark*

**Cause/s of Action:**      Breach of covenant to repair

**Tribunal and Judge:**     Lambeth County Court – HHJ James

**Where Reported:**         March 1992 LAB 14

**Date of Award:**          January 17, 1992

**Brief Facts of Case:**    Ts and 4 other members of the family occupied a 5- bedroom property on 3 floors. Penetrating damp in 1979 spread to all floors by 1985. In 1988 severe disrepair resulted in collapsed plaster and dampness. Out of the 5 bedrooms 3 were uninhabitable. Ts were rehoused in 1988.

Ts brought proceedings in 1990 and claimed that over a period of 4 years family members suffered from chest, throat and ear infections. T1 was on renal dialysis.

**Award:**                  Damages agreed at £14,500.

**General Damages:**        £14,500

**Value of Award of £14,500 as at April 2004: £19,857**

*Property – Housing – Breach of covenant to repair*

---

**Name of Case:**           *Gething v Evans*

**Cause/s of Action:**      Breach of covenant to repair

**Tribunal and Judge:**     CC (Skegness) - District Judge Moore

**Where Reported:**         [1997] CLY 1753; May 1997 LAB 18

**Date of Award:**          March 21,1996

**Brief Facts of Case:**    Between May 1988 and June 1994 G and daughter occupied dwelling with defects which were reported at the outset of the tenancy, including cracked WC bowl, rotting floorboards, disintegrating kitchen units, damp wall and broken immersion heater. E only replaced one floorboard in 6 months, G carried out installation of kitchen and bathroom at own expense.

**Award:** Total: £15,093 (excluding interest) including:

£1,148 for diminution in value – 20% for first 6 months and 15% thereafter

£2,000 for discomfort, distress and inconvenience

£1,000 each for inconvenience, distress and discomfort up to August 1993 (£790 each for the remainder of the tenancy)

£3,000 for value of minor repairs and decorations

£150 and £500 personal injury damages for exacerbation of asthma suffered

(Special damages: £1,729 for costs of works carried out by T and £400 special damages to property.)

**General Damages:** £3,000

**Value of Award of £3,000 as at April 2004: £3,677**

*Property – Landlord and Tenant – Breach of covenant to repair*

---

**Name of Case:** *Hallett v Camden LBC*

**Cause/s of Action:** Breach of implied covenant to repair under s11 Landlord and Tenant Act 1985

**Tribunal and Judge:** Central London County Court – Recorder Behar

**Where Reported:** August 1994 LAB 17

**Date of Award:** May 4, 1994

**Brief Facts of Case:** T complained to the Council of cracks to walls and ceilings and defective windows to the Victorian house which disrepair had been outstanding for 2½ years. The Council maintained that the minor cracks could be filled and redecorated by T and the windows would be addressed in their cycle of external redecoration.

**Award:** £750 for the windows (£300 per annum) which led the premises to be draughty.

(No award for the cracks which were so minor as not to be actionable having regard to the age, character and prospective life of the house.)

**General Damages:** £750

**Value of Award of £300 per annum as at April 2004: £385 per annum**

*Property – Housing – Breach of covenant to repair*

---

**Name of Case:** *Hardy v Maund*

**Cause/s of Action:** Breach of implied covenant to repair under s11 of Landlord and Tenant Act 1985

**Tribunal and Judge:** Stockport County Court – The District Judge

**Where Reported:** December 1995 LAB 22

**Date of Award:** August 21, 1995

**Brief Facts of Case:** T occupied a bed-sit as an assured shorthold tenant for 6 months before leaving. Her rent was £75 per week. She claimed damages in respect of rising and penetrating damp in most parts of the property. In the bedroom the conditions were so bad that apart from a 2-week period T had to sleep on a sofa bed in the living room.

**Award:** £975 damages for loss of value (50% of rent for 26 weeks)

£1,500 general damages for discomfort and inconvenience (£3,000 pa)

**General Damages:**          £1,500

**Value of Award of £3,000 per annum as at April 2004: £3,716**

*Property – Landlord & Tenant – Breach of covenant to repair*

---

**Name of Case:**          *Hickey v A Gayden Properties Ltd*

**Cause/s of Action:**          Breach of covenant to repair

**Tribunal and Judge:**          Birmingham County Court – Assistant Recorder Corbett

**Where Reported:**          May 1998 LAB 23

**Date of Award:**          December 19,1997

**Brief Facts of Case:**          T occupied 2 successive bed-sits in an old house. There were partially collapsing ceilings, roof leaks, penetrating dampness and defective windows and heaters.

**Award:**          £6,000 damages for diminution in value and discomfort (£2,000 per year for 6 years where conditions had been bad for ½ of each year).

**General Damages:**          £6,000

**Value of Award of £2,000 per annum as at April 2004: £2,321 p.a.**

*Property – Landlord & Tenant – Breach of covenant to repair*

---

**Name of Case:**          *Homes v Lambeth LBC*

**Cause/s of Action:**          Breach of covenant to repair

**Tribunal and Judge:**          Wandsworth County Court – DJ Gittens

**Where Reported:**          May 1997 LAB 19

**Date of Award:**          February 2, 1997

**Brief Facts of Case:**    T occupied a 1-bedroom council flat between May 1995 and September 1996. T was in her fifties and suffered from a condition causing pain in her back, arms and neck. The disrepair included penetrating dampness due to a defective roof, gutter and rainwater goods, defective windows and water heater. She had to use buckets to catch the water in heavy rain.

L agreed in December 1995 to carry out works but these were not started until June 1886 when a court order was obtained. T was asked to move out temporarily and alternative accommodation was not provided. On her return in July 1996 the work and not been completed and some of her personal effects ad been damaged in the process.

**Award:**                  £4,342.40 comprising:

Diminution in value @ 50% of rent for 16 weeks (May to September 1995)

30% of rent for 38 weeks (September 95 - June 96)

100% for 4 weeks (June to July 1996)

50% for 8 weeks (July to September 1996)

£2,000 general damages

(Special damages: £500.)

**General Damages:**        £2,000

**Value of Award of £2,000 as at April 2004: £2,396**

*Property – Housing – Breach of covenant to repair*

| | |
|---|---|
| **Name of Case:** | *Hooker-Goodman v Cohane and Cohane* |
| **Cause/s of Action:** | Breach of covenant to repair, action for specific performance under s17 Landlord and Tenant Act 1985 |
| **Tribunal and Judge:** | West London County Court – HHJ Charles |
| **Where Reported:** | September 1992 LAB 22 |
| **Date of Award:** | March 30, 1992 |
| **Brief Facts of Case:** | T brought proceedings for disrepair against L. The judge ordered that Ts were to receive an interim payment of £7,400 to fund remedial works in lieu of specific performance, with liberty to apply for further amounts. This was on the basis that mandatory orders would be difficult to enforce as Ls were outside the jurisdiction.<br><br>(Special damages additional to the award.) |
| **Award:** | £3,480 general damages (in lieu of specific performance). |
| **General Damages:** | £3,480 |

**Value of Award of £3,480 as at April 2004: £4,727**

*Property – Landlord & Tenant – Breach of covenant to repair – Damages in lieu of specific performance*

---

| | |
|---|---|
| **Name of Case:** | *Hubble v London Borough of Lambeth* |
| **Cause/s of Action:** | Disrepair under s32 Housing Act 1961, Occupier's Liability Act 1957 and Defective Premises Act 1972 |
| **Tribunal and Judge:** | Wandsworth County Court – The Circuit Judge |
| **Where Reported:** | April 1986 LAB 50 |

**Date of Award:**          October 28, 1985

**Brief Facts of Case:**    Ts and his wife rented a ground floor flat in a Council house between 1972 and 1983 on a weekly tenancy. Ts had complained continuously about the following disrepairs: defective down pipes and guttering; defective and dangerous electrical fittings, wiring and plaster; rotten floorboard joists in bedroom resulting in Ts wife injuring her leg.

**Award:**                  £4,000 total damages (by consent). General damages awarded to both T and his wife in respect of discomfort caused by the living conditions leading to ill health and leg injury.

                            (Special damages: £740 for furniture and carpets; £600 for clothing; £320 for other expenses.)

**General Damages:**        £4,000

**Value of Award of £4,000 as at April 2004: £7,773**

*Property – Housing – Disrepair*

---

**Name of Case:**           *Hughes v Liverpool CC*

**Cause/s of Action:**      Breach of covenant to repair

**Tribunal and Judge:**     Liverpool County Court – Recorder Stockdale

**Where Reported:**         August 1999 LAB 27

**Date of Award:**          February 19, 1999

**Brief Facts of Case:**    T occupied a house in which most of the rooms were affected by either penetrating or rising dampness. Fungus grew on the kitchen wall. The dampness affected carpets curtains and clothing and attracted vermin. Sometimes rainwater penetration was so bad T had to stay with relatives.

**Award:**                     £15,000 general damages (6 x £2,500 per year).

**General Damages:**     £15,000

**Value of Award of £2,500 per annum as at April 2004: £2,836**

*Property – Housing – Breach of covenant to repair*

---

**Name of Case:**         *Ireland v Sheffield City Council*

**Cause/s of Action:**     Breach of covenant to repair

**Tribunal and Judge:**    Sheffield County Court – HHJ Henham

**Where Reported:**       December 1987 LAB 16

**Date of Award:**        September 2, 1987

**Brief Facts of Case:**   T had occupied property as a council tenant since
                          1978. There was extensive disrepair including
                          damp and rainwater penetration which affected
                          T's health. An independent environmental health
                          officer certified the property as unfit for
                          habitation and a statutory nuisance.

**Award:**                £5,000 damages.

**General Damages:**     £5,000

**Value of Award of £5,000 as at April 2004: £9,067**

*Property – Housing – Breach of covenant to repair*

---

**Name of Case:**         *Islam (T/A Eurasia Property Services) v Begum*

**Cause/s of Action:**     Breach of covenant to repair

**Tribunal and Judge:**    CC (Bow) – District Judge Gregory

**Where Reported:**       [2000] CLY 3938

**Date of Award:**          February 22, 2000

**Brief Facts of Case:**    B lived with 5 children in house between March and December 1996. Prior to her occupation L had agreed to provide carpets and mend defective windows but failed to do so. B was without hot water and heating for half the tenancy, the kitchen was damp and water leaked from the bathroom. In June 1996 L removed bathroom fittings without replacing them.

**Award:**                  Total £3,930.80 - including:

£2,160 general damages for removal of bath, WC and basin (30% diminution in rental value);

£400 for distress and inconvenience

£360 (5% diminution in value) for failure to provide carpets

£760.80 interest

(Special damages: £250.)

**General Damages:**        £2,560

**Value of Award of £2,560 as at April 2004: £2,838**

*Property - Landlord & Tenant – Breach of covenant to repair*

---

**Name of Case:**           *Islington LBC v Spence*

**Cause/s of Action:**      Breach of covenant to repair

**Tribunal and Judge:**     Clerkenwell County Court – DDJ Stary

**Where Reported:**         July 2001 LAB 26

**Date of Award:**          September 6, 2000

**Brief Facts of Case:** L issued possession proceedings for rent arrears. T counterclaimed for damages for disrepair. T had had to stay with a friend for 3 months because his flat had no hot water or heating for the first 6 months of his tenancy. The radiators were inefficient and the gas fire defective. T was without a gas cooker and unable to cook for a period. The window in the living room was ill-fitting leading to draughts and damp penetration.

**Award:** £5,660 total damages including:

£4,250 general damages (£1,500 for the first 6 months and £1,100 thereafter)

(Special damages: £1,199 for carpets, decoration, extra gas, cost of buying cooked food.)

**General Damages:** £4,250

**Value of Award of £3,000 per annum as at April 2004: £3,245**

**Value of Award of £2,200 per annum as at April 2004: £2,379**

*Property – Housing – Breach of covenant to repair*

---

**Name of Case:** *John-Baptiste v Ayvaliouglu*

**Cause/s of Action:** Breach of covenant to repair

**Tribunal and Judge:** Edmonton County Court – HHJ Tibber

**Where Reported:** May 1998 LAB 23

**Date of Award:** February 17, 1997

**Brief Facts of Case:** Ts were joint tenants living with 2 young children in the premises for 2 years and 4 months. There was disrepair from the outset of the tenancy including dampness, defective windows and plaster. The Council served 5 notices under Building Act 1984 s76 for urgent remedial works. If L had not ignored the notices a flood could have been avoided. Damage from the flood forced the family to live in temporary accommodation for 5 weeks.

**Award:**              £20,020 total damages including:

£11,070 diminution in value (50% of weekly rent throughout tenancy)

£1,250 for discomfort caused up until the flood

£1,750 for discomfort caused by the flood and after

£5,000 exemplary damages

**General Damages:**    £3,000

**Value of Award of £3,000 as at April 2004: £3,594**

**Value of Award of £5,000 exemplary damages as at April 2004: £5,990**

*Property – Landlord & Tenant – Breach of covenant to repair*

---

| | |
|---|---|
| **Name of Case:** | *Johnson v Sheffield City Council* |
| **Cause/s of Action:** | Breach of covenant of repair |
| **Tribunal and Judge:** | Sheffield County Court – Mr Recorder Bullock |
| **Where Reported:** | [1994] CLY 1445; August 1994 LAB 16 |
| **Date of Award:** | February 15, 1994 |
| **Brief Facts of Case:** | House occupied by J suffered severe condensation, resulting in black mould and damp. Gas heaters were inadequate and one considered dangerous. J complained Council had breached obligation in tenancy agreement to provide dwelling "fit to live in" under s604 Housing Act 1985 and failed to repair under Landlord and Tenant Act 1985. |

(Special damages: £200 for cost of extra heating £500 for damage to curtains and carpets, £100 for extra decoration.)

**Award:**                £1,500 general damages per winter. Total £3,000.

**General Damages:**      £3,000

**Value of Award of £3,000 as at April 2004: £3,920**

*Property - Housing – Breach of covenant to repair*

---

**Name of Case:**         *Joyce v Liverpool City Council*

**Cause/s of Action:**    Breach of implied covenant to repair

**Tribunal and Judge:**   Court of Appeal – Sir Thomas Bingham MR and Hirst and Aldous LJJ

**Where Reported:**       (1995) 27 HLR 548

**Date of Award:**        April 28,1995

**Brief Facts of Case:**  J was a weekly tenant bringing proceedings against the Council for breach of repairing covenant despite notice of the disrepair and specific performance. She claimed damages for inconvenience, discomfort and distress not exceeding £5,000. District Judge awarded £50 general damages. J unsuccessfully appealed the order on costs.

**Award:**                £50 (appeal dismissed.)

**General Damages:**      £50

**Value of Award of £50 as at April 2004: £62**

*Property – Housing – Breach of covenant to repair*

---

**Name of Case:**     *Khan v Cory*

**Cause/s of Action:**     Breach of covenant to repair

**Tribunal and Judge:**     Birmingham County Court – HHJ Nicholls

**Where Reported:**     September 1995 LAB 14

**Date of Award:**     October 12, 1993

**Brief Facts of Case:**     L commenced possession proceedings against T an assured tenant on the ground of waste. T counterclaimed for breach of covenant to repair. Proceedings were settled with T moving out temporarily whilst L carried out repair works but L sold the property instead.

**Award:**     £30,000 damages under ss27-28 Housing Act 1988 (reduced by 50% due to T's untenant-like behaviour).

(£5,221.28 damages for waste were set off against T's award) leaving £9,778.72 for T.

*Property – Landlord & Tenant – Breach of covenant to repair*

---

**Name of Case:**     *Kinch v London Borough of Lambeth*

**Cause/s of Action:**     Breach of covenant to repair

**Tribunal and Judge:**     Wandsworth County Court – Recorder Russell

**Where Reported:**     June 1988 LAB 20

**Date of Award:**     March 15, 1988

**Brief Facts of Case:**     T occupied a council house suffering from disrepair for a period of 10 years. Environmental health officers had served repair notices and the property was found to be a dangerous structure. It was certified as unfit for habitation by 1986.

**Award:**                    £7,000 general damages.

                              (Special damages: £550.)

**General Damages:**          £7,000

**Value of Award of £7,000 as at April 2004: £12,487**

*Property – Housing – Breach of covenant to repair*

---

**Name of Case:**             *Kurland v London Borough of Camden*

**Cause/s of Action:**        Nuisance by noise – Breach of covenant to repair

**Tribunal and Judge:**       Bloomsbury County Court – HHJ Quarren Evans

**Where Reported:**           December 1991 LAB 22

**Date of Award:**            October 14, 1991

**Brief Facts of Case:**      T was disturbed over a 3-year period by noise from a faulty central heating boiler outside her flat. She also suffered from periods without heat, hot water or running water and developed depression, anxiety and then agoraphobia (to which she had a predisposition).

**Award:**                    £8,500 damages.

**Value of Award of £8,500 as at April 2004: £11,684**

*Property – Housing – Nuisance by noise – Breach of covenant to repair*

---

**Name of Case:**             *Lally v Whiteley*

**Cause/s of Action:**        Breach of covenant to repair – breach of covenant for quiet enjoyment

**Tribunal and Judge:**       Liverpool County Court – HHJ Downey

**Where Reported:**           [1995] CLY 1852

**Date of Award:**        December 21, 1994

**Brief Facts of Case:**  T (who lived alone) was required to vacate a 4-bedroom property for 8 weeks whilst L carried out works of repair. Local authority placed him in a 1-bedroom flat which was cramped due to storage of T's furniture.

**Award:**                £500 general damages for the inconvenience of having to live in flat for 8 weeks.

**General Damages:**      £500

**Value of Award of £500 as at April 2004: £636**

*Property – Landlord & Tenant – Breach of covenant to repair – Breach of covenant for quiet enjoyment*

---

**Name of Case:**         *Lambeth LBC v DeFreitas*

**Cause/s of Action:**    Breach of covenant to repair

**Tribunal and Judge:**   Central London County Court – HHJ Diamond QC

**Where Reported:**       March 1995 LAB 15

**Date of Award:**        November 8, 1994

**Brief Facts of Case:**  The Council commenced possession proceedings on the basis of rent arrears and T counterclaimed for damages for disrepair. The property was affected by penetrating damp caused by defective, blocked or broken rainwater pipes, failure of the hot water and heating system and leaking radiators. Between 1985 and 1993 both the living rooms of the flat were affected by severe damp.

**Award:**                Total of £12,785 including:

£2,500 for the period September 1984 to August 1988 @ £12 per week

£6,500 for the period August 1988 to August 1993 @ £25 per week (when T's 2 children were living at the property and conditions became much worse)

£500 for the inconvenience of removal to and from temporary accommodation whilst flat was repaired

(£1,200 for injury to health i.e. anxiety, depression and respiratory illness aggravated by the conditions)

(Special damages: £878.)

**General Damages:**          £11,585

**Value of Award of £500 as at April 2004: £639**

**Value of Award of £12 per week as at April 2004: £15 per week**

**Value of Award of £25 per week as at April 2004: £32 per week**

*Property – Housing – Breach of covenant to repair*

---

**Name of Case:**          *Lambeth LBC v Guerrero*

**Cause/s of Action:**          Breach of covenant to repair

**Tribunal and Judge:**          Wood Green Trial Centre – HHJ Beddard

**Where Reported:**          March 1993 LAB 14

**Date of Award:**          November 12, 1992

**Brief Facts of Case:**          L issued proceedings for possession and rent arrears. T occupied council house with his wife and 3 children. T counterclaimed for disrepair since 1981. A notice had been served in 1984 by the Council's environmental health officer due to damp and mould growth. In 1987 T obtained an injunction requiring rehousing within 3 months but this did not take place until 1988. T's wife suffered from asthma.

**Award:**

£15,982 total damages (against which £3,500 rent arrears were set off):

£8,000 general damages for ill-health and inconvenience over 7 years

6,000 for diminution in value (less the rent arrears)

(Special damages: £1,098 removal expenses; £600 for damage to goods.)

**General Damages:**       £8,000

**Value of Award of £8,000 as at April 2004: £10,634**

*Property – Housing – Breach of covenant to repair*

| | |
|---|---|
| **Name of Case:** | *Lambeth LBC v Martin* |
| **Cause/s of Action:** | Breach of covenant to repair . |
| **Tribunal and Judge:** | Lambeth County Court – HHJ Cox |
| **Where Reported:** | August 1999 LAB 26 |
| **Date of Award:** | January 27, 1999 |
| **Brief Facts of Case:** | L brought possession proceedings for arrears of rent. T counterclaimed for damages for disrepair. T lived with four children in council maisonette from March 1995. At least three parts of the maisonette were affected by dampness throughout the tenancy. There was also water build-up on a defective balcony which flooded the premises in 1997. |

**Award:**                        Total £10,021.44 including:

                                  £4,500 general damages for 2 ¼ years of tenancy

                                  £3,500 general damages for 18 months (from flooding to trial).

                                  (Special damages: £1,950 comprising £455 for extra heating costs; £750 for redecoration; £745 for damaged possessions.)

**General Damages:**              £8,000

**Value of Award of £8,000 as at April 2004: £9,092**

**Value of Award of £2,000 per annum as at April 2004: £2,273**

**Value of Award of £2,333 per annum as at April 2004: £2,651**

*Property – Housing – Breach of covenant to repair*

---

**Name of Case:**                 *Lambeth London Borough Council v Stables*

**Cause/s of Action:**            Breach of covenant to repair

**Tribunal and Judge:**           Wandsworth County Court – HH Judge Compston

**Where Reported:**               [1994] CLY 1453; December 1994 LAB 18

**Date of Award:**                September 27, 1994

**Brief Facts of Case:**          T had been tenant of a six-bedroom house since 1976 and was in poor health in 1993. L brought possession proceedings against T for rent arrears and T counterclaimed for disrepair of the property.

**Award:**                        £7,181.07 damages for diminution in the value of tenancy of 50% of rent for 1984 and 1988-1994.

General damages of £2,000 for 1994 (defective plastering by L on 4 occasions); £1,000 for 1984 and £1,500 per annum 1988-1994

Total: £11,500.

(Special damages: £100.)

**General Damages:**        £4,500

**Value of Award of £4,500 as at April 2004: £5,763**

**Value of Award of £2,000 per annum as at April 2004: £2,561**

**Value of Award of £1,500 per annum as at April 2004: £1,921**

**Value of Award of £1,000 per annum as at April 2004: £1,281**

*Property - Housing – Breach of covenant of repair*

---

| | |
|---|---|
| **Name of Case:** | *Lambeth LBC v Wright* |
| **Cause/s of Action:** | Breach of covenant to repair – Nuisance by infestation |
| **Tribunal and Judge:** | Wood Green Trial Centre – HHJ Medawar |
| **Where Reported:** | August 1994 LAB 18 |
| **Date of Award:** | December 10, 1993 |
| **Brief Facts of Case:** | T occupied a council flat in a pre-war block affected by cockroach infestation over a 30-month period. L brought possession proceedings for rent arrears. T counterclaimed for damages for disrepair and nuisance. |
| **Award:** | £3,600 total damages comprising: |
| | Damages for loss of value @ £40 per month |

Damages for inconvenience and distress @ £80 per month

**General Damages:**     £3,600

**Value of Award of £3,600 as at April 2004: £4,711**

**Value of Award of £960 per annum as at April 2004: £1,256**

*Property – Housing – Breach of covenant to repair – Nuisance –
Cockroach infestation*

---

**Name of Case:**     *Larksworth Investments Ltd v Temple House Ltd*

**Cause/s of Action:**     Breach of covenant to repair

**Tribunal and Judge:**     Court of Appeal

**Where Reported:**     August 1999 LAB 26

**Date of Award:**     January 18,1999

**Brief Facts of Case:**     T was a solicitors' firm occupying premises as offices. L had failed to repair over 50% of the property and the kitchen and associated room became unusable and the entire premises became unpleasant. At first instance T was awarded £37,500 – for diminution in value and general damages for inconvenience over 5 years.

**Award:**     Reduced to £25,000 on appeal on a rent-related mathematical approach.

**General Damages:**     £25,000

**Value of Award of £25,000 as at April 2004: £28,412**

*Property – Landlord & Tenant – Breach of covenant to repair*

| | |
|---|---|
| **Name of Case:** | *Laskey v Webb* |
| **Cause/s of Action:** | Breach of covenant to repair |
| **Tribunal and Judge:** | Pontypridd County Court – HHJ Robert |
| **Where Reported:** | March 1993 LAB 14 |
| **Date of Award:** | 19 January 1993 |
| **Brief Facts of Case:** | T was an assured tenant of a house for an 8 month period, which he occupied with his wife, new born baby and 7 year-old daughter. There was a leaking roof, rotten windows and defective electrical installations. The entire house was in disrepair and the upper storey became uninhabitable. The property was certified as unfit and T was rehoused. |
| **Award:** | £4,477 total damages over 8 months: |
| | £1,052 (80% diminution on rent of £40 for 8 months) |
| | £1,000 general damages for ill-health and inconvenience |
| | £1,500 exemplary damages |
| | (Special damages: £300.) |
| **General Damages:** | £1,000 |

**Value of Award of £1,000 as at April 2004: £1,347**

**Value of Award of £1,500 exemplary damages as at April 2004: £2,020**

*Property – Landlord & Tenant – Breach of covenant to repair*

**Name of Case:**        *London Borough of Islington v Bakari*

**Cause/s of Action:**    Breach of covenant to repair

**Tribunal and Judge:**   Clerkenwell County Court – The Circuit Judge

**Where Reported:**      March 1992 LAB 11

**Date of Award:**       November 5, 1991

**Brief Facts of Case:**  Council brought possession proceedings based on £3,800 arrears of rent. T was unrepresented and although he stated that the flat was damp he did not enter a defence or counterclaim. A suspended possession order was made of which he was later in breach and possession recovered. T applied to set aside the possession order on the grounds that the arrears were only £2,200 and these would be covered by the damages on a disrepair counterclaim. The judge set aside the possession order on the basis that the T may not have understood the proceedings (not having a good command of the English language). T then entered a defence and counterclaim.

**Award:**               £6,000 agreed damages to be set off against the arrears and a money judgment. Possession action discontinued.

**Value of Award of £6,000 as at April 2004: £8,217**

*Property – Housing – Breach of covenant to repair*

---

**Name of Case:**        *Lessey v Lambeth London Borough Council*

**Cause/s of Action:**    Breach of covenant to repair

**Tribunal and Judge:**   Wandsworth County Court – Recorder Susman

**Where Reported:**      [1995] CLY 1573; December 1995 LAB 22

**Date of Award:**       August 18, 1995

**Brief Facts of Case:** L lived with 12 children as a council tenant of an 8-bedroom 4-storey house. Water penetration between 1983 and 1985 on the top floor rendered the floor uninhabitable – there was damp in the basement and ingress of water due to rotten windows. Between 1985 and 1986 a series of contractors sent to repair the property left it in a dirty state. Between 1987 and 1995 some repair work was carried out but the kitchen remained unusable and the windows in disrepair. L and her family moved into temporary accommodation from 1993.

**Award:** £1,500 per annum general damages from 1983 - 1985 and 1987-1995;

£4,000 per annum general damages for 15 months between 1985 and 1987 when contractors were in attendance.

Total (with interest): £50,850.

(Special damages: £14,000.)

**General Damages:** £19,000

**Value of Award of £1,500 per annum as at April 2004: £1,858**

**Value of Award of £267 per month as at April 2004: £331 per month**

*Property - Housing – Breach of covenant to repair*

---

**Name of Case:** *Lewin (Alphonso) v Brent London Borough Council*

**Cause/s of Action:** Breach of covenant to repair

**Tribunal and Judge:** Central London County Court – HHJ Diamond QC

**Where Reported:** [1995] CLY 1574; March 1995 LAB 15

**Date of Award:** 1995

**Brief Facts of Case:** L purchased council flat under right to buy scheme. Council covenanted to keep common parts and curtilage of block in repair and to provide facilities for rubbish collection, cleaning and caretaking. Between 1987 and 1994 the service areas were dirty, the grass areas were not kept clean and the rubbish collection ineffective. An overflow of manholes for a period of 2 years left sewage on lawn and pathways.

**Award:** £500 per annum for 2 years in respect of overflow of sewers

£300 per annum for remaining 5 years and 4 months

£1,500 for diminution in value of the lease

Total less set-off for service charges unpaid by L was £2,636 (excluding interest).

(Special damages: £375.67.)

**General Damages:** £2,600

**Value of Award of £2,600 as at April 2004: £3,206**

**Value of Award of £500 per annum as at April 2004: £617**

**Value of Award of £300 per annum as at April 2004: £370**

*Property – Landlord & Tenant – Breach of covenant to repair – disrepair of common parts*

---

**Name of Case:** *Lewisham LBC v Al-Aziz*

**Cause/s of Action:** Breach of covenant to repair

**Tribunal and Judge:** Bromley County Court

**Where Reported:** June 1990 LAB 16

**Date of Award:**       January 10, 1990

**Brief Facts of Case:**       Ts and their 5 children occupied a house suffering from a leaking and sagging roof, gaps between the walls and roof, defective and cracked windows and windowsills, blocked gutters, crumbling plaster, dampness and rainwater penetration. In an action by Ls for possession on rent arrears, Ts counterclaimed for disrepair.

**Award:**       £9,500 general damages in respect of 8 years of disrepair (c £1,200 per annum) and £3,000 for personal injury by way of respiratory illness.

(Special damages: £500.)

**General Damages:**       £9,500

**Value of Award of £9,500 as at April 2004: £14,763**

**Value of Award of £1,200 per annum as at April 2004: £1,865**

*Property – Housing – Breach of covenant to repair*

---

**Name of Case:**       *Lloyd v Rees*

**Cause/s of Action:**       Breach of covenant to repair

**Tribunal and Judge:**       Pontypridd County Court – HHJ Moreton

**Where Reported:**       [1996] CLY 3725; (1996) H&HI (1) 2:7; May 1997 LAB 19

**Date of Award:**       September 12, 1996

**Brief Facts of Case:**       T occupied a 2-bedroom flat between January 1993 and August 1994. Throughout the tenancy the flat was affected by penetrating dampness, condensation dampness and mould growth. Works carried out in September 1993 only remedied the conditions in part. T had to spend most weekends and daytime away from her home because it caused her son's asthma to worsen and he suffered from frequent colds.

**Award:**          Damages for diminution in value @ 30% of rent for May – August 1993

General damages for inconvenience, discomfort and ill-health @ £100 per month for 15 months. (Special damages were awarded.)

**General Damages:**          £1,500

**Value of Award of £1,500 as at April 2004: £1,811**

**Value of Award of £100 per month as at April 2004: £121 per month**

*Property – Landlord & Tenant – Breach of covenant to repair*

---

**Name of Case:**          *Loria v Hammer*

**Cause/s of Action:**          Breach of covenant to repair; damage by ingress of rainwater, damp and growth of rot

**Tribunal and Judge:**          Chancery Division – Mr John Lindsay QC sitting as deputy judge

**Where Reported:**          [1989] 2 EGLR 249

**Date of Award:**          July 31, 1989

**Brief Facts of Case:**          In 1986 T acquired the long lease of one of five flats into which L's property had been converted. T alleged L's breach of repairing obligations had caused deterioration to all flats. Ingress of rainwater through cracks in flat roof of extension caused dampness and growth of dry and wet rot. When L did not respond to complaints by T, she carried out the remedial works at her own expense between July and November 1987 over which period she had to move into alternative accommodation.

(Special damages: £16,931.25.)

**Award:**                    £900 general damages.

**General Damages:**      £900

**Value of Award of £900 as at April 2004: £1,447**

*Property – Landlord & Tenant – Breach of covenant to repair –*
*inconvenience*

---

**Name of Case:**         *Lubren v London Borough of Lambeth*

**Cause/s of Action:**    Breach of covenant to repair

**Tribunal and Judge:**   Court of Appeal – Parker LJ and Caulfield J

**Where Reported:**       (1988) 20 HLR 165; June 1998 LAB 20

**Date of Award:**        November 12, 1987

**Brief Facts of Case:**  T had been a council tenant of the property since
1973. The local authority was to keep the
premises in repair. In 1979 defects began to
appear. T complained, refusing two offers of
alternative accommodation and by 1984 the
premises were in an appalling condition.

During proceedings issued by T in 1984 the
Council undertook to carry out the repairs within 3
months and provide alternative accommodation. T
moved out on this basis but was unable to return
until 14 months later.

The Council appealed against the award of
general damages comprising £800 per year
between 1979 and Oct 1984 for inconvenience,
discomfort and damage to health and £500 per
year from Oct 1984 to 1985 for inconvenience
when T was in alternative accommodation.

|  |  |
|---|---|
| **Award:** | (Special damages: £500.) |
|  | £4,500 general damages award upheld. |

**General Damages:**     £4,500

**Value of Award as at April 2004: £8,082**

**Value of Award of £800 per annum as at April 2004: £1,437**

**Value of Award of £500 per annum as at April 2004: £898**

*Property – Housing – Breach of covenant to repair*

---

**Name of Case:**        *Maguire v Tower Hamlets LBC*

**Cause/s of Action:**    Breach of covenant to repair - Negligently
                         conducted repairs

**Tribunal and Judge:**   Queens Bench Division (Official Referee's
                         Court) – HHJ Lloyd

**Where Reported:**       June 1991 LAB 16

**Date of Award:**        April 16, 1991

**Brief Facts of Case:**  Council contractors replaced windows in a flat
                         occupied by M. In doing so they disturbed
                         asbestos panels and contaminated the flat with
                         asbestos fibres requiring M and her children to
                         vacate and abandon their belongings before they
                         were rehoused.

**Award:**                £40,000 damages.

**General Damages:**      £40,000

**Value of Award of £40,000 as at April 2004: £55,808**

*Property – Housing – Breach of covenant to repair - Negligent repairs*

---

**Name of Case:** *Mainsbridge v Zanco Int Ltd and others*

**Cause/s of Action:** Breach of covenant to repair

**Tribunal and Judge:** Reading County Court – HHJ Kenny

**Where Reported:** May 1997 LAB 18

**Date of Award:** March 7, 1996

**Brief Facts of Case:** Ts occupied a 3-bedroom house under a joint assured tenancy between August 1990 and June 1994 (when they were rehoused temporarily). L had notice throughout the tenancy that there was rising/penetrating damp, structural cracking and rotten windows and doors.

**Award:** £9,800 damages (£40 per week up to June 1994). Damages after vacation assessed at 100% of rent until repairs completed.

(Special damages: £180.)

**General Damages:** £9,800

**Value of Award of £9,800 as at April 2004: £12,012**

**Value of Award of £40 per week as at April 2004: £49**

*Property – Landlord & Tenant – Breach of covenant to repair*

---

**Name of Case:** *M'Boge v London Borough of Hackney*

**Cause/s of Action:** Breach of covenant to repair; nuisance by infestation

**Tribunal and Judge:** Shoreditch County Court

**Where Reported:** December 1991 LAB 22

**Date of Award:** July 12, 1991

| | |
|---|---|
| **Brief Facts of Case:** | T occupied flat in a tower block affected by damp penetration and cockroach infestation. T made counterclaim for disrepair. |
| **Award:** | £4,260 general damages. |
| **General Value:** | £4,260 |

**Value of Award of £4,260 as at April 2004: £6,020**

*Property – Housing – Breach of covenant to repair - Nuisance – cockroach infestation*

---

| | |
|---|---|
| **Name of Case:** | *McCarthy v Khosla* |
| **Cause/s of Action:** | Breach of covenant to repair |
| **Tribunal and Judge:** | Bristol County Court – DJ Stuart Brown |
| **Where Reported:** | (1996) H&HI (2) 1:3; May 1997 LAB 19 |
| **Date of Award:** | 1996 |
| **Brief Facts of Case:** | T occupied a 3-bedroom flat on an assured shorthold tenancy for almost three years. Throughout the tenancy the flat was subject to defective windows and central heating, leaking radiators and toilet, dampness in the kitchen, defective electrical installations. |
| **Award:** | Total £8,654 damages including: |
| | £2,238 for diminution in value (20% of rent for period of tenancy) |
| | £2,062 general damages for inconvenience (@ £750 per year) |
| | £4,000 general damages for ill-health (a depressive disorder) |

**General Damages:** £2,062

**Value of Award of £2,062 as at April 2004: £2,488**

**Value of Award of £750 per annum as at April 2004: £904 per annum**

*Property – Landlord & Tenant – Breach of covenant to repair*

---

| | |
|---|---|
| **Name of Case:** | *McDermott v Southwark LBC* |
| **Cause/s of Action:** | Breach of covenant to repair |
| **Tribunal and Judge:** | Lambeth County Court – HHJ Pearce |
| **Where Reported:** | December 1986 LAB 167; June 1987 LAB 21 |
| **Date of Award:** | November 5, 1986 |
| **Brief Facts of Case:** | The Council placed T in compulsorily purchased property in August 1981. There was disrepair by way of a leaking roof, defective wiring and damp in most of the rooms. |
| **Award:** | £7,000 total damages between August 1981 and May 1983; general damages of £4,200. |
| | (NB: The court also gave effect to an additional £2,305 damages (comprising £1,900 general damages) awarded by the local arbitration unit for the period December 1983-1985) |
| | (Special damages: £2,300 to include £1,600 for furniture and £400 extra fuel costs.) |

**General Damages:** £4,200

**Value of Award of £4,200 as at April 2004: £7,854**

*Property – Housing – Breach of covenant to repair*

---

**Name of Case:**        *McGorrian v Liverpool City Council*

**Cause/s of Action:**        Breach of covenant to repair

**Tribunal and Judge:**        Liverpool County Court – HH Judge Urquart

**Where Reported:**        [1994] CLY 1452

**Date of Award:**        February 15, 1994

**Brief Facts of Case:**        M lived in council house suffering from disrepair for 6 years. Defective pipework and guttering caused pooling of water in wet weather which made the rear walls damp. Broken rear windows remained boarded up by the Council. Defective window frames led to either draughts or a lack of ventilation. Hot water tap in bathroom dripped continuously – T was forced to use local public baths due to lack of hot water.

**Award:**        £550 per annum general damages for discomfort and inconvenience; total £3,250.

**General Damages:**        £3,250

**Value of Award of £3,250 as at April 2004: £4,247**

**Value of Award of £550 per annum as at April 2004: £719 per annum**

*Housing – Breach of covenant to repair*

---

**Name of Case:**        *McLarty v London Borough of Islington*

**Cause/s of Action:**        Breach of covenant to repair

**Tribunal and Judge:**        Clerkenwell County Court – HHJ Aaron Owen

**Where Reported:**        October 1992 LAB 22

**Date of Award:**        July 10, 1992

**Brief Facts of Case:**        T was a secure tenant of a converted one-bedroom council flat. Between August 1989 and December

1991 when the repair works were completed the flat was in disrepair. The whole flat was damp and wet. There was a burst water pipe in the kitchen – the kitchen and bathroom floors were saturated with water. Water poured down the walls of the kitchen and bathroom from the flat above which had faulty plumbing. T received an electric shock from a toaster and water pored onto a deep fat fryer and her arm was burnt by the hot fat. The back door would not shut due to damp and she could not sleep due to the door being open. The whole flat suffered from a dank musty smell due to damp.

**Award:** £8,315 total damages:

£4,000 damages for discomfort, distress and inconvenience

£1,900 for damages to health

£250 for burns and shock

(Special damages: £1,825.)

**General Damages:** £4,000

**Value of Award of £4,000 as at April 2004: £5,352**

*Property – Housing – Breach of covenant to repair*

---

**Name of Case:** *McManus v Landfarm Properties Ltd*

**Cause/s of Action:** Breach of covenant to repair

**Tribunal and Judge:** Liverpool County Court – HHJ Stannard

**Where Reported:** December 1990 LAB 17

**Date of Award:** March 20, 1989

**Brief Facts of Case:** T brought proceedings for L's breach of repairing obligations.

**Award:**                    £1,000 general damages for 2 ½ years' disrepair.

(£2,225 interim damages award for cost of agreed works on the basis that a subsequent supplementary award could meet the balance necessary for completion of the works)

**General Damages:**          £1,000

**Value of Award of £1,000 as at April 2004: £1,654**

**Value of Award of £400 per annum as at April 2004: £661**

*Property – Landlord & Tenant – Breach of covenant to repair*

---

**Name of Case:**             *Meah v Mayor and Burgesses of the London Borough of Tower Hamlets*

**Cause/s of Action:**        Breach of covenant to repair

**Tribunal and Judge:**       Bow County Court – Registrar Platt

**Where Reported:**           [1987] CLY 1127; October 1986 LAB 135

**Date of Award:**            August 14, 1986

**Brief Facts of Case:**      T and her 3 children occupied a council flat over a period of 3 ½ years. The property was affected by damp (aggravated by condensation) during the last 2 years of the tenancy. The living room and kitchen ceilings were cracked and stained due to a leaking roof. Penetrating damp through the window frames led to black mould growth in the kitchen, living room and 2 of the 3 bedrooms. T felt unable to use the kitchen for the remaining 3 months of the tenancy due to an infestation of black beetles. Owing to the coldness of the other rooms the family lived in one bedroom.

**Award:**                    Total damages of £3,284 including: £1,750 general damages for ill-health and inconvenience suffered by M and her family for loss of enjoyment (£500 per annum).

(Special damages: £1,534 in respect of: the diminution in the value of the property caused by the disrepair @ 70% of rent for last year of tenancy and 30% for the previous year and damage by damp to furniture and clothing at 75% of cost of acquisition.)

**General Damages:**       £1,750

**Value of Award as at April 2004: £3,323**

**Value of Award of £500 per annum as at April 2004: £949 per annum**

*Property – Housing – Breach of covenant to repair*

---

| | |
|---|---|
| **Name of Case:** | *Minchburn Ltd v Peck* |
| **Cause/s of Action:** | Breach of covenant to repair |
| **Tribunal and Judge:** | Court of Appeal – Dillon and Bingham LJJ |
| **Where Reported:** | (1988) 15 EG 97; [1988] 1 EGLR 53; June 1988 LAB 21 |
| **Date of Award:** | November 2, 1987 |
| **Brief Facts of Case:** | L appealed against county court award of general damages for inconvenience and discomfort on the basis that T could have mitigated by giving notice of defects to L earlier. |
| **Award:** | General damages sum reduced from £800 to £700. |
| **General Damages:** | £700 |

**Value of Award of £700 as at April 2004: £1,257**

*Property – Landlord & Tenant – Breach of covenant to repair – Failure to mitigate loss*

**Name of Case:**          *Moodie v Hackney LBC*

**Cause/s of Action:**     Breach of covenant to repair

**Tribunal and Judge:**    Shoreditch County Court – HHJ Clapham

**Where Reported:**        June 1987 LAB 21

**Date of Award:**         February 6, 1987

**Brief Facts of Case:**   T occupied a council property. Between 1980 and 1985 defective windows let in rainwater, damp and cold conditions resulting from the penetration of rainwater and/or defective cold-bridging.

**Award:**                 Total: £2,845.

                           General damages of £2,200 for the period between 1980 and 1985 and £375 for 1985 to date of trial.

                           (Special damages: £250 for injury to T's health resulting in an upper respiratory tract infection and £20 for damage to furniture.)

**General Damages:**       £2,575

**Value of Award of £2,575 as at April 2004: £4,763**

*Property – Housing – Breach of covenant to repair*

---

**Name of Case:**          *Mullen v Hackney LBC*

**Cause/s of Action:**     Breach of covenant to repair

**Tribunal and Judge:**    Shoreditch County Court – HHJ Graham QC

**Where Reported:**        May 1997 LAB 18

**Date of Award:**       March 4,1996

**Brief Facts of Case:**       T occupied a council house affected by extensive dampness, defective windows and plasterwork. T brought proceedings in 1988 for damages and specific performance which were compromised in July 1994 when L agreed to pay damages of £19,500 and gave an undertaking to start works before December 1994 and complete them by March 1995. L failed to start the work and in October 1995 T issued committal proceedings.

**Award:**       A further £6,000 damages and an undertaking to complete works within 14 weeks.

**General Damages:**       £6,000

**Value of Award as at April 2004: £7,354**

*Property – Housing – Breach of covenant to repair*

---

**Name of Case:**       *Mulligan v Halton BC*

**Cause/s of Action:**       Breach of covenant to repair

**Tribunal and Judge:**       St Helens County Court – Deputy Judge Bennett

**Where Reported:**       [1999] CLY 3674; July 2001 LAB 26

**Date of Award:**       1999

**Brief Facts of Case:**       T occupied a 3-bedroom house affected by penetrating dampness through a defective window, draughts through an ill-fitting door, perished plaster, a defective electrical socket and heating system leaving T without hot water for up to 3 weeks a time. T claimed damages for personal injury for aggravation of asthma and for inconvenience and distress.

**Award:**                          £2,750 general damages (£1,750 per year)

                                    (£1,000 per annum personal injury for 1½ years)

**General Damages:**        £2,750

**Value of Award of £2,750 as at April 2004: £3,084**

**Value of Award of £1,750 per annum as at April 2004: £1,962**

*Property – Housing – Breach of covenant to repair*

---

**Name of Case:**           *Muzira v Lewisham LBC*

**Cause/s of Action:**      Breach of covenant to repair

**Tribunal and Judge:**     Bromley County Court – HHJ Russell Vick

**Where Reported:**         August 1999 LAB 27

**Date of Award:**          April 29, 1998

**Brief Facts of Case:**    T and family rented a 2-bedroom top floor flat on 11th floor. It was affected by condensation dampness and from 1992 also was subject to penetrating dampness through the failure of the original flat roof. Water penetrated in times of heavy rainfall.

**Award:**                  Total: £6,354:

                            £1,000 per annum for discomfort and inconvenience

                            £800 per annum for loss of value averaged over 3 years

                            (Special damages: £954 for replacement carpets and redecoration.)

**General Damages:**        £5,400

**Value of Award of £5,400 as at April 2004: £6,167**

**Value of Award of £1,000 per annum as at April 2004: £1,142**

*Property – Housing – Breach of covenant to repair*

| | |
|---|---|
| **Name of Case:** | *Newham LBC v Hewitt* |
| **Cause/s of Action:** | Breach of covenant to repair |
| **Tribunal and Judge:** | Bow County Court – Mr Recorder White |
| **Where Reported:** | June 1995 LAB 23 |
| **Date of Award:** | March 28, 1995 |
| **Brief Facts of Case:** | Council installed new heating system in property occupied by T (a frail man in his late fifties) in 1989. The radiators in the bedrooms and hallway never worked and one out of the three in the living room was defective. Over a period of 4 years the house was so cold that T wore his coat in the living room and slept in his clothes. |
| **Award:** | £3,400 total damages for discomfort and inconvenience @ £850 pa (taking into account that loss occurred only over 6 months during winter). |
| | £600 due to the cold causing the Ts bad foot to feel 'dead' |
| **General Damages:** | £3,400 |

**Value of Award of £3,400 as at April 2004: £4,281**

**Value of Award of £850 per annum as at April 2004: £1,070**

*Property – Housing – Breach of covenant to repair*

**Name of Case:**          *Ngo v London Borough of Lewisham*

**Cause/s of Action:**          Breach of covenant to repair

**Tribunal and Judge:**          Bromley County Court – District Judge Brett

**Where Reported:**          [1999] CLY 1390; August 1999 LAB 27

**Date of Award:**          February 2, 1999

**Brief Facts of Case:**          N lived with 4 children in semi-detached council house. Ingress of water to top floor bedroom due to roof leaks and rotten window frames from winter 1991-1995 when repaired by LBC. Rising damp in ground floor bedroom experienced 1991-May 1988 when N was re-housed.

**Award:**          £1,750 per annum general damages from 1991-1998, total £12,250.

**General Damages:**          £12,250

**Value of Award of £12,250 as at April 2004: £13,896**

**Value of Award of £1,750 per annum as at April 2004: £1,985**

*Property – Housing – Breach of covenant to repair*

---

**Name of Case:**          *O'Beirne v Lambeth LBC*

**Cause/s of Action:**          Breach of covenant to repair

**Tribunal and Judge:**          Central London County Court – HHJ Colin Smith QC

**Where Reported:**          July 2001 LAB 26

**Date of Award:**          March 8, 2000

**Brief Facts of Case:**          T's occupied a converted flat under a joint tenancy from September 1993. The roof and windows allowed water to penetrate. T's put holes in the ceiling in the kitchen in order to collect the rainwater that had accumulated. The bedrooms, toilet, bathroom, living room and landing were also affected. T's internal decorations were damaged and they were embarrassed about its state. There was also loss of hot water and heating intermittently.

**Award:**                   £17,400 total damages including:

£7,550 general damages for each T for inconvenience and distress (discounted by 20 % because T's were in a relationship where they gave each other support) from October 1993 to the date of the trial.

(Special damages: £ 2,000 agreed for décor and carpets.)

**General Damages:**    £7,550

**Value of Award of £7,550 as at April 2004: £8,326**

*Property – Housing – Breach of covenant to repair*

| | |
|---|---|
| **Name of Case:** | *O'Connor v Birmingham CC* |
| **Cause/s of Action:** | Breach of covenant to repair |
| **Tribunal and Judge:** | Birmingham County Court – HHJ Potter |
| **Where Reported:** | [1997] CLY 2642; May 1997 LAB 19 |
| **Date of Award:** | November 7, 1996 |
| **Brief Facts of Case:** | T occupied a council house and complained to L of severe rising dampness exacerbating condensation and mould growth. L failed in its attempts to address the condition between 1988 and 1989. Eventually a damp proof course was inserted and one ceiling and plasterwork were taken down. |

**Award:**                     £10,500 general damages over 7 years (£1,500 per year).

(Special damages: £5,707.)

**General Damages:**    £10,500

**Value of Award of £10,500 as at April 2004: £12,670**

**Value of Award of £1,500 per annum as at April 2004: £1,810 p.a.**

*Property – Housing – Breach of covenant to repair*

---

**Name of Case:**          *Ogefere v Islington BC*

**Cause/s of Action:**     Breach of covenant to repair

**Tribunal and Judge:**    CC (Clerkenwell) – District Judge Southcombe

**Where Reported:**        [1999] CLY 1391; August 1999 LAB 26

**Date of Award:**         April 22, 1999

**Brief Facts of Case:**   O lived with daughter in council flat between August 1996 and April 1999. Damp affected all rooms save the living room. There was damage to carpets, decorations and plaster. Conditions caused O and daughter to sleep on living room floor. She suffered from depression, coughs and colds and worried about her daughter's health. In April 1999 she was rehoused.

**Award:**                 Total £8,415 including damages for diminution in value at 30% for the first year of tenancy, 50% for 6 months thereafter and 60% for the last year;

£1,250 damages for inconvenience and discomfort for 1st year, £700 for the next 6 months and £1,500 for the last year;

£750 for ill-health suffered

(Special damages: £1,918.70.)

**General Damages:** £1,950

**Value of Award of £1,950 as at April 2004: £2,192**

**Value of Award of £1,250 per annum as at 2004: £1,405 p.a.**

**Value of Award of £1,400 per annum as at 2004: £1,574 p.a.**

**Value of Award of £1,500 per annum as at 2004: £1,686 p.a**

*Property – Housing – Breach of covenant to repair*

---

**Name of Case:** *Palmer v Sandwell MBC*

**Cause/s of Action:** Breach of implied covenant to repair

**Tribunal and Judge:** Court of Appeal – Slade and Balcombe LJJ

**Where Reported:** (1987) 284 EG 1487, [1987] 2 EGLR 79, [1988] 20 HLR 74; March 1988 LAB 19

**Date of Award:** October 8, 1987

**Brief Facts of Case:** L appealed against county court award of damages on basis that the repairing covenant had not been properly implied. The Court set aside the award but substituted damages in respect of actual disrepair caused by condensation dampness including crumbling plaster and damage to window frames.

**Award:** £2,000 award set aside and £200 damages award substituted in respect of disrepair caused by condensation dampness.

**General Damages:** £200

**Value of Award of £200 as at April 2004: £361**

*Property – Housing – Breach of covenant to repair*

**Name of Case:**          *Paolucci v Parfitt and Gasgoine*

**Cause/s of Action:**     Breach of covenant to repair

**Tribunal and Judge:**    Wood Green Trial Centre – Mr Recorder Leach

**Where Reported:**        March 1993 LAB 14

**Date of Award:**         January 19, 1993

**Brief Facts of Case:**   Ts counterclaimed in a possession action that:

1) they had been forced to stay in temporary accommodation for a year longer than necessary while L carried out repairs;

2) L's workmen, once Ts were back in occupation, had cut a large hole in the living room wall in order to treat dry rot for 4 weeks posing a threat to their security; and

3) dry rot had then been treated with a foul smelling chemical while they were in residence over 3-4 days.

**Award:**                 General damages for      1) £1,000

                                                    2) £1,000

                                                    3) £60

**General Damages:**       £2,060

**Value of Award of £2,060 as at April 2004: £2,774**

*Property – Landlord & Tenant – Breach of covenant to repair*

---

**Name of Case:**          *Parrish v Leslie*

**Cause/s of Action:**     Breach of covenant to repair

**Tribunal and Judge:**    Lowestoft County Court – HHJ Mellor

**Where Reported:** August 1994 LAB 17

**Date of Award:** March 25,1994

**Brief Facts of Case:** T and her 2 children under the age of 10 occupied a 3-bedroom house over a period of 8 months. The property was subject to a leaking roof, rising damp and inefficient water heating. The gas fire had been condemned and removed but had not been replaced. The drainage system was blocked which led to the garden being flooded with waste water.

**Award:** £1,200 for diminution in value (50% of the contractual rent)

£800 damages for distress and inconvenience

(Special damages: £430.)

**General Damages:** £800

**Value of Award of £800 as at April 2004: £1,043**

*Property – Landlord & Tenant – Breach of covenant to repair*

---

**Name of Case:** *Pierce v City of Westminster*

**Cause/s of Action:** Breach of covenant to repair

**Tribunal and Judge:** CC (Willesden) – HH Judge Sich

**Where Reported:** [2001] CLY 431; July 2001 LAB 27

**Date of Award:** January 18, 2001

**Brief Facts of Case:** P occupied council house. For 10 years subsidence had caused cracks in ceilings and walls. Plaster fell down and prevented decoration. There was a problem of heat loss due to draughts. Damages for disrepair sought under s.11 of Landlord and Tenant Act 1985.

**Award:**                   £5,450 damages for disruption of T's comfort
                             and enjoyment @ £500 - £1,000 over 7 years.

**General Damages:**         £5,450

**Value of Award of £5,450 as at April 2004: £5,915**

**Value of Award of £500 per annum as at April 2004: £543**

**Value of Award of £1,000 per annum as at April 2004: £1,085**

*Property – Housing – Breach of covenant to repair*

---

**Name of Case:**            *Pierre v Gasper*

**Cause/s of Action:**       Breach of covenant to repair

**Tribunal and Judge:**      Bow County Court – HHJ Goldstein

**Where Reported:**          May 1997 LAB 18

**Date of Award:**           March 7, 1996

**Brief Facts of Case:**     T occupied a small bed-sit which was subject to a
                             leaking sink, broken gutter causing dampness, a
                             leaking kitchen roof, peeling wallpaper and
                             mould on the carpet. Conditions had deteriorated
                             over 6 years and it was on the border of being
                             uninhabitable.

**Award:**                   £10,000 total damages (£1,500 per year).

                             (Special damages were awarded.)

**General Damages:**         £10,000

**Value of Award of £10,000 as at April 2004: £12,257**

**Value of Award of £1,500 per annum as at April 2004: £1,839**

*Property – Landlord & Tenant – Breach of covenant to repair*

---

**Name of Case:**          *Pillay v Farahani*

**Cause/s of Action:**     Breach of covenant to repair - nuisance by infestation

**Tribunal and Judge:**    Wandsworth County Court – HHJ Compston

**Where Reported:**        May 1998 LAB 23

**Date of Award:**         January 29, 1998

**Brief Facts of Case:**   T (a tenant of a bed-sit) complained of damp, cockroach infestation and defects in parts of the premises shared with other tenants (defective heater in the bathroom, damp walls, crumbling plaster, defective kitchen sink). The council served a disrepair notice under s190(1) of HA 1985 before remedial work was carried out.

**Award:**                 £10,046 total damages including:

£7,000 for diminution in value over 7 years (at a discounted rate of £1,000 per year to reflect T's failure to co-operate)

£1,500 for discomfort and inconvenience

£1,200 for cockroach infestation (2 years @ £600 per year)

(Special damages: £346.)

**General Damages:**       £2,700

**Value of Award of £2,700 as at April 2004: £3,144**

**Value of Award of £1,500 as at April 2004: £1,746**

**Value of Award of £600 per annum as at April 2004: £699**

*Property – Landlord & Tenant – Breach of covenant to repair - Nuisance by infestation*

**Name of Case:**        *Polnik v Tomlinson*

**Cause/s of Action:**   Breach of covenant to repair

**Tribunal and Judge:**  Hastings County Court – HHJ Kennedy

**Where Reported:**      May 1997 LAB 18

**Date of Award:**       July 11, 1995

**Brief Facts of Case:**  T occupied a converted upper floor flat under a long lease. Damage was sustained in the great storm of October 1987 and the flat was left in substantial disrepair. By April 1993 the flat was uninhabitable – L's builder had abandoned remedial work after heavily using T's services. T vacated and put his possessions into storage.

**Award:**               £19,478 total damages including:

£6,000 for discomfort and inconvenience

(Special damages: £1,067 – electricity charges £1,131 – gas; £413 – water and telephone; £10,366 for more than 3 years' commercial storage charges for T's possessions; £500 for alternative accommodation (T had spent most of the time house-sitting rent-free).)

**General Damages:**     £6,000

**Value of Award of £6,000 as at April 2004: £7,473**

*Property – Landlord & Tenant – Breach of covenant to repair*

---

**Name of Case:**        *Rayson v Sanctuary Housing Association Ltd*

**Cause/s of Action:**   Breach of covenant to repair

**Tribunal and Judge:**  Ipswich County Court – HHJ Brandt

**Where Reported:**      March 1996 LAB 15

**Date of Award:**          January 17, 1996

**Brief Facts of Case:**    T moved into new house in 1979 and noticed structural cracks. By 1983 the cracking had worsened and by 1991 the internal doorframes were distorted. L failed to carry out remedial works despite T's complaints. She became anxious over the condition of the property.

**Award:**                  £4,750 for the 2 years when the worst cracking had taken place.

                            (Special damages: £1,250.)

**General Damages:**        £4,750

**Value of Award of £4,750 as at April 2004: £5,873**

**Value of Award of £2,375 per annum as at April 2004: £2,936**

*Property – Housing – Breach of covenant to repair*

---

**Name of Case:**           *Rees v Davies*

**Cause/s of Action:**      Breach of covenant to repair

**Tribunal and Judge:**     Swansea County Court – The District Judge

**Where Reported:**         September 1987 LAB 12

**Date of Award:**          1987

**Brief Facts of Case:**    Ts occupying property suffering from extensive disrepair over a period of 4 years. Problems included a leaking roof, a ceiling falling in, decayed wet plaster, penetrating and rising damp leaving one room uninhabitable for a 6 month period. L carried out works over 5 months with Ts in occupation. Works included replastering and the removal of the roof and ceilings.

**Award:**                    £4,000 general damages for inconvenience, distress and hardship.

(Special damages: £398 for furnishings and costs of redecoration.)

**General Damages:**          £4,000

**Value of Award of £4,000 as at April 2004: £7,428**

*Property – Landlord & Tenant – Breach of covenant to repair*

---

**Name of Case:**             *Satchwell v Martinvale Developments Ltd*

**Cause/s of Action:**        Breach of covenant to repair

**Tribunal and Judge:**       Birmingham County Court – HHJ Durman

**Where Reported:**           August 1994 LAB 17

**Date of Award:**            March 18, 1994

**Brief Facts of Case:**      T occupied house since 1936. L acquired property in 1983 when it was already in a state of disrepair. Conditions declined. There was penetrating dampness, the roof leaked, the windows were rotten and the gutters leaked. The mortar between the brickwork was missing.

**Award:**                    Total £13,875 including:

£1,500 per year over 4 ½ years for inconvenience and loss of value

£2,500 for costs of redecoration

(There was no claim for ill-health.)

(No claim for special damages was made.)

**General Damages:**      £9,250

**Value of Award of £9,250 as at April 2004: £12,054**

**Value of Award of £1,500 as at April 2004: £1,955**

*Property – Landlord & Tenant – Breach of covenant to repair*

---

**Name of Case:**         *Savage and Savage v Harscott Ltd*

**Cause/s of Action:**    Breach of covenant to repair

**Tribunal and Judge:**   Lambeth County Court – HHJ Macnair

**Where Reported:**       September 1987 LAB 12

**Date of Award:**        June 11, 1987

**Brief Facts of Case:**  Ts (2 adults and 2 children) occupied a ground floor flat. Extensive rising damp and dry rot made one room uninhabitable. L arranged for damp proof course to be inserted whilst Ts were in occupation. They were forced to leave due to the mess and fumes of the work and were unable to resume occupation until 3 months after completion of the works as the property required redecoration and clearing up.

(Special damages: £747 in respect of accommodation costs, cleaning and redecoration.)

**Award:**                £3,000 general damages.

**General Damages:**      £3,000

**Value of Award of £3,000 as at April 2004: £5,467**

*Property – Landlord & Tenant – Breach of covenant to repair*

---

**Name of Case:**       *Savoury v Southwark LBC*

**Cause/s of Action:**     Breach of covenant to repair

**Tribunal and Judge:**    Lambeth County Court

**Where Reported:**      March 1987 LAB 19

**Date of Award:**      October 3, 1986

**Brief Facts of Case:**    Ts occupied a 2-bedroom property that had been in disrepair over a period of 2 years. The Ts chest infections and rheumatism was aggravated by the conditions. The diminution in the value of the property by the end of the tenancy was calculated to be as much as 90 per cent.

(Special damages: £600-£700 estimated.)

**Award:**          £4,000 damages.

**General Damages**      £4,000

**Value of Award as at April 2004: £7,452**

*Property – Housing – Breach of covenant to repair*

---

**Name of Case:**       *Sealey v Hammersmith and Fulham LBC*

**Cause/s of Action:**     Breach of covenant to repair

**Tribunal and Judge:**    Central London County Court – HHJ Ryland

**Where Reported:**      [1997] CLY 2641; May 1998 LAB 23

**Date of Award:**      April 24, 1997

**Brief Facts of Case:**    T and her 4 children each sought damages for inconvenience and ill-health caused by disrepair of their home. They had had no hot water for 3 weeks and lost the use of the bath and WC for 8

days. For over 3 years there were difficulties with the hot water boiler and heating.

**Award:**            Settlement at £1,400 for T and £100 for each of 4 children.

**General Damages:**   £1,800

**Value of Award of £1,800 as at April 2004: £2,139**

*Property – Housing – Breach of covenant to repair*

---

**Name of Case:**       *Shields v Hussain*

**Cause/s of Action:**  Breach of covenant to repair

**Tribunal and Judge:** Leeds County Court – DJ Heath

**Where Reported:**     [1996] CLY 3726; May 1997 LAB 18

**Date of Award:**      March 19, 1996

**Brief Facts of Case:** Ts occupied an old terraced house under an assured joint tenancy between May 1991 and May 1994. From the outset L had notice that the toilet leaked, the cellars and kitchen floor were damp, most windows were rotten and there was penetrating damp in 2 bedrooms and the attic rooms. L's workmen part installed new attic windows in August 1993 and did not return. During the winter rain and snow penetrated the attic and entire house.

**Award:**              £15,092 total damages including:

£7,260 diminution in value – 50 % of rent from May 1991- August 1993, 75% thereafter

£1,750 per T for discomfort and inconvenience

£3,000 costs of Ts' decoration and repair

£650 damages for personal injury (aggravation of asthma)

(Special damages: £400.)

**General Damages:**       £1,750

**Value of Award of £1,750 as at April 2004: £2,145**

*Property – Landlord & Tenant – Breach of covenant to repair*

---

**Name of Case:**          *Southwark LBC v Bente*

**Cause/s of Action:**     Breach of covenant to repair

**Tribunal and Judge:**    Lambeth County Court – HHJ Cox

**Where Reported:**        [1998] CLY 2986; May 1998 LAB 23

**Date of Award:**         December 10, 1997

**Brief Facts of Case:**   T and her 6 children occupied a 5-bedroom 3-storey council house for 5 years. Disrepair included leaks and dampness. The garden wall was so dangerous the children could not play outside.

(Special damages: £2,000 representing two thirds of the replacement costs of ruined goods.)

**Award:**                 £2,500 per year for 5 years

**General Damages:**       £12,500

**Value of Award of £12,500 as at April 2004: £14,058**

**Value of Award of £2,500 per annum as at April 2004: £2,902**

*Property – Housing – Breach of covenant to repair*

---

**Name of Case:**          *Staves & Staves v Leeds City Council*

**Cause/s of Action:**     Breach of covenant to repair

**Tribunal and Judge:**    Court of Appeal – Lloyd LJ and Ewbank J

**Where Reported:**        December 1990 LAB 17; march 1991 LAB 15;
                           (1991) 23 HLR 107

**Date of Award:**         October 4, 1990

**Brief Facts of Case:**   From 1981 P and three children occupied council
                           property. From the start of the tenancy it was
                           damp and P complained on several occasions.
                           Proceedings were commenced in 1985. In 1988
                           the Council cured the damp.

                           Judge found the damage caused by the defective
                           plasterwork had commenced before 1984. There
                           was progressive deterioration between 1986 and
                           1987 and it needed to be renewed.

                           Judge found the renewal of the plasterwork was a
                           repair and awarded £5,000 general damages. The
                           Council appealed.

**Award:**                 £5,000 award upheld. (Appeal dismissed.)

**General Damages:**       £5,000

**Value of Award of £5,000 as at April 2004: £7,126**

*Property – Housing – Breach of covenant to repair*

---

**Name of Case:**          *Steel v London Borough of Newham*

**Cause/s of Action:**     Breach of covenant to repair

**Tribunal and Judge:**    Bow County Court

**Where Reported:**        December 1985 LAB 171

**Date of Award:**          June 22, 1985

**Brief Facts of Case:**    Council in breach of covenant to repair –
                            insulation of flank wall.

**Award:**                  £925 damages

**Value of Award of £925 as at April 2004: £1,801**

*Property – Housing – Breach of covenant to repair*

---

**Name of Case:**           *Stratton and Porter v Arakpo and Southwark
                            LBC*

**Cause/s of Action:**      Breach of covenant to repair

**Tribunal and Judge:**     Mayor's and City of London County Court –
                            HHJ Byrt QC

**Where Reported:**         June 1991 LAB 16; December 1991 LAB 22

**Date of Award:**          June 14, 1990

**Brief Facts of Case:**    Ts occupied rooms in a derelict house in multiple
                            occupation owned by D1.The property was
                            subsequently taken over by the council pursuant
                            to a control order. The property was in an
                            appalling condition. The property was found to
                            be unsafe and a health hazard.

**Award:**                  Over £5,000 total damages for T1 comprising
                            diminution in value of 90% rent and £1,000 per
                            year for inconvenience and ill-health

                            £6,000 total damages for T2 comprising
                            diminution in value of 90% rent and £1,000 per
                            year for inconvenience and ill-health

                            £2,000 exemplary damages awarded against the
                            Council for failure to comply with its statutory
                            obligations after the control order

**General Damages:**      £1,000 per person per annum.

**Value of Award of £1,000 as at  April 2004: £1,466**

**Value of Award of £2,000 exemplary damages as at April 2004: £2,931**

*Property – Housing – Breach of covenant to repair*

---

**Name of Case:**        *Stockley v Knowsley MBC*

**Cause/s of Action:**   Negligence – Breach of covenant to repair

**Tribunal and Judge:**  Court of Appeal – Neill and Nicholls LJJ

**Where Reported:**      (1986) 279 EG 677; [1986] 2 EGLR 141;  March 1987 LAB 20

**Date of Award:**       June 11, 1986

**Brief Facts of Case:** T telephoned L twice to warn of frozen pipes but was not told to turn off the stopcock or where it might be found. The pipes burst and the severity of the flooding resulted in her having to vacate for one night and part of the property remained unusable for a period of 10 months.

**Award:**               £250 general damages for Ls breach of duty of care; £100 general damages for failure to repair window under 1961 Act.

                         (Special damages £75.)

**General Damages:**     £350

**Value of Award of £250 as at April 2004: £475**

**Value of Award of £100 as at April 2004: £190**

*Property – Housing – Negligence – Breach of covenant to repair*

---

**Name of Case:** *Stone and Stone (a minor) v Redair Mersey Agencies*

**Cause/s of Action:** Breach of covenant to repair

**Tribunal and Judge:** Liverpool County Court – DJ Knopf

**Where Reported:** May 1997 LAB 18

**Date of Award:** March 7, 1996

**Brief Facts of Case:** T occupied a converted upper floor flat in a Victorian house for 4 years. Throughout the tenancy L had notice that all rooms were subject to penetrating damp, windows were draughty, electrical installations faulty and sewage overflowed due to drainage problems. T and her young daughter suffered from chest infections and their asthma was aggravated by the conditions.

**Award:** £12,000 total damages including:

£10,000 for T (£2,500 per year)

£2,000 for child (£500 per year)

**General Damages** £12,000

**Value of Award of £12,000 as at April 2004: £14,709**

**Value of Award of £2,500 per annum as at April 2004: £3,064**

**Value of Award of £500 per annum as at April 2004: £613**

*Property – Landlord & Tenant – Breach of covenant to repair*

---

**Name of Case:** *Sturolson & Co v Mauroux*

**Cause/s of Action:** Breach of covenant to repair

**Tribunal and Judge:** Court of Appeal – Glidewell and Taylor LJJ

| | |
|---|---|
| **Where Reported:** | (1988) 20 HLR 332; March 1988 LAB 19; (1988) *Times, Independent* 27 January, CA |
| **Date of Award:** | January 25, 1988 |
| **Brief Facts of Case:** | T occupied flat since 1963. L's predecessor in title had failed to carry out repairs in breach of covenant. From 1973 the property was registered for a fair rent. In 1982 T's wife died and he became statutory tenant under the Rent Act 1977. L brought proceedings in 1973 for arrears of rent of £1,020. T pleaded set off and counterclaim of breach of covenant to repair. |

Judge entered judgment for rent arrears and dismissed claim for possession.

He awarded £5,895 in total (£1,345 for diminution in value to premises caused by breach of covenant and £4,550 for inconvenience, discomfort and injury to health).

L appealed on the ground that the registration of a fair rent must have taken account of the disrepair and that T had failed to mitigate the loss by failing to carry out minor repairs.

| | |
|---|---|
| **Award:** | £5,895 upheld. (Appeal dismissed.) |
| **General Damages:** | £4,550 |

**Value of Award of £4,550 as at April 2004: £8,179**

*Property – Landlord & Tenant – Breach of covenant to repair*

---

| | |
|---|---|
| **Name of Case:** | *Sullivan v Johnson* |
| **Cause/s of Action:** | Breach of covenant to repair |
| **Tribunal and Judge:** | Queens Bench Division – Master Turner |
| **Where Reported:** | March 1992 LAB 13 |

**Date of Award:**          November 21, 1991

**Brief Facts of Case:**    T (96 years old) occupied a property which was formerly his family home. L acquired house in 1975. The conditions had worsened and L carried out no works of repair. Only 2 rooms were habitable.     There was penetrating damp, collapsed ceiling and plaster, rising damp and rot.

**Award:**                  Between 1977-84 total damages of £2,100 (£300 per year)

Between 1984-91 (a period of the worst conditions) total damages of £7,000 (£1,000 per year)

£1,500 general damages for ill-health

(Special damages: £1,495.)

**General Damages:**        £9,100

**Value of Awards of £9,100 as at April 2004: £12,462**

**Value of Award of £1,000 per annum as at April 2004: £1,369**

**Value of Award of £300 per annum as at April 2004: £411**

*Property – Landlord & Tenant – Breach of covenant to repair*

---

**Name of Case:**           *Switzer v Law*

**Cause/s of Action:**      Breach of covenant to repair

**Tribunal and Judge:**     Southport County Court –HHJ Morgan

**Where Reported:**         [1998] CLY 3624; August 1999 LAB 26

**Date of Award:**          1998

**Brief Facts of Case:**    T occupied property which was affected by severe condensation dampness. The wall plaster had disintegrated. The cause was the lack of a system of ventilation which could be remedied by the installation of extractor fans. There were also rotten windows, open mortar joints, defects to gutters and penetrating dampness in the lounge.

**Award:**                £5,500 general damages for discomfort and inconvenience over 8 years.

(Special damages: £150.)

**General Damages:**      £5,500

**Value of Award of £5,500 as at April 2004: £6,251**

*Property – Landlord & Tenant – Breach of covenant to repair*

---

**Name of Case:**         *Symons v Warren*

**Cause/s of Action:**    Breach of covenant to repair˙

**Tribunal and Judge:**   Clerkenwell County Court – District Judge Armon Jones

**Where Reported:**       [1995] CLY 3039

**Date of Award:**        1995

**Brief Facts of Case:**  L sought possession of property let on assured shorthold tenancy. T counterclaimed for damages for disrepair. Bathroom had no natural light, electric light or ventilation for 5 months of tenancy. L failed to repair despite 3 requests from T.

**Award:**                £1,000 damages for diminution in value of his tenancy of £ 17.50 per week (representing 10% of the weekly rent) on basis that T could only make partial use of bathroom (20% of the flat); £30 per week general damages.

**General Damages:**      £1,600

**Value of Award of £1,600 as at April 2004: £1,983**

**Value of Award of £30 per week as at April 2004: £37 per week**

*Property – Landlord & Tenant – Breach of covenant to repair*

---

**Name of Case:**          *Thompson v Birmingham CC*

**Cause/s of Action:**     Breach of covenant to repair

**Tribunal and Judge:**    Birmingham County Court – HHJ Gosling

**Where Reported:**        September 1990 LAB 8; December 1990 LAB 17

**Date of Award:**         July 11, 1990

**Brief Facts of Case:**   T occupied an old terraced council house suffering from severe rising damp for which the remedy was insertion of a damp proof course. Council maintained that having regard to the age, character and locality of house repair should not be required. In the alternative it requested that the court should fix a low level of damages taking into account the fact that T was unemployed and on a low income.

**Award:**                 £4,500 damages including:

£3,028 general damages (17 x 184 weeks)

£1,200 for cost of redecoration after repair

(Special damages: £150.)

**General Damages:**       £3,028

**Value of Award of £3,028 as at April 2004: £4,435**

**Value of Award of £17 per week as at April 2004: £25 per week**

*Property – Housing – Breach of covenant to repair*

---

**Name of Case:**          *Toff v McDowell*

**Cause/s of Action:**     Breach of covenant to repair – Nuisance by noise

**Tribunal and Judge:**    Chancery Division – Evans-Lombe J

**Where Reported:**        (1993) 25 HLR 650; (1995) 69 P&CR 535

**Date of Award:**         July 19, 1993

**Brief Facts of Case:**   In 1987 T took an assignment of a lease of a basement flat in a house which had been converted into 4 flats. He experienced noise nuisance from the ground floor flat from 1987 which worsened in 1990 when the lessee of the ground floor flat, M, removed the floor covering and then let it out to a group of noisy tenants. The lease contained a covenant for the lessor to keep the main structure of the building in repair and a covenant for the lessee to keep the flat in repair. In 1991 T commenced proceedings. The Judge allowed the claim against M the lessee of the ground floor flat. The floor was not the responsibility of the lessor.

**Award:**                 Total of £6,000: £1,000 for diminution in T's enjoyment of the flat for the 6 month period between July 1990 and January 1991 (when the ground floor was occupied by the noisy tenants) and £5,000 from June 1990 to date of judgment. Damages to be increased by £12,000 (the cost of installing a hung ceiling) if M failed to replace the floor covering within 3 months. (£12,000 contingent special damages.)

**General Damages:**       £6,000

**Value of Award of £6,000 as at April 2004: £7,919**

*Property – Landlord & Tenant – Breach of covenant to repair*

*and*

*Nuisance by noise*

| | |
|---|---|
| **Name of Case:** | *Trevantos v McCullogh* |
| **Cause/s of Action:** | Breach of covenant to repair |
| **Tribunal and Judge:** | Court of Appeal – Nicholls and Mann LJJ |
| **Where Reported:** | September 1991 LAB 17; December 1991 LAB 22; (1991) 19 EG 18; [1991] 1 EGLR 123 |
| **Date of Award:** | December 4, 1990 |
| **Brief Facts of Case:** | T, a Rent Act tenant of a ground floor flat since 1975 withheld rent due to L's failure to repair. L issued possession proceedings based on rent arrears of £2,274. T counterclaimed for breach of repair. HHJ Hill-Smith awarded T damages to cover a period of 10 months but made an order for possession. L appealed against general damages award. |
| **Award:** | County Court award not interfered with. Damages to cover period of tenancy since 1985.

£2,700 total damages including:

£1,700 general damages

(Special damages: £1,000 in respect of cleaning curtains and carpets, loss of frozen food etc.) |
| **General Damages:** | £1,700 |

**Value of Award of £1,700 as at April 2004: £2,490**

*Property – Landlord and tenant – Breach of covenant to repair*

---

| | |
|---|---|
| **Name of Case:** | *Trustees of Calthorpe Edgbaston Estate v Routledge* |
| **Cause/s of Action:** | Breach of covenant to repair |
| **Tribunal and Judge:** | Birmingham County Court |

**Where Reported:** December 1991 LAB 22

**Date of Award:** 1990

**Brief Facts of Case:** T made counterclaim for damages for disrepair. T occupied an old house affected by disrepair and permeating dampness. T suffered 6 years' discomfort and inconvenience and 3 years' personal injury by way of asthma colds and coughs. Judge found that repairs should have been carried out 7 years earlier.

**Award:** £4,186 general damages (£750 for personal injury).

**General Damages:** £4,186

**Value of Award of £4,186 as at April 2004: £6,135**

*Property – Landlord & Tenant – Breach of covenant to repair*

---

**Name of Case:** *Tuoma v Raad*

**Cause/s of Action:** Breach of covenant to repair

**Tribunal and Judge:** Central London County Court – HHJ Hallgarten

**Where Reported:** August 1994 LAB 17

**Date of Award:** May 26, 1994

**Brief Facts of Case:** T occupied a 1-bedroom flat paying rent of £150 per week. Water began to drip through bathroom ceiling in 1991. In 1992 the plaster fell off the ceiling and he was without a light fitting. A notice was served on L by the Council in November 1992. Repair was carried out in March 1993 by L but proved ineffective.

**Award:**　　£3 per week damages for loss of value for the first year, £10 per week thereafter; £9 per week damages for inconvenience for second year, £25 per week thereafter.

**Value of Award of £9 per week as at April 2004: £11.55 per week**

**Value of Award of £25 per week as at April 2004: £32 per week**

*Property – Landlord & Tenant – Breach of covenant to repair*

---

**Name of Case:**　　*Turnbull v Much*

**Cause/s of Action:**　　Breach of covenant to repair

**Tribunal and Judge:**　　Liverpool County Court – HHJ Bernstein

**Where Reported:**　　March 1995 LAB 15

**Date of Award:**　　November 10, 1994

**Brief Facts of Case:**　　Since 1981 T had occupied 2 rooms in a Victorian house with shared use of a bathroom and toilet under a Rent Act protected tenancy. Upon occupation L had agreed to carry out repair works but failed to do so. From 1989 there was extensive rising and penetrating damp in the rooms together with dry rot, lack of guttering and a defective roof. The judge found the property to be derelict.

**Award:**　　£7,590 general damages @ £30 per week for 253 weeks. (Special damages: £477.)

**General Damages:**　　£7,590

**Value of Award of £7,590 as at April 2004: £9,700**

**Value of Award of £30 per week as at April 2004: £38**

*Property – Landlord & Tenant – Breach of covenant to repair*

| | |
|---|---|
| **Name of Case:** | *Ujima HA v Aboasu* |
| **Cause/s of Action:** | Breach of covenant to repair |
| **Tribunal and Judge:** | Willesden County Court – HHJ Copley |
| **Where Reported:** | July 2001 LAB 26 |
| **Date of Award:** | April 27, 2000 |

**Brief Facts of Case:** L brought possession proceedings for rent arrears. T counterclaimed damages for disrepair. T occupied a house that had been subject to structural disrepair and damp. The children's bedrooms only were affected by damp for a certain period. Thereafter for 12 months and 2 weeks both of the 2 bedrooms and hall were affected and the family had to sleep in the living room. The family then had to be moved to other temporary accommodation with no garden while work took place. They had been told it would take 3 months but it actually took 22 months.

**Award:** £1,500 for the period when the children's bedrooms were affected

£2,250 for the period when the family had to sleep in the living room

£1,000 for the period in temporary accommodation

(Special damages: £3,467 for cost of new clothing and furnishings and extra transport costs whilst in temporary accommodation.)

**General Damages:** £4,750

**Value of Award of £4,750 as at April 2004: £5,186**

*Property – Housing – Breach of covenant to repair*

**Name of Case:**      *Vass v Pank*

**Cause/s of Action:**      Unlawful eviction – Breach of covenant to repair

**Tribunal and Judge:**      Court of Appeal – Pill LJ, Sir Anthony Evans.

**Where Reported:**      July 2001 LAB 25

**Date of Award:**      November 14, 2000

**Brief Facts of Case:**      T brought proceedings for disrepair and unlawful eviction. L counterclaimed for unpaid rent. The district judge awarded damages. T applied for permission to appeal.

**Award:**      £500 damages. Application dismissed.

**General Damages:**      £500

**Value of Award of £500 as at April 2004: £540**

*Property – Landlord & Tenant – Unlawful eviction – Breach of covenant to repair*

---

**Name of Case:**      *Vaughan v Lambeth LBC*

**Cause/s of Action:**      Breach of covenant to repair

**Tribunal and Judge:**      Lambeth County Court – HHJ James

**Where Reported:**      May 1997 LAB 18

**Date of Award:**      February 9, 1996

**Brief Facts of Case:**      T occupied a 5-bedroom council house which was affected by penetrating dampness. Between 1976 and 1994 (when the roof was repaired) there was a severe leak in 1 bedroom and dampness in another.

**Award:**                    £12,000 damages.

**General Damages:**          £12,000

**Value of Award of £12,000 as at April 2004: £14,767**

*Property – Housing – Breach of covenant to repair*

---

**Name of Case:**         *Vergara v Lambeth LBC and Hyde Southbank Homes*

**Cause/s of Action:**    Breach of covenant to repair

**Tribunal and Judge:**   Lambeth County Court – HHJ Cox

**Where Reported:**       LAB August 2002 30

**Date of Award:**        September 5, 2001

**Brief Facts of Case:**  Ts (together with their elderly mother and 2 sons) lived in 3-bedroom ground floor flat (in a converted terrace house) owned by first the Council and then HSH. They claimed damages for disrepair from July 1994 in respect of water penetration, disrepair of windows, failed hot water supply to kitchen and bathroom, lack of service of living room gas heater. In 1997 the tenants remaining in the terrace had vacated and Ts were the sole occupiers. The properties had been allowed to fall into a state of disrepair with squatting, rubbish accumulation, blocked drains and rat infestations.

**Award:**                £25,000 total damages assessed on the basis of progressive deterioration plus £625 interest comprising:

                          3 years @ £2,500 per year

                          2 years @ £3,500 per year

2 years @ £4,500 per year

£1,500 for 6 months' inconvenience in temporary accommodation

**General Damages:**          £25,000

**Value of Award of £25,000 as at April 2004: £26,589**

**Value of Award of £2,500 per annum as at April 2004: £2,659**

**Value of Award of £3,000 per annum as at April 2004: £3,191**

**Value of Award of £3,500 per annum as at April 2004: £3,723**

**Value of Award of £4,500 per annum as at April 2004: £4,786**

*Property – Housing – Breach of covenant to repair*

---

**Name of Case:**          *Wakefield v Lambeth LBC*

**Cause/s of Action:**          Breach of covenant of repair

**Tribunal and Judge:**          Lambeth County Court – HHJ Gibson

**Where Reported:**          August 1999 LAB 25

**Date of Award:**          November 13, 1998

**Brief Facts of Case:**          Under express term of tenancy agreement L covenanted to repair fences. The fence which was rotten fell down in high winds and although notice was given to the Council it was not repaired. Months later a vicious dog entered the garden and bit T and damaged his garden furniture.

**Award:**          £5,000 damages agreed (to include damages for personal injury).

(Special damages were awarded.)

**General Damages:** £5,000

**Value of Award of £5,000 as at April 2004: £5,648**

*Property – Housing – Breach of covenant to repair*

---

| | |
|---|---|
| **Name of Case:** | *Walker v Andrews* |
| **Cause/s of Action:** | Breach of covenant to repair |
| **Tribunal and Judge:** | Manchester County Court – DJ Fairclough |
| **Where Reported:** | (1996) H&HI (2) 1:12; May 1997 LAB 19 |
| **Date of Award:** | 1996 |
| **Brief Facts of Case:** | T and her 3 children occupied her 7-roomed flat for 18weeks in the winter of 1994/5. The flat was affected by extensive rising and penetrating dampness. The family were forced to live and sleep in one room only. The Council had served an abatement notice under the Environmental Protection Act 1990. |
| **Award:** | £850 damages for diminution in value (six sevenths of the rent) |
| | £1,200 general damages for discomfort and inconvenience |
| **General damages:** | £1,200 |

**Value of Award of £1,200 as at April 2004: £1,448**

*Property – Landlord & Tenant – Breach of covenant to repair*

---

| | |
|---|---|
| **Name of Case:** | *Walker v Lambeth LBC* |
| **Cause/s of Action:** | Breach of covenant to repair |
| **Tribunal and Judge:** | Lambeth County Court –HHJ James |
| **Where Reported:** | September 1992 LAB 21 |
| **Date of Award:** | October 18, 1991 |
| **Brief Facts of Case:** | T occupied a council flat on the 15$^{th}$ floor of a 21-storey block. Two lifts and a staircase served the block and for 18 months one or other of the lifts was out of order whilst the remaining lift was prone to regularly breakdown. The working lift was often used by Council workmen to carry their materials. T had been trapped in the lift on occasion and at other times was forced to use the stairs. This was at a time when she was pregnant and had a 2-year old child. |
| **Award:** | £3,750 general damages. |
| **General damages:** | £3,750 |

**Value of Award of £3,750 as at April 2004: £5,155**

*Property – Housing – Breach of covenant to repair*

---

| | |
|---|---|
| **Name of Case:** | *Wallace v Manchester City Council* |
| **Cause/s of Action:** | Breach of covenant to repair under s11 Landlord and Tenant Act 1985 – Breach of duty of care under s4 Defective Premises Act 1972 |
| **Tribunal and Judge:** | Court of Appeal – Kennedy and Morritt LJJ |
| **Where Reported:** | (1998) 30 HLR 1111 |
| **Date of Award:** | July 7, 1998 |

**Brief Facts of Case:**    From 1989 T was the secure tenant of a council house. In 1996 surveyors reported defects including a collapsed wall, rotten window, mould, defective plaster and skirting board and leaky rainwater pipe. T had complained of the coldness of the rooms and rats from 1994.

In 1997 T issued proceedings. The Judge awarded damages to T's children and to T for her distress and inconvenience but declined to make a separate award reflecting the diminution in the value of the tenancy based on the amount of rent paid.

T appealed on the basis that the Judge should have made an award for diminution in value and that the award was too low.

The Court of Appeal held that the judge was not bound to assess damages under 2 separate heads and declined to interfere with the award.

**Award:**                  £2,000 to each of T's 2 children, £3,500 for distress, inconvenience and disruption to T's lifestyle.

(Special damages: £780.)

**General Damages:**        £7,500

**Value of Award of £7,500 as at April 2004: £8,544**

**Value of Award of £2,000 per annum as at April 2004: £2,279**

**Value of Award of £3,500 per annum as at April 2004: £3,987**

*Property – Housing – Breach of covenant to repair*

**Name of Case:**      *Walton v Lewisham LBC*

**Cause/s of Action:**      Breach of covenant to repair under s11 of Landlord and Tenant Act 1985

**Tribunal and Judge:**      Tunbridge Wells County Court – HHJ Hargrove

**Where Reported:**      May 1997 LAB 20

**Date of Award:**      August 1996

**Brief Facts of Case:**      On 13 February 1995 L removed T's roof to replace it using a temporary cover. On 20 February 1995 rain poured in. The next day a roofer put his foot through the ceiling. On 28 February 1995 there was a further flood. The re-roofing work was completed weeks later and the redecoration not completed until June 1995.

**Award:**      £750 general damages.

**General Damages:**      £750

**Value of Award of £750 as at April 2004: £910**

*Property – Housing – Breach of covenant to repair*

---

**Name of Case:**      *Webb v Tower Hamlets LBC*

**Cause/s of Action:**      Breach of covenant to repair

**Tribunal and Judge:**      Wood Green Civil Trial Centre – The Circuit Judge

**Where Reported:**      August 1994 LAB 17

**Date of Award:**      January 31, 1994

**Brief Facts of Case:**      Council house suffered from serious disrepair including water penetration through the roof, defective windows, rotten floorboards, defective plumbing.

**Award:**  Agreed damages of £5,750 for diminution in value between 1987-1994 (rent discounted at between 50%-100% per year)
£9, 250 agreed damages for inconvenience

($1,000$ for the 1$^{st}$ year and £1,500 thereafter).

**General Damages:**  £9,250

**Value of Award of £9,250 as at April 2004: £12,157**

**Value of Award of £1,000 per annum as at April 2004: £1,314**

**Value of Award of £1,500 per annum as at April 2004: £1,971**

*Property – Housing – Breach of covenant to repair*

---

**Name of Case:**  *Weller v London Borough of Lewisham*

**Cause/s of Action:**  Breach of covenant to repair – Breach of duty of care under section 4 Defective Premises Act 1972

**Tribunal and Judge:**  Bromley County Court

**Where Reported:**  September 1988 LAB 15

**Date of Award:**  January 18, 1988

**Brief Facts of Case:**  T brought proceedings on the basis of an independent environmental health officer's report. The property was declared unfit for human habitation under the Housing Act 1985 before trial. Council agreed to waive county court limit for damages.

**Award:**  £6,250 damages (to include special damages).

(Special damages: £1,107.60.)

**General Damages:**  £5,142.40

**Value of Award of £5,142.40 as at April 2004: £9,244.37**

*Property – Housing – Breach of covenant to repair*

| | |
|---|---|
| **Name of Case:** | *Welsh v Greenwich London Borough Council* |
| **Cause/s of Action:** | Breach of covenant to repair |
| **Tribunal and Judge:** | Court of Appeal – Robert Walker and Latham LJJ and Bell J |
| **Where Reported:** | [1999] CLY 3738; August 1999 LAB 23; [2000] EGCS 84; (2000) *Times* 4 August, CA; (2001) 81 P & CR 144; January 2001 LAB 24 |
| **Date of Award:** | June 27, 2000 |
| **Brief Facts of Case:** | W was a secure tenant of a council flat which did not have thermal insulation, where she lived with 3 children aged 13, 5 and 3 years old when she left the premises. Between 1990 and 1994 the flat suffered from damp and condensation due to lack of proper insulation resulting in severe black spot and mould growth around windows, on walls, soft furnishings and under carpets. |
| | Parties agreed quantum of general damages and trial fought on liability only. |
| | Judge found that lack of insulation and excessive condensation constituted the condition of the dwelling and council had been in breach of covenant to keep flat in good condition |
| **Award:** | £9,000 (agreed) damages award upheld. (Appeal dismissed.) |
| **General Damages:** | £9,000 |

**Value of Award of £9,000 as at April 2004: £9,768**

*Property – Housing – Breach of covenant to repair*

**Name of Case:**        *Wetherall v London Borough of Lambeth*

**Cause/s of Action:**   Breach of covenant to repair

**Tribunal and Judge:**  Wood Green Trial Centre (Lambeth County Court) – Recorder Bridges-Adams

**Where Reported:**      December 1991 LAB 22

**Date of Award:**       March 13, 1991

**Brief Facts of Case:** T occupied a 2-bedroom flat. There was window disrepair from 1984 and a leaking flat roof from 1985. Works to roof were carried out in 1989 but were not effective. At trial damages limitation removed.

**Award:**               Total: £12,640:

                         £2,600 damages for diminution in value over 6 years (25% of rent for first 3 years, %0% of rent for last 3 years)

                         £6,000 general damages

                         £2,000 exemplary damages for failure to comply with Council's environmental health officer's notice

                         £1,000 for disrepair thereafter

**General Damages:**     £6,000

**Value of Award of £6,000 as at April 2004: £8,479**

*Property – Housing – Breach of covenant to repair*

**Name of Case:**        *Willis and Willis v Fuller*

**Cause/s of Action:**    Breach of covenant to repair

**Tribunal and Judge:**    Hastings County Court – Recorder Gault

**Where Reported:**    (1996) H&HI (1) 3:0; May 1997 LAB 20

**Date of Award:**    1996

**Brief Facts of Case:**    T occupied a 2-bedroom ground floor flat under a Rent Act tenancy. Plasterwork had perished and the flat was in substantial disrepair.

**Award:**    £1,000 per year general damages.

**General Damages:**    £1,000

**Value of Award of £1,000 per annum as at April 2004: £1,207**

*Property – Landlord & Tenant – Breach of covenant to repair*

---

**Name of Case:**    *Yilmaz v Hackney LBC*

**Cause/s of Action:**    Breach of covenant to repair

**Tribunal and Judge:**    Shoreditch County Court – HHJ Graham QC

**Where Reported:**    March 1995 LAB 15

**Date of Award:**    November 29, 1994

**Brief Facts of Case:**    T (the sole tenant) occupied a flat (with his wife and 2 children) which was in disrepair for 5 years. All members of the family suffered anxiety and depression caused in part by the disrepair of the property.

**Award:**    For T £5,000 general damages for inconvenience

For each adult £500 in respect of psychiatric damage

For each child £1,000 in respect of psychiatric damage

(Special damages: £750 for T.)

**General Damages:**      £5,000

**Value of Awards of £5,000 as at April 2004: £6,390**

*Property – Housing – Breach of covenant to repair*

---

**Name of Case:**         *Yorston and Yorston v Crewfield Ltd and Festal International Ltd*

**Cause/s of Action:**    Breach of covenant to repair

**Tribunal and Judge:**   Clerkenwell County Court – HHJ Krickler

**Where Reported:**       July 1985 LAB 102

**Date of Award:**        April 19, 1985

**Brief Facts of Case:**  Ps were long lessees of a top floor flat in a converted house. D1 owned the freehold from May 1983 but sold it to D2 in March 1985. Ps issued proceedings for breach of Ds repairing covenant. A defective roof caused rainwater seepage through the ceiling of the flat; there was dry rot to the roof beams. Holes which had been made in the ceilings by dry rot consultants (employed by Ps) prior to D1s acquisition of the freehold, had not been filled by the Ds. This exacerbated water seepage, caused further plaster to fall and amplified outside noise disturbing Ps sleep and leading them to sleep in the living room. A defective boiler left Ps without hot water for 2 months.

**Award:**                £2,250 general damages against D1 (including a sum of £500 in respect of the estimated cost of redecoration/replastering of the holes) in respect of the hardship to the Ps over a 22 month period.

**General Damages:**      £2,250

**Value of Award of £2,250 as at April 2004: £2,804**

*Property – Landlord & Tenant – Breach of covenant to repair*

---

**Name of Case:**        *Zone Properties Ltd v Painter*

**Cause/s of Action:**   Breach of covenant to repair

**Tribunal and Judge:**  Edmonton County Court – HHJ Tibber

**Where Reported:**      June 1987 LAB 21

**Date of Award:**       April 13, 1987

**Brief Facts of Case:** T had to use buckets over a period of 3 years to keep the property habitable. At first the leaking roof let water into one room but all other rooms were subsequently affected.

**Award:**               £2,000 general damages for distress and inconvenience. (Special damages were awarded.)

**General Damages:**     £2,000

**Value of Award of £2,000 as at April 2004: £2,376**

*Property – Landlord & Tenant – Breach of covenant to repair*

---

# Trespass to Land

| | |
|---|---|
| **Name of Case:** | *Bernadt v Dhatariya* |
| **Cause/s of Action:** | Boundary dispute – Trespass |
| **Tribunal and Judge:** | Dartford County Court – HH Judge Russell-Vick |
| **Where Reported:** | [1990] CLY 1517 |
| **Date of Award:** | May 15,1990 |
| **Brief Facts of Case:** | D removed and destroyed a boundary fence owned by B without consent. D replaced the fence with a 2 metre-high brick wall which encroached on B's land. |
| **Award:** | £2,000 for distress and inconvenience suffered by B for 2-year period up to judgment. |
| | Special damages £14,735: D ordered to pay cost of replacement fencing. |
| **General Damages:** | £2,000 |

**Value of Award of £2,000 as at April 2004: £2,943**

*Property – Trespass – Boundary dispute*

---

| | |
|---|---|
| **Name of Case:** | *Branchett v Beaney, Coster & Swale Borough Council* |
| **Cause/s of Action:** | *Trespass* |
| **Tribunal and Judge:** | Court of Appeal – Balcombe and Ralph Gibson LJJ |
| **Where Reported:** | (1992) 24 HLR 348 |
| **Date of Award:** | January 31, 1992 |
| **Brief Facts of Case:** | Appellant succeeded to her mother's tenancy of the property in 1969 and became a statutory tenant. In 1973 due to disrepair the council made a demolition order on the house. In 1983 B purchased the house – it became a listed |

building and the demolition order was revoked and replaced by a closing order. In 1986 B began to build an access to serve a new house they intended to build – part of appellant's garden was bulldozed. In 1987 the closing order was rescinded by the Council. In 1988 B was granted planning permission subject to their agreement to repair the appellant's house and not to use access until a new by-pass had been built. B transferred property to C who started to use the access across the appellant's garden. In 1990 the Council made a closing order on the property. Appellant brought proceedings against B and C.

**Award:**           For trespass only £3,250 exemplary damages against B and nominal general damages against C.

Exemplary Damages:    £3,250

**Value of Award for trespass as at April 2004: £4,451**

*Property – Trespass*

---

| | |
|---|---|
| **Name of Case:** | *Griffiths v Kingsley-Stubbs* |
| **Cause/s of Action:** | Trespass to land |
| **Tribunal and Judge:** | Court of Appeal |
| **Where Reported:** | [1987] CLY 1227 |
| **Date of Award:** | June 3, 1986 |
| **Brief Facts of Case:** | D's bathroom extension encroached on P's neighbouring land which had the benefit of outline planning permission for the erection of a dwelling-house. The development potential of P's land was not affected and P was awarded damages of £1,250 in lieu of an injunction. D appealed on basis that the damages should be nominal. |

**Award:**               Damages reduced from £1,250 to £400. The
                         encroachment was an inconvenience in the
                         planning for development – compensated for by a
                         reasonable award of damages.

**General Damages:**     £400

**Value of Award of £400 as at April 2004: £760**

*Property - Trespass*

---

**Name of Case:**        *Haque v Chopra*

**Cause/s of Action:**   Trespass

**Tribunal and Judge:**  Leeds County Court – HH Judge Hoffman

**Where Reported:**      [1993] CLY 1383

**Date of Award:**       July 5, 1993

**Brief Facts of Case:** C – to prevent risk of subsidence to his property
                         – cut one-third off height of 12 trees on boundary
                         line with neighbouring property (owned by H)
                         without H's consent. C mistakenly believed the
                         trees were his. Only 3 trees needed attention – the
                         remainder had been wrongfully interfered with.

**Award:**               £200 to make good damage to the trees; and
                         £1,800 for loss of visual amenity and distress and
                         inconvenience suffered by H.

                         (Special damages: £200.)

**General Damages:**     £1,800

**Value of Award of £1,800 as at April 2004: £2,376**

*Trespass – Wrongful interference to trees*

**Name of Case:**        *Jaggard v Sawyer and another*

**Cause/s of Action:**   Trespass to land – Breach of restrictive covenant

**Tribunal and Judge:**  Court of Appeal – Sir Thomas Bingham MR,
                         Kennedy and Millett LJJ

**Where Reported:**      [1994] EGCS 139

**Date of Award:**       July 18, 1994

**Brief Facts of Case:** Ds owned property (No 5) at end of cul-de-sac
                         and constructed a dwelling (No 5A) on land
                         adjacent to it, pursuant to planning permission.
                         Ds believed road was a public highway but were
                         aware of a covenant restricting use of the land to
                         a private garden. P owned part of land over
                         which the road ran and claimed that Ds did not
                         have a right of way over it for the benefit of No
                         5A. Ds sold No 5 and moved into No 5A. P
                         sought an injunction restraining trespass on P's
                         part of the road and alternatively damages in lieu
                         of an injunction.

                         High Court Judge refused injunction but awarded
                         damages for right of way and release of
                         restrictive covenant representing the amount P
                         could reasonably have expected to receive.

**Award:**               £6,250 damages. (Appeal dismissed.)

**General Damages:**     £6,250

**Value of Award of £6,250 as at April 2004: £8,060**

*Property – Trespass – Breach of restrictive covenant*

---

**Name of Case:**        *JS Bloor (Measham) Ltd v Calcott*

**Cause/s of Action:**   Trespass - breach of covenant for quiet
                         enjoyment

**Tribunal and Judge:**  Chancery Division – Hart J

**Where Reported:**  [2002] 09 EG 222

**Date of Award:**  November 23, 2001

**Brief Facts of Case:**  B purchased 38 acres of agricultural land with planning permission from W for £2.5 million on 1 July 1997.On 28 July1997 B entered the land to start development and learnt of an agricultural tenancy of the land granted to C by W in 1993. The tenancy was protected by the Agricultural Holdings Act 1986 and had been intended for the period 1 November 1992 to 31 November 1993 but owing to C's delay in signing the agreement less than 12 months of the term remained by June 1993.C commenced proceedings against B in August claiming damages for trespass (including aggravated damages) and an injunction restraining entry and requiring the removal of B's equipment and an interlocutory injunction to restrain B from continuing to work on the land. B's counterclaim was for the rescission of the 1993 agreement. C recovered £1,200 damages from B for trespass (not including aggravated damages) in the county court but the judge found that C was not entitled to equitable relief due to its deceit in avoiding signing the 1993 agreement and encouraging W to act to its detriment and not take steps to end the tenancy. C's claim for an injunction and B's counterclaim were dismissed.

B served a notice to quit terminating C's tenancy on June 2000 and in October 1997 commenced proceedings seeking a declaration that it was entitled to occupy the land and continue development on the basis that a proprietary estoppel had arisen due to C's behaviour. C counterclaimed for damages for breach of covenant for quiet enjoyment and trespass arguing that a 1986 Act tenancy could not be defeated by proprietary estoppel.

Held claim allowed. B entitled to possession between October 1997 and June 2000. The equitable remedy of proprietary estoppel was not barred by county court order. Nothing in 1986 Act prevented B from asserting claim either positively (by claiming the right to use the land) or negatively (in denying C's damages for such use). In trespass claimant elects to recover damages representing either loss to him or value of benefit to defendant.

**Award:** If so entitled to damages C would have been entitled to the tenancy rental value between October 1997 and June 2000.

*Property – Agricultural tenancy –Trespass – Breach of covenant for quiet enjoyment*

---

**Name of Case:** *Ketley v Gooden*

**Cause/s of Action:** Trespass to neighbouring land by building works

**Tribunal and Judge:** Court of Appeal – Hirst and Pill LJJ

**Where Reported:** (1997) 73 P & CR 305

**Date of Award:** February 29, 1996

**Brief Facts of Case:** Parties owned adjacent properties – G carried out works to provide access to block of flats built on his land. Some works were carried out on path of which K were the registered owners, other works involved interference with the access to K's property. K sought a mandatory injunction and damages.

HHJ Corrie granted K a mandatory injunction requiring G to remove works and restore access way to original form and granted £1,500 general damages and £750 aggravated damages. On the basis that he might be wrong to grant an injunction he assessed general damages at £6,650, aggravated damages at £1,000 and exemplary damages at £1,500.

**Award:**          Sum of £6,650 general damages was an appropriate overall award – exemplary damages were not appropriate – injunction should not have been granted.

**General damages:**     £6,650

**Value of Award of £6,650 as at April 2004: £8,184**

*Property – Trespass to land*

---

**Name of Case:**        *Lawson v Hartley-Brown*

**Cause/s of Action:**   Breach of covenant for quiet enjoyment – Trespass - derogation from grant

**Tribunal and Judge:**  Court of Appeal – Hirst and Aldous LJJ and Forbes J

**Where Reported:**      (1996) 71 P&CR 242

**Date of Award:**       November 8, 1995

**Brief Facts of Case:** T was tenant of retail premises which L was to redevelop by adding 2 additional floors. T sought possession of roof and air space over unit by bringing proceedings in the County Court which were consolidated with proceedings in the High Court. In 1998 L served notice to terminate the tenancy under s25 Landlord and Tenant Act 1954. T applied for the grant of a new tenancy. This was subsequently withdrawn and T vacated in 1992. L brought proceedings for arrears of rent which were consolidated with the other proceedings.

T appealed against County Court Judge's award of £20 nominal damages for trespass by L of flat roof which had been demised to T.

**Award:** £8,100 damages for trespass (equivalent to 1½ years rent) based on the bargain that may have been struck by a willing lessor and lessee taking into account the advantage to L, the disturbance and potential loss of profit to T.(Appeal allowed in part.)

**General Damages:** £8,100

**Value of Award of £8,100 as at April 2004: £10,041**

*Property – Breach of Covenant for Quiet Enjoyment – Derogation from Grant – Trespass*

# Interference with Goods

| | |
|---|---|
| **Name of Case:** | *Adams v Vickers* |
| **Cause/s of Action:** | Breach of covenant for quiet enjoyment – Harassment – Trespass to goods |
| **Tribunal and Judge:** | Manchester County Court – The Circuit Judge |
| **Where Reported:** | June 1994 LAB 11 |
| **Date of Award:** | January 11, 1994 |
| **Brief Facts of Case:** | T occupied bed and breakfast accommodation. L evicted her by locking her out of her room and she had to stay in a hostel for 2 months before finding alternative accommodation. |
| **Award:** | £3,250 general damages for breach of covenant including £1,750 in respect of the harassment in the week prior to being evicted |
| | £250 for trespass to goods (interference with mail and going without her toiletries for 3 days after the eviction) |
| | £1,250 aggravated damages |
| **General Damages:** | £3,250 |

**Value of Award of General Damages as at 2004: £4,271**

*Property – Landlord & Tenant – Breach of covenant for quiet enjoyment – Harassment – Trespass to goods*

---

| | |
|---|---|
| **Name of Case:** | *Ayari v Jethi* |
| **Cause/s of Action:** | Unlawful eviction – Trespass – Breach of covenant for quiet enjoyment |
| **Tribunal and Judge:** | West London County Court |
| **Where Reported:** | December 1990 LAB 13; March 1991 LAB 16 |
| **Date of Award:** | November 24, 1989 |
| **Brief Facts of Case:** | T occupied a flat under a Rent Act protected tenancy. One Friday evening L changed the lock |

       and removed T's possessions in dustbin bags. T regained possession of the flat the following Tuesday after obtaining an *ex parte* injunction but failed to recover most of her possessions.

**Award:**     £15,733 total damages (it was agreed that the county court's jurisdiction limit be waived) including £1,250 general damages.

       Special damages: £11,472 on the basis that L was responsible for the loss of T's belongings.

**General Damages:**  £1,250

**Value of Award of General Damages as at April 2004: £2,553**

*Property – Landlord & Tenant – Unlawful eviction*

---

| | |
|---|---|
| **Name of Case:** | *Burchett and Strugnell v Vine* |
| **Cause/s of Action:** | Breach of covenant for quiet enjoyment – interference with goods |
| **Tribunal and Judge:** | Southampton County Court – Recorder Boyle |
| **Where Reported:** | [1997] CLY 3284; September 1997 LAB 17 |
| **Date of Award:** | December 12, 1996 |
| **Brief Facts of Case:** | T owed 2 weeks' rent. L changed locks and threw T's possessions in a horsebox damaging some of them and kept the television and microwave against unpaid rent. T and his licensee had to stay with their parents before they were able to secure alternative accommodation. |
| **Award:** | £1,000 general damages for inconvenience and indignity |
| | £50 for detention of goods |
| **General Damages:** | £1050 |

**Value of Award of £1,000 as at April 2004: £1,203**

**Value of Award of £50 as at April 2004: £60**

*Property – Landlord & Tenant – Breach of covenant for quiet enjoyment – Interference with goods*

| | |
|---|---|
| **Name of Case:** | *Burke v Berioit* |
| **Cause/s of Action:** | Unlawful eviction – Breach of covenant for quiet enjoyment – Trespass to goods – Assault |
| **Tribunal and Judge:** | Central London County Court – Mr Recorder Hockman QC |
| **Where Reported:** | [1995] CLY 1572; March 1995 LAB 13 |
| **Date of Award:** | September 25, 1994 |
| **Brief Facts of Case:** | L liable for breach of covenant for quiet enjoyment and trespassing his goods and person. |
| **Award:** | £100 per day general damages for T's 2 months of homelessness – total £6,000 |
| | £1,500 exemplary damages for threats and violence |
| | £500 damages for trespass to goods |
| | £250 aggravated damages |
| | Total £8,250 exceeded statutory damages assessed at £5,000. |
| **General Damages:** | £8,250 |

**Value of Award of £100 per day as at April 2004: £145**

**Value of Award of Exemplary Damages of £1,500 as at April 2004: £1,921**

**Value of Award of £500 damages for trespass to goods as at April 2004: £640**

**Value of £250 Aggravated Damages of £250 as at April 2004: £320**

*Property – Landlord and Tenant – Unlawful eviction – Breach of covenant for quiet enjoyment and Landlord and Tenant – trespass to goods – assault*

**Name of Case:**          *Cyril Morgan (Holdings) v Dyer*

**Cause/s of Action:**      Interference with goods - removal of goods by owner in breach of walking possession agreement after distress for rent

**Tribunal and Judge:**    Pontypridd County Court – HH Judge Price QC

**Where Reported:**       [1995] CLY 1594

**Date of Award:**         September 19,1995

**Brief Facts of Case:**     Bailiff levied distress upon shop goods at premises let to T as rent in arrear. A walking possession agreement was entered into. T then removed all goods against which distress had been levied and emptied the shop.

**Award:**                 Under the Distress for Rent Act 1689 damages of treble £2,000 (the value of the goods seized) and the costs of levying the distress awarded.
Total: £6,100.37.

**Statutory Damages:**     £2,000

**Value of Award of £2,000 as at April 2004: £2,466**

*Property - Landlord & Tenant – interference with goods*

---

**Name of Case:**          *Daniel v Harty*

**Cause/s of Action:**      Unlawful eviction - Breach of covenant for quiet enjoyment - Trespass to goods

**Tribunal and Judge:**    Edmonton County Court – DJ Morley

**Where Reported:**       September 1995 LAB 14

**Date of Award:**         May 26, 1995

**Brief Facts of Case:**  T an assured tenant was evicted by L. He had been threatened and accused of drug-dealing and theft. L's agent had forced entry and his shower had been broken, his furniture and belongings removed. He found that someone had also urinated on his bed linen. He was too frightened to stay at the property.

**Award:**     £22,040 total damages including:

£14,000 damages under ss27-28 of Housing Act 1988

£4,675 damages for trespass to goods

£1,500 for breach of covenant for quiet enjoyment over 5 months

£1,250 for aggravated damages for trespass

£280 for disrepair to shower

£250 for return of deposit

**General Damages:**  £2,030

**Value of Award of £1,500 general damages as at April 2004: £1,862**

**Value of £1,250 aggravated damages as at April 2004: £1,552**

*Property – Landlord & Tenant – Unlawful eviction – Breach of covenant for quiet enjoyment – Trespass to goods*

---

**Name of Case:**   *Ditchfield v Devlin*

**Cause/s of Action:**  Unlawful eviction – Trespass to goods

**Tribunal and Judge:**  Chester County Court – District Judge Newman

**Where Reported:**  [1995] CLY 1849; December 1995 LAB 20

**Date of Award:**   May 22, 1995

**Brief Facts of Case:** T occupied a flat under a tenancy agreement providing for 6 months notice to quit. L demanded immediate possession, threatening violence with baseball bat, entered unlawfully and left T's belongings on lawn, some of which were stolen. T lived in hostel for the homeless for 11 weeks before being rehoused.

**Award:** £2,500 general damages to include aggravated damages.

(Special damages: £2,414.)

**General Damages:** £2,500

**Value of £2,500 as at April 2004: £3,103**

*Property – Landlord & Tenant – Unlawful eviction*

*and*

*Property - Landlord & Tenant – Trespass to goods*

---

**Name of Case:** *Fairweather v Ghafoor*

**Cause/s of Action:** Unlawful eviction – Conversion of goods

**Tribunal and Judge:** CC (Rawtenstall) – District Judge Geddes

**Where Reported:** [2001] CLY 421

**Date of Award:** September 14, 2000

**Brief Facts of Case:** G permanently excluded F from property let under assured shorthold tenancy due to rent arrears. F unable to collect possessions (of which some had belonged to her young son who had died). F suffered anxiety and depression for between 18 months and 2 years following eviction.

**Award:** £3,300 statutory damages under ss27-28 of Housing Act 1988;

£300 aggravated damages made for G's conduct in withholding her belongings and at the hearing.

**Aggravated Damages:** £300

**Value of Award of £300 as at April 2004: £324**

*Property – Landlord & Tenant – Unlawful eviction – Trespass to goods – Conversion*

---

**Name of Case:**      *Ghanie v Brade*

**Cause/s of Action:**      Unlawful eviction – Breach of covenant for quiet enjoyment – Trespass to goods

**Tribunal and Judge:**      Mayor's and City of London County Court – HHJ Byrt QC

**Where Reported:**      December 1997 LAB 14

**Date of Award:**      September 2, 1997

**Brief Facts of Case:**      T was an assured tenant. L's father harassed and intimidated him and then evicted him causing him personal injury. T was unable to recover any of his possessions.

**Award:**      £5,000 statutory damages

£3,000 for breach of covenant for quiet enjoyment

£1,000 aggravated damages

£750 damages for personal injury

£1,500 aggravated damages against L's father

£6,500 damages for trespass to goods

**General Damages:**      £3,000

**Value of Award of £3,000 general damages as at April 2004: £3,497**

**Value of Award of £1,000 aggravated damages as at April 2004: £1,167**

**Value of Award of £1,500 aggravated damages as at April 2004: £1,749**

*Property – Landlord & Tenant – Unlawful eviction – Breach of covenant for quiet enjoyment – Trespass to goods*

| | |
|---|---|
| **Name of Case:** | *Kinsella v Bi and Rashid* |
| **Cause/s of Action:** | Unlawful eviction – trespass to goods |
| **Tribunal and Judge:** | Birmingham County Court – HHJ Harris |
| **Where Reported:** | September 1994 LAB 13 |
| **Date of Award:** | April 13, 1994 |
| **Brief Facts of Case:** | L changed lock to T's home following delays in the payment of T's housing benefit. T was unable to resume occupation. Only some of his possessions were returned following the grant of an injunction. |
| **Award:** | £12,850 total damages comprising: |
| | £11,000 statutory damages (representing the difference between the value of the house tenanted and with vacant possession) |
| | £450 for loss of use of personal effects |
| | £500 for distress |
| | (Special damages: £900.) |
| **General Damages:** | £950 |

**Value of Award of £500 as at April 2004: £644**

*Property – Landlord & Tenant – Unlawful eviction – Trespass to goods*

**Name of Case:**        *Pillai v Amendra*

**Cause/s of Action:**      Unlawful eviction – Trespass to goods

**Tribunal and Judge:**    Central London County Court – HHJ Green QC

**Where Reported:**       October 2000 LAB 24

**Date of Award:**        July 27, 2000

**Brief Facts of Case:**    T occupied a 1-bedroom flat as a weekly assured tenant. He refused to leave to allow L to avoid a benefit fraud investigation in respect of a previous tenant. L locked out T when he returned from holiday and deposited his belongings in the garden. His windscreen was smashed and he was left a threatening note. The police secured his re-entry and he was then locked out again and his effects thrown out again. L failed to comply with an injunction and T was too frightened to return. He stayed with a friend for 6 months and lost his job because of the amount of time he had to take off.

**Award:**             £36,000 total damages including:

                      £6,000 general damages

                      £10,000 aggravated and exemplary damages for trespass to land

                      £3,000 aggravated damages for trespass to goods

                      (Special damages: £17,000 for loss of goods and other expenditure.)

**General Damages:**      £6,000

**Value of Award of £6,000 as at April 2004: £6,535**

**Value of Award of £3,000 aggravated damages as at April 2004: £3,267**

**Value of Award of £10,000 aggravated and exemplary damages as at April 2004: £10,892**

*Property – Landlord & Tenant – Unlawful eviction – Trespass to goods*

**Name of Case:**          *Rahman v Erdogan*

**Cause/s of Action:**     Breach of covenant for quiet enjoyment –
                           Trespass –Trespass to goods

**Tribunal and Judge:**    Edmonton County Court/ Central London Civil
                           trial Centre – HHJ Previte QC

**Where Reported:**        June 1998 LAB 14

**Date of Award:**         February 11, 1998

**Brief Facts of Case:**   L issued possession proceedings against T and
                           her husband alleging arrears of rent under an
                           assured shorthold tenancy. The proceedings were
                           adjourned and within 1 month L evicted T while
                           she was out and put her possessions in black bin
                           bags. She was unable to gain access for 1 ½
                           hours and only able to retrieve her possessions
                           for about 8 hours.

**Award:**                 £750 for breach of covenant and trespass

                           £250 for trespass to goods

                           £2,000 aggravated damages

                           £1,000 exemplary damages

                           (Special damages: £340.)

**General Damages:**       £1,000

**Value of Award of £1,000 as at April 2004: £1,158**

**Value of Award of £2,000 aggravated damages as at April 2004: £2,317**

**Value of Award of £1,000 exemplary damages as at April 2004: £1,158**

**Value of Award of £250 as at April 2004: £290**

*Property – Landlord & Tenant – Breach of covenant for quiet enjoyment
– Trespass – Trespass to goods*

| | |
|---|---|
| **Name of Case:** | *Silva v Coelho* |
| **Cause/s of Action:** | Unlawful eviction – Breach of covenant for quiet enjoyment – Trespass to goods |
| **Tribunal and Judge:** | Wandsworth County Court – DJ Gittens |
| **Where Reported:** | March 1998 LAB 13 |
| **Date of Award:** | January 5, 1998 |
| **Brief Facts of Case:** | T was an assured tenant of a bed-sit. L gave T 20 days' notice to quit. Later in the month he put T's possessions in the street, front garden and common hallway. The door was removed from its hinges. T was allowed re-entry when the police were called but his belongings and the door were not replaced. L was advised about the Protection from Eviction Act 1977 by a tenancy relations officer but proceeded to remove the remaining possessions from the room. T and his family vacated and had to spend 1 month in B&B accommodation and 6 months in a temporary flat before being rehoused. |
| **Award:** | £6,264.88 total damages (taking into account compensation order in criminal proceedings): |
| | £3,500 general damages for breach of covenant for quiet enjoyment and trespass to goods |
| | £1,500 aggravated damages |
| | £1,500 exemplary damages |
| | (Special damages: £514.88.) |
| **General Damages:** | £3,500 |

**Value of Award of £3,500 as at April 2004: £4.075**

**Value of Award of £1,500 exemplary/aggravated damages as at April 2004: £1,746**

*Property – Landlord & Tenant – Unlawful eviction – Breach of covenant for quiet enjoyment – Trespass to goods*

**Name of Case:**          *Sullman v Little, Little & Little*

**Cause/s of Action:**     Trespass to goods –Unlawful eviction

**Tribunal and Judge:**    Canterbury County Court – HH Judge Peppitt QC

**Where Reported:**        [1993] CLY 1604; March 1994 LAB 13

**Date of Award:**         July 23, 1993

**Brief Facts of Case:**   S occupied an annexe owned by L under an oral agreement with L's wife. S was evicted and his possessions removed. S had breached the agreement by keeping cats on the premises and refusing to leave on a date previously agreed between the parties.

**Award:**                 Statutory damages of £3,000 (reduced by four-fifths under s 27(7)(a) of Housing Act 1988 in respect of S's conduct); £250 for trespass to goods. No award of aggravated damages.

**General Damages:**       £250

**Value of Award of £250 as at April 2004: £330**

*Property - Landlord & Tenant – Unlawful eviction – Trespass to goods*

---

**Name of Case:**          *White v Lambeth LBC*

**Cause/s of Action:**     Breach of covenant for quiet enjoyment – Trespass

**Tribunal and Judge:**    Lambeth County Court – Recorder Rylance

**Where Reported:**        June 1995 LAB 20

**Date of Award:**         March 6, 1995

**Brief Facts of Case:** An absolute possession order had been obtained against T (a secure tenant) but was subsequently set aside. The Council, in the mistaken belief that the order was still in force and that T had abandoned the flat, instructed contractors to force entry to carry out works. T returned to the flat to find that most of his belongings had been removed and the flat was like a building site. T was without accommodation for 15 weeks before he was able to gain access to another flat that had been offered by the Council.

**Award:** £ 18,000 statutory damages under ss27-28 Housing Act 1988

£1,500 damages for interference with goods

£8,000 damages for trespass to land and breach of covenant for quiet enjoyment

£2,000 aggravated damages

(Award limited to £19,500 total damages.)

**General Damages:** £9,500

**Value of Award of £9,500 as at April 2004: £11,960**

**Value of Award of £8,000 as at April 2004: £10,072**

**Value of Award of £1,500 as at April 2004: £1,888**

**Value of Award of £2,000 aggravated damages as at April 2004: £2,518**

*Property – Housing – Breach of covenant for quiet enjoyment – interference with goods*

# Breach of restrictive covenant

| | |
|---|---|
| **Name of Case:** | *Amec Developments Limited v Jury's Hotel Management (UK) Limited* |
| **Cause/s of Action:** | Breach of restrictive covenant |
| **Tribunal and Judge:** | HCJ Chancery Division – Anthony Mann QC |
| **Where Reported:** | (2001) 82 P & CR 286 |
| **Date of Award:** | November 17, 2000 |
| **Brief Facts of Case:** | Ds owned land subject to a restrictive covenant in favour of the claimant's adjoining land not to build beyond a line A-B. Ds constructed a hotel on their land which encroached the line by 3.9 metres. |
| **Award:** | £375,000 damages in lieu of injunction, assessed on the basis of a hypothetical negotiation as to the sum that the claimant's might have demanded from Ds for permitting the encroachment. |
| **General Damages:** | £375,000 |

**Value of Award as at April 2004: £404,634**

*Property – Breach of restrictive covenant*

---

| | |
|---|---|
| **Name of Case:** | *Gafford v Graham* |
| **Cause/s of Action:** | Breach of restrictive covenants |
| **Tribunal and Judge:** | Court of Appeal – Nourse, Pill and Thorpe LJJ |
| **Where Reported:** | (1998) 76 P & CR D18; [1999] 3 EGLR 75 |
| **Date of Award:** | April 8, 1998 |
| **Brief Facts of Case:** | D was alleged to be in breach of restrictive covenants which a) restricted use of land for |

livery yard, stabling of horses, 1 residential bungalow and no more than 1 caravan and b) prevented building without the submission to and approval of detailed plans by P.

P alleged that bungalow converted, barn extended and indoor riding school constructed without the submission of plans, business of riding school carried out, up to 3 caravans placed on land and holding of car boot sales on land all in breach of the restrictive covenants.

P granted an injunction to prevent operation of riding school and restrain land from being used other than as livery and stabling for horses and was awarded damages of £250 for riding school, £750 for barn extension and £20,000 for bungalow conversion.

**Award:**     Awards of damages for barn extension and bungalow conversion discharged on basis of P's acquiescence.

£25,000 damages in lieu of injunction held to be appropriate remedy on the basis that this sum could have reasonably been demanded by P for his consent.

**General Damages:**     £25,000

**Value of Award of £25,000 as at April 2004: £28,552**

*Property – Breach of Restrictive Covenant – Damages in lieu of injunction*

**Name of Case:**            *In Jillas' Application*

**Cause/s of Action:**       Application to modify restrictive covenant, grounds (a) (aa) and (c) of s84(1) Law of Property Act 1925, whether restriction applied to extension of original building, determination of compensation payable

**Tribunal and Judge:**      Lands Tribunal – Mr George Bartlett QC, President

**Where Reported:**          [2000] 2 EGLR 99

**Date of Award:**           November 30, 1999

**Brief Facts of Case:**     Applicants sought discharge/modification of a restrictive covenant in a conveyance of 1969 to permit the erection of an extension to their property in accordance with planning permission granted on appeal. The covenant restricted the erection of a house or other building until plans and specifications had been submitted to and approved by the vendors or successors in title. The successor in title to the original vendor objected contending a reduction in the value of her property by £32,500 - £65,000.

**Award:**                   £10,000 compensation awarded. (Appeal allowed under paragraph (aa) of 1925 Act. Effect of breach of covenant on value of property was 11.5% - not of substantial value/advantage in terms of property worth £650,000.)

**Value of Award of £10,000 as at April 2004: £11,140**

*Property – Compensation for modification of restrictive covenant*

**Name of Case:**            *Jaggard v Sawyer and another*

**Cause/s of Action:**       Trespass to land – Breach of restrictive covenant

**Tribunal and Judge:**      Court of Appeal – Sir Thomas Bingham MR, Kennedy and Millett LJJ

**Where Reported:**          [1994] EGCS 139

**Date of Award:**           July 18, 1994

**Brief Facts of Case:**     Ds owned property (No 5) at end of cul-de-sac and constructed a dwelling (No 5A) on land adjacent to it, pursuant to planning permission. Ds believed road was a public highway but were aware of a covenant restricting use of the land to a private garden. P owned part of land over which the road ran and claimed that Ds did not have a right of way over it for the benefit of No 5A. Ds sold No 5 and moved into No 5A. P sought an injunction restraining trespass on P's part of the road and alternatively damages in lieu of an injunction.

High Court Judge refused injunction but awarded damages for right of way and release of restrictive covenant representing the amount P could reasonably have expected to receive.

**Award:**                   £6,250 damages. (Appeal dismissed.)

**General Damages:**         £6,250

**Value of Award of £6,250 as at April 2004: £8,060**

*Property – Trespass – Breach of restrictive covenant*

**Name of Case:**  *Re Marcello Developments Ltd's Application*

**Cause/s of Action:**  Restrictive Covenants – Compensation

**Tribunal and Judge:**  Lands Tribunal – George Bartlett QC

**Where Reported:**  (2002) 9 CL 428; [2002] RVR 146

**Date of Award:**  May 16, 2001

**Brief Facts of Case:**  M (a developer) had been granted planning permission for the redevelopment of a site occupied by a 2-storey block of flats with detached houses, garages and two 3-storey blocks of flats with car parking. Covenants had been imposed in conveyances dated 1923 and 1925 restricting use to residential and imposed controls in relation to frontage and building line. M sought to discharge or modify them on the basis that they were obsolete.

Application granted on basis that frontage restriction obsolete, building line restriction could not be met and the use restriction did not refer to density or design and matched the character of the area.

**Award:**  £2,500 compensation to each of 8 local residents/objectors for their personal disadvantage. No compensation due to the local authority as the rights conferred no benefit.

**Value of Award of £2,500 as at April 2004: £2,665**

*Property – Restrictive covenants – Compensation*

# Nuisance by Noise

| | |
|---|---|
| **Name of Case:** | *Bird v Hackney LBC* |
| **Cause/s of Action:** | Breach of covenant to repair – Nuisance by noise |
| **Tribunal and Judge:** | Central London County Court – Recorder Lawson QC |
| **Where Reported:** | July 2001 LAB 25 |
| **Date of Award:** | June 15, 2000 |

**Brief Facts of Case:**

T was granted a secure tenancy of a flat in a tower block which was destined for demolition. The remainder of the estate was being redeveloped and the block was in the middle of a building site. There was serious disrepair. The windows and balcony doors were ill-fitting leaving the flat cold in winter and allowing in dust and noise. The heating system frequently broke down and between December 1996 and February 1997 there was no heating. There were holes in the floor of the flat and a gap under the front door. The neighbouring tower block was covered by plastic sheeting which made a noise when windy and prevented T's family from sleeping.

The judge found L liable for breach of repair under s11 of Landlord and Tenant Act 1985 until remedial work took place in January 1998 and in nuisance for the noise.

**Award:**

£2,500 general damages for December 1996 to November 1997 to include the problems of heating and noise

£1,800 damages per annum for the remaining period between commencement and repair

(£2,500 per child for respiratory problems)

(Special damages: £780 for extra heating costs – £5 per week for 6 months of the year for 6 years.)

**General Damages:**      £2,500 and £1,800 per annum

**Value of Award of £2,500 as at April 2004: £2,713**

**Value of Award of £1,800 per annum as at April 2004: £1,954**

*Property – Housing – Breach of covenant to repair – Nuisance by noise*

---

**Name of Case:**           *Kurland v London Borough of Camden*

**Cause/s of Action:**      Nuisance by noise – Breach of covenant to repair

**Tribunal and Judge:**     Bloomsbury County Court – HHJ Quarren Evans

**Where Reported:**         December 1991 LAB 22

**Date of Award:**          October 14, 1991

**Brief Facts of Case:**    T was disturbed over a 3-year period by noise from a faulty central heating boiler outside her flat. She also suffered from periods without heat, hot water or running water and developed depression, anxiety and then agoraphobia (to which she had a predisposition).

**Award:**                  £8,500 damages.

**Value of Award of £8,500 as at April 2004: £11,684**

*Property – Housing – Nuisance by noise – Breach of covenant to repair*

---

**Name of Case:**          *Power v Hammersmith LBC*

**Cause/s of Action:**     Nuisance by noise

**Tribunal and Judge:**    Central London County Court – HHJ Hunter

**Where Reported:**        March 1993 LAB 14

**Date of Award:**         January 28, 1993

**Brief Facts of Case:**   T occupied a basement flat in a converted house with no sound insulation. Domestic sound from the flat above caused a nuisance. T had first complained to the Council in February 1987.

**Award:**                 £5,500 general damages @ £1,000 per year for 5 ½ years

**General Damages:**       £5,500

**Value of Award of £5,500 as at April 2004: £7,406**

**Value of Award of £1,000 per annum as at April 2004: £1,347**

*Property – Housing – Nuisance by noise*

---

**Name of Case:**          *Saunders v Community Housing Association*

**Cause/s of Action:**     Nuisance by noise

**Tribunal and Judge:**    Central London County Court – HHJ Coltran

**Where Reported:**        December 1997 LAB 12

**Date of Award:**         October 14, 1997

**Brief Facts of Case:**   L acquired row of terrace houses and converted into flats. T of first floor flat claimed disturbance from the ordinary domestic activities of the other tenants due to inadequate sound insulation. (No special damages)

**Award:**                    £1,000 damages per year for 3 ½ years

**General Damages:**          £3,500

**Value of Award of £1,000 per annum as at April 2004: £1,164**

*Property – Housing – Nuisance by noise*

| | |
|---|---|
| **Name of Case:** | *Toff v McDowell* |
| **Cause/s of Action:** | Breach of covenant to repair – Nuisance by noise |
| **Tribunal and Judge:** | Chancery Division – Evans-Lombe J |
| **Where Reported:** | (1993) 25 HLR 650; (1995) 69 P&CR 535 |
| **Date of Award:** | July 19, 1993 |
| **Brief Facts of Case:** | In 1987 T took an assignment of a lease of a basement flat in a house which had been converted into 4 flats. He experienced noise nuisance from the ground floor flat from 1987 which worsened in 1990 when the lessee of the ground floor flat, M, removed the floor covering and then let it out to a group of noisy tenants. |
| | The lease contained a covenant for the lessor to keep the main structure of the building in repair and a covenant for the lessee to keep the flat in repair. In 1991 T commenced proceedings. |
| | The Judge allowed the claim against M the lessee of the ground floor flat. The floor was not the responsibility of the lessor. |
| **Award:** | Total of £6,000: £1,000 for diminution in T's enjoyment of the flat for the 6 month period between July 1990 and January 1991 (when the ground floor was occupied by the noisy tenants) and £5,000 from June 1990 to date of judgment. Damages to be increased by £12,000 (the cost of |

installing a hung ceiling) if M failed to replace the floor covering within 3 months.

(£12,000 contingent special damages.)

**General Damages:**      £6,000

**Value of Award of £6,000 as at April 2004: £7,919**

*Property – Landlord & Tenant – Breach of covenant to repair*
*and*
*Nuisance by noise*

---

**Name of Case:**         *Wilson v Southwick Contractors*

**Cause/s of Action:**    Nuisance by noise and noxious fumes

**Tribunal and Judge:**   CC (Central London) – District Judge Hasan

**Where Reported:**       [1996] CLY 2157

**Date of Award:**        May 3, 1996

**Brief Facts of Case:**  W lived in a flat in a residential mews above garage workshop. She endured loud machine noise smoke and smells, and shouting at weekends and at night, interference with her water supply and blocking of access to the property. W suffered headaches, insomnia, sore throats and nausea due to the nuisance for 2½ years before vacating.

(Special damages: £2,500.)

**Award:**                £3,000 general damages.

**General Damages:**      £3,000

**Value of Award of £3,000 as at April 2004: £3,644**

*Nuisance – noise, noxious fumes*

---

# Nuisance by Infestation

| | |
|---|---|
| **Name of Case:** | *Brent LBC v Roberts* |
| **Cause/s of Action:** | Nuisance by infestation |
| **Tribunal and Judge:** | Willesden County Court – HHJ Lowe |
| **Where Reported:** | December 1990 LAB 16; April 1991 LAB 21 |
| **Date of Award:** | October 9, 1990 |

**Brief Facts of Case:** The Council sought possession of a council tenancy on the basis of £5,000 rent arrears. Ts (joint tenants living with their 5 children in a 3-bedroom council flat) brought a counterclaim for the Council's failure to deal with a cockroach infestation over a period of 4 years.

The infestation affected every room except the main bedroom and was particularly bad in the living room and kitchen. Ts first complained in 1986 when the problem started. Despite attempts made by the Council to treat it by spraying the flat, the problem continued.

**Award:** £6,205 total damages assessed as follows:

£5,200 general damages for anxiety and inconvenience (£25 per week for 4 years).

Special damages: £500 for insecticide sprays (£2.40 per week for 4 years); £280 for damaged wallpaper; £200 for loss of food; £25 for loss of photos of the children (cockroaches had made their homes behind them.)

**General Damages:** £5,200

**Value of Award of £25 per week as at April 2004: £36**

*Property – Housing – Nuisance by cockroach infestation*

**Name of Case:**  *Clark v London Borough of Wandsworth*

**Cause/s of Action:**  Nuisance by infestation

**Tribunal and Judge:**  Wandsworth County Court – HHJ Sumner

**Where Reported:**  June 1994 LAB 15; August 1994 LAB 18

**Date of Award:**  April 21, 1994

**Brief Facts of Case:**  T (a single mother with 2 children aged 10 and 3) occupied a 2-bedroom maisonette in a block since June 1985. The block had ducted warm-air heating. Between January 1991 and June 1992 the premises were affected by a severe infestation of cockroaches.

**Award:**  £3,500 general damages for the physical, mental and emotional effects on the family over a 1-year period. (Special damages: £100.)

**General Damages:**  £3,500

**Value of Award of £3,500 as at April 2004: £4,507**

*Property – Housing – Nuisance – Cockroach infestation*

---

**Name of Case:**  *Dadd v Christian Action (Enfield) Housing Association*

**Cause/s of Action:**  Breach of covenant to repair – Nuisance by infestation

**Tribunal and Judge:**  Central London County Court – DJ Langley

**Where Reported:**  December 1994 LAB 18

**Date of Award:**  September 28, 1994

**Brief Facts of Case:**  T was a single parent occupying a 2-bedroom flat in a converted house with her 2 children aged 2

and 4 years between November 1990 and May 1993. The house was infested with rats throughout the tenancy. The rats did not enter the flat but could be heard at night. When treated with poison the rotting carcasses attracted flies and the rats returned a few weeks later. There was dampness in the kitchen and the heating and hot water supply was defective.

**Award:**              £7,476 total damages including:

£3,250 general damages (£1,300 per year)

£790 per year damages for diminution in value (40% of rent)

(Special damages: £1,950.)

**General Damages:**    £3,250

**Value of Award of £1,300 per annum as at April 2004: £1,665**

*Property – Housing – Breach of covenant to repair – Nuisance – Infestation by rats*

---

**Name of Case:**        *Dolan v Sefton MBC*

**Cause/s of Action:**   Nuisance by infestation

**Tribunal and Judge:**  Liverpool County Court – HHJ Urqhart

**Where Reported:**      July 2001 LAB 27

**Date of Award:**       January 20, 2000

**Brief Facts of Case:** T occupied a property affected by severe cockroach infestation for 3 years. She vacated the property and left her belongings, to sleep on her mother's floor for 2 years. L's rent arrears claim was dismissed and 2 of her children were awarded damages for personal injury (infected insect bites and HSP disease causing rashes, swollen joints and abdominal pains).

**Award:** £16,000 damages (£2,000 for each child for personal injury).

**General Damages:** £12,000

**Value of £4,000 per annum as at April 2004: £4,458**

*Property – Housing – Nuisance by infestation*

---

**Name of Case:** *Hodder v Tower Hamlets London Borough Council*

**Cause/s of Action:** Nuisance by cockroach infestation

**Tribunal and Judge:** Shoreditch County Court – District Judge Silverman

**Where Reported:** [1993] CLY 1371; August 1994 LAB 17

**Date of Award:** September 3, 1993

**Brief Facts of Case:** H suffered severe cockroach infestation in council flat

**Award:** Total general damages: £10,500 (£1,500 per annum general damages for 7 years due to H's distress and embarrassment).

(Special damages: £1,056 for the cost of insecticide sprays and redecoration.)

**General Damages:** £10,500

**Value of Award of £1,500 as at April 2004: £1,963**

*Nuisance – cockroach infestation*

*and*

*Property – Housing – Nuisance – infestation*

---

**Name of Case:**        *Hudson v Royal Borough of Kensington and Chelsea*

**Cause/s of Action:**        Nuisance by infestation

**Tribunal and Judge:**        Bloomsbury and Marylebone County Court - HHJ Honig

**Where Reported:**        December 1985 LAB 171

**Date of Award:**        October 9, 1985

**Brief Facts of Case:**        T brought proceedings against the Council in respect of its failure to deal with a severe cockroach infestation on an estate.

**Award:**        £1,000 damages awarded for Ts discomfort over a substantial period of time.

**Value of Award of £1,000 as at April 2004: £1,943**

*Property – Housing – Nuisance by infestation*

---

**Name of Case:**        *Joyce v Southwark LBC*

**Cause/s of Action:**        Breach of covenant to collect refuse

**Tribunal and Judge:**        Lambeth County Court – DJ Lacey

**Where Reported:**        May 1997 LAB 20

**Date of Award:**        February 20, 1996

**Brief Facts of Case:**        Ts were joint council tenants claiming damages for breach of express and implied terms of their tenancy agreement for the collection and removal of refuse. Between 1979-81 refuse from 16 flats had been collected infrequently from only 8 dustbins. For 11 years refuse was stored and infrequently removed from a converted washroom also used by schoolchildren for smoking and urinating. Fires had been started in the refuse including a serious fire one night under Ts' flat. For the last 2 years the wheelie bins had been infrequently emptied. For over 16 years the refuse had smelled and attracted pests. Ts were unable to open their windows or use the garden.

**Award:**             £12,250 total damages including:

£600 per year general damages for 16 years

£1,000 for fear and sleeping difficulties in connection with the serious fire

(Special damages were awarded.)

**General Damages:**   £1,600

**Value of Award of £600 per annum as at April 2004: £738**

*Property – Housing – Breach of covenant*

---

**Name of Case:**          *Lambeth LBC v Wright*

**Cause/s of Action:**     Breach of covenant to repair – Nuisance by infestation

**Tribunal and Judge:**    Wood Green Trial Centre – HHJ Medawar

**Where Reported:**        August 1994 LAB 18

**Date of Award:**         December 10, 1993

**Brief Facts of Case:**   T occupied a council flat in a pre-war block affected by cockroach infestation over a 30-month period. L brought possession proceedings for rent arrears. T counterclaimed for damages for disrepair and nuisance.

**Award:**                 £3,600 total damages comprising:

Damages for loss of value @ £40 per month

Damages for inconvenience and distress @ £80 per month

**General Damages:**          £3,600

**Value of Award of £3,600 as at April 2004: £4,711**

**Value of Award of £960 per annum as at April 2004: £1,256**

*Property – Housing – Breach of covenant to repair – Nuisance – Cockroach infestation*

---

| | |
|---|---|
| **Name of Case:** | *Lowbridge v London Borough of Hackney* |
| **Cause/s of Action:** | Nuisance by infestation |
| **Tribunal and Judge:** | Shoreditch County Court |
| **Where Reported:** | February 1991 LAB 23 |
| **Date of Award:** | November 26, 1990 |
| **Brief Facts of Case:** | The Council had been convicted in 1989 for allowing L's premises to become prejudicial to public health under the Public Health Act 1936. The Council then failed to comply with the magistrates' court order which required that repair works be carried out at L's flat and that a programme be implemented to eradicate cockroaches in the block. In May 1990 L issued proceedings claiming that the Council had caused adopted or continued a nuisance due to cockroaches entering her flat from the retained parts within the Council's control and by failing to eliminate the infestation. |
| **Award:** | £4,000 damages. |
| **General Damages:** | £4,000 |

**Value of Award of £4,000 as at April 2004: £5,714**

*Property – Housing – Nuisance – Cockroach Infestation*

---

| | |
|---|---|
| **Name of Case:** | *M'Boge v London Borough of Hackney* |
| **Cause/s of Action:** | Breach of covenant to repair; nuisance by infestation |
| **Tribunal and Judge:** | Shoreditch County Court |
| **Where Reported:** | December 1991 LAB 22 |
| **Date of Award:** | July 12, 1991 |
| **Brief Facts of Case:** | T occupied flat in a tower block affected by damp penetration and cockroach infestation. T made counterclaim for disrepair. |
| **Award:** | £4,260 general damages. |
| **General Value:** | £4,260 |

**Value of Award of £4,260 as at April 2004: £6,020**

*Property – Housing – Breach of covenant to repair-* **Nuisance –**
**cockroach infestation**

---

| | |
|---|---|
| **Name of Case:** | *McGuigan v Southwark LBC* |
| **Cause/s of Action:** | Nuisance by infestation |
| **Tribunal and Judge:** | Central London Court – Recorder Rose |
| **Where Reported:** | March 1996 LAB 14 |
| **Date of Award:** | September 15, 1995 |
| **Brief Facts of Case:** | T's flat had been subject to severe ant infestation since 1986. There were ants in food, sheets, towels and clothes. The ants were eradicated by the Council after a year. |

A cockroach infestation also began in 1986 about which the Council was aware. By 1990 there was severe infestation with cockroaches in the food, fridge, freezer and oven. T was unable to eat in the property and no food could be stored there. T stopped heating the property to discourage an increase in the infestation. By mid 1991 T was sleeping on others' floors and had become depressed and suicidal about the conditions and was referred to a psychiatrist. She moved in December 1991 as soon as alternative accommodation was offered but was unable to take her belongings with her for fear of the infestation spreading.

**Award:**          £28,650 total damages including:

General damages:
| £2,000 | 1986-87 |
| £1,000 | 1987-88 |
| £5,000 | 1988-90(£2,500 per year) |
| £7,000 | 1990-91(£3,500 per year) |

(for the period without replacement furniture)

£1,500          1991-95(£500 per year)

(Special damages: £9,000.)

**General Damages:**     £16,500

**Value of Award of £16,500 as at April 2004: £20,346**

**Value of Award of £1,000 per annum as at April 2004: £1,233**

**Value of Award of £2,000 per annum as at April 2004: £2,466**

**Value of Award of £2,500 per annum as at April 2004: £3.083**

**Value of Award of £3,500 per annum as at April 2004: £4,316**

*Property – Housing – Nuisance – infestation*

**Name of Case:**          *Pillay v Farahani*

**Cause/s of Action:**     Breach of covenant to repair - nuisance by
                           infestation

**Tribunal and Judge:**    Wandsworth County Court – HHJ Compston

**Where Reported:**        May 1998 LAB 23

**Date of Award:**         January 29, 1998

**Brief Facts of Case:**   T (a tenant of a bed-sit) complained of damp,
                           cockroach infestation and defects in parts of the
                           premises shared with other tenants (defective
                           heater in the bathroom, damp walls, crumbling
                           plaster, defective kitchen sink). The council
                           served a disrepair notice under s 190(1) of HA
                           1985 before remedial work was carried out.

**Award:**                 £10,046 total damages including:

                           £7,000 for diminution in value over 7 years (at a
                           discounted rate of £1,000 per year to reflect T's
                           failure to co-operate)

                           £1,500 for discomfort and inconvenience
                           £1,200 for cockroach infestation (2 years @ £600
                           per year)

                           (Special damages: £346.)

**General Damages:**       £2,700

**Value of Award of £2,700 as at April 2004: £3,144**

**Value of Award of £1,500 as at April 2004: £1,746**

**Value of Award of £600 per annum as at April 2004: £699**

*Property – Landlord & Tenant – Breach of covenant to repair - Nuisance
by infestation*

**Name of Case:**          *Southwark LBC v Long*

**Cause/s of Action:**     Nuisance by smell and infestation – Breach of
                           covenant to maintain common parts

**Tribunal and Judge:**    Court of Appeal – Arden LJ

**Where Reported:**        [2002] EWCA Civ 403; [2002] 47 EG 150;
                           *Times*, April 16, 2002; 2002 5 CL 426; August
                           2002 LAB 27

**Date of Award:**         March 27, 2002

**Brief Facts of Case:**   L was awarded damages for breach of landlord's
                           obligations under a tenancy agreement namely a
                           failure to keep the common parts clean and tidy and
                           a failure to keep the refuse facilities in repair. L was
                           a secure tenant of a flat adjacent to a large bin and
                           rubbish chute which was inadequate to deal with
                           volume of rubbish produced by the block on the
                           estate. L complained of maggot infestation, smells
                           and noise by tenants using chute and leaving
                           rubbish outside the bin. S appealed arguing that it
                           had fulfilled its obligation by engaging contractors
                           to clean the common parts and had taken reasonable
                           steps to prevent tenants from using the rubbish
                           chute inappropriately by written notice.

                           Held that the obligation to clean the common
                           parts could only be satisfied if there was an
                           adequate system in place for monitoring
                           performance by the contractors. S had been put
                           on notice by L's complaints that function not
                           exercised properly therefore failure to adequately
                           supervise constituted a breach of covenant. In
                           considering whether S had taken reasonable steps
                           its provision of low cost housing had to be taken
                           into account. There was no proviso that the
                           landlord should have the resources to fund the
                           steps to achieve a basic standard of cleanliness.
                           Notifying the tenants regarding proper use of the
                           chute was not sufficient as there was a likelihood
                           that a high proportion of tenants would ignore the
                           notice. There was no breach of the implied

covenant of quiet enjoyment, or the repair obligation under the tenancy agreement, but there was evidence of liability in nuisance.

**Award:** Appeal dismissed. £13,500 damages upheld (£2,500 per year between 1993 and 1995 and £1,500 per year for the next 5 ½ years).

**General Damages:** £13,500

**Value of Award of £13,500 as at April 2004: £14,366**

**Value of Award of £2,500 per annum as at April 2004: £2,660**

**Value of Award of £1,500 per annum as at April 2004: £1,596**

*Property – Housing – Breach of covenant to maintain common parts – Nuisance by smell and infestation*

---

**Name of Case:** *Syrett v Carr and Neave*

**Cause/s of Action:** Surveyor's negligence - Nuisance by infestation

**Tribunal and Judge:** Queens Bench Division – Judge Peter Bowsher QC

**Where Reported:** December 1990 LAB 17

**Date of Award:** July 1990

**Brief Facts of Case:** Home owner purchased property which suffered from a death watch beetle infestation in respect of which her surveyors had failed to report.

**Award:** £8,000 general damages for inconvenience over a period of less that 2 years.

**General Damages:** £8,000

**Value of Award of £8,000 as at 2004: £11,716**

*Surveyor's negligence – Infestation by beetles*

---

## Nuisance by Noxious Smell

| | |
|---|---|
| **Name of Case:** | *Bone and another v Seale* |
| **Cause/s of Action:** | Nuisance by noxious smells |
| **Tribunal and Judge:** | Court of Appeal – Stephenson, Scarman and Ormrod LLJ |
| **Where Reported:** | [1975] 2 EGLR 117 |
| **Date of Award:** | November 26, 1974 |
| **Brief Facts of Case:** | Appeal from a decision of Walton J in the Chancery Division granting an injunction to restrain S from pig farming in such a manner as to cause a nuisance by smell and awarding each plaintiff damages of £6,000 in respect of nuisance suffered over period of 12 years. Smell emanated from manure and the boiling of swill for 700 pigs. |
| **Award:** | £1,000 damages for each plaintiff in respect of inconvenience and discomfort. (Award of £6,000 too high – parallel drawn with personal injury awards for loss of sense of smell.) |
| **General Damages:** | £1,000 |

**Value of Award as at April 2004: £6,361**

*Nuisance – Noxious smell – inconvenience and discomfort*

---

| | |
|---|---|
| **Name of Case:** | *Southwark LBC v Long* |
| **Cause/s of Action:** | Nuisance by smell and infestation – Breach of covenant to maintain common parts |
| **Tribunal and Judge:** | Court of Appeal – Arden LJ |
| **Where Reported:** | [2002] EWCA Civ 403; [2002] 47 EG 150; *Times*, April 16, 2002; 2002 5 CL 426; August 2002 LAB 27 |

**Date of Award:**     March 27, 2002

**Brief Facts of Case:**     L was awarded damages for breach of landlord's obligations under a tenancy agreement namely a failure to keep the common parts clean and tidy and a failure to keep the refuse facilities in repair. L was a secure tenant of a flat adjacent to a large bin and rubbish chute which was inadequate to deal with volume of rubbish produced by the block on the estate. L complained of maggot infestation, smells and noise by tenants using chute and leaving rubbish outside the bin. S appealed arguing that it had fulfilled its obligation by engaging contractors to clean the common parts and had taken reasonable steps to prevent tenants from using the rubbish chute inappropriately by written notice.

Held that the obligation to clean the common parts could only be satisfied if there was an adequate system in place for monitoring performance by the contractors. S had been put on notice by L's complaints that function not exercised properly therefore failure to adequately supervise constituted a breach of covenant. In considering whether S had taken reasonable steps its provision of low cost housing had to be taken into account. There was no proviso that the landlord should have the resources to fund the steps to achieve a basic standard of cleanliness. Notifying the tenants regarding proper use of the chute was not sufficient as there was a likelihood that a high proportion of tenants would ignore the notice. There was no breach of the implied covenant of quiet enjoyment, or the repair obligation under the tenancy agreement, but there was evidence of liability in nuisance.

**Award:**     Appeal dismissed. £13,500 damages upheld (£2,500 per year between 1993 and 1995 and £1,500 per year for the next 5 ½ years).

**General Damages:**   £13,500

**Value of Award of £13,500 as at April 2004: £14,366**

**Value of Award of £2,500 per annum as at April 2004: £2,660**

**Value of Award of £1,500 per annum as at April 2004: £1,596**

*Property – Housing – Breach of covenant to maintain common parts –*
*Nuisance by smell and infestation*

---

| | |
|---|---|
| **Name of Case:** | *Wilson v Southwick Contractors* |
| **Cause/s of Action:** | Nuisance by noise and noxious fumes |
| **Tribunal and Judge:** | CC (Central London) – District Judge Hasan |
| **Where Reported:** | [1996] CLY 2157 |
| **Date of Award:** | May 3, 1996 |
| **Brief Facts of Case:** | W lived in a flat in a residential mews above garage workshop. She endured loud machine noise smoke and smells, and shouting at weekends and at night, interference with her water supply and blocking of access to the property. W suffered headaches, insomnia, sore throats and nausea due to the nuisance for 2½ years before vacating. |
| | (Special damages: £2,500.) |
| **Award:** | £3,000 general damages. |

**General Damages:**   £3,000

**Value of Award of £3,000 as at April 2004: £3,644**

*Nuisance – noise, noxious fumes*

---

# Statutory Nuisance and Environmental Protection

**Name of Case:** *R v The Liverpool Crown Court, ex p. Cooke*

**Cause/s of Action:** Statutory nuisance, property prejudicial to health under s82 Environmental Protection Act 1990

**Tribunal and Judge:** Divisional Court, Queen's Bench Division – Leggatt LJ and Sir Iain Glidewell

**Where Reported:** (1997) 29 HLR 249

**Date of Award:** April 3, 1996

**Brief Facts of Case:** P was tenant of a local authority flat. She brought proceedings against the landlord under s82 of Environmental Protection Act 1990. In December 1994 the Local Authority pleaded guilty and was ordered to carry out works to abate the nuisance and pay £3,000 compensation (on the assumption that the nuisance had continued for 2 ½ years).

The Local Authority appealed. The Crown Court reduced the award of compensation but imposed a fine of £500 on basis that the summons only alleged nuisance from November 1994 so that compensation should be confined to that period.

P appealed for Judicial Review of Crown Court's decision.

**Award:** Compensation award reduced by the Crown Court to £250. (Application for Judicial Review dismissed.)

**Value of Award of £250 as at April 2004: £304**

*Nuisance – Statutory Nuisance – Environmental Protection*

# Right to Light

**Name of Case:**    *Carr-Saunders v Dick McNeil Associates Ltd & others*

**Cause/s of Action:**    Nuisance – Obstruction of Light

**Tribunal and Judge:**    Chancery Division – Mr Justice Millett

**Where Reported:**    [1986] 2 EGLR 181

**Date of Award:**    February 24, 1986

**Brief Facts of Case:**    Easement of light, obstruction of light by development owing to subdivision of rooms behind ancient windows. D had erected 2 additional storeys opposite ancient windows. Space affected had been sub-divided into 2 rooms which were in use as part of a suite of rooms for alternative therapy.

**Award:**    £8,000 general damages for a substantial interference with C-S's enjoyment of its property taking into account loss of amenity generally and the parties' relative bargaining positions.

**General Damages:**    £8,000

**Value of Award of £8,000 as at April 2004: £15,379**

*Property – Nuisance – obstruction of light*

---

**Name of Case:**    *Deakins v Hookings*

**Cause/s of Action:**    Nuisance – Obstruction of light

**Tribunal and Judge:**    Mayors & City of London County Court – HHJ Cooke

**Where Reported:**    [1994] 1 EGLR 190

**Date of Award:**          September 24, 1993

**Brief Facts of Case:**    Interference with right of light by building
                            extension. D had lived for 40 years in a terraced
                            cottage with a small courtyard at rear. Windows
                            of the property facing the courtyard had acquired
                            easements of light. H owned adjoining property
                            and constructed a rear extension. D brought
                            action that the light to the windows of her kitchen
                            and living room was affected.

**Award:**                  Mandatory injunction appropriate but damages
                            the judge would have awarded in the alternative
                            to an injunction assessed at £4,500 (being 15% of
                            the benefit of the development to H. Interference
                            with right of light to living room only.)

**General Damages if awarded:** £4,500

**Value of Award of £4,500 as at April 2004: £5,889**

*Property – Nuisance – Obstruction of light – Damages in lieu of injunction*

---

**Name of Case:**           *Marine & General Mutual Life Assurance
                            Society v St James' Real Estate Co Ltd*

**Cause/s of Action:**      Nuisance - Obstruction of light

**Tribunal and Judge:**     Mayors and City of London Court – His Honour
                            Judge JG Ross-Martyn

**Where Reported:**         [1991] 2 EGLR 178; [1991] 38 EG 230; [1992]
                            CLY 1793

**Date of Award:**          April 4, 1991

**Brief Facts of Case:**    Easement of light, obstruction of ancient lights
                            by proposed new building, relief under ss3 & 4 of
                            Prescription Act 1832, doctrine of lost modern
                            grant. M was freehold owner of office block. S
                            was leaseholder of the adjoining property. An

open space between the two properties caused a light well. The effect of a proposed reconstruction project by S was to remove the light well and raise the wall and roof of S's property.

**Award:**          £18,000 general damages for actual loss of light and the general deteriorating quality of the environment taking into account the parties' bargaining positions.

**General Damages:**      £18,000

**Value of Award of £18,000 as at April 2004: £25,113**

*Property – Nuisance – Obstruction of light*

# Tree Root

| | |
|---|---|
| **Name of Case:** | *Bridges & others v Harrow London Borough* |
| **Cause/s of Action:** | Nuisance – tree root damage |
| **Tribunal and Judge:** | Queen's Bench Division – Mr Justice Stuart-Smith |
| **Where Reported:** | [1981] 2 EGLR 143 |
| **Date of Award:** | June 11, 1981 |
| **Brief Facts of Case:** | B and neighbours owned a pair of semi-detached houses. The roots of 2 trees standing in front of their houses had caused cracks in their properties necessitating substantial repairs. H liable to both B and neighbour for damages in nuisance. |
| **Award:** | £750 general damages to B only for disturbance and loss of amenity between 1973 and 1976 while waiting for repairs and during 3 month period of carrying out permanent repairs to the house. |
| | Special damages: £7,287.36 and £6,350.35 awarded to B and neighbour respectively for the agreed cost of repairs. |
| **General Damages:** | £750 |

**Value of Award of £750 as at April 2004: £1,858**

*Property – Nuisance – Tree root damage and Tree root damage – Nuisance*

---

| | |
|---|---|
| **Name of Case:** | *Masters v Brent London Borough Council* |
| **Cause/s of Action:** | Nuisance - Tree root damage |
| **Tribunal and Judge:** | Queen's Bench Division – Mr Justice Talbot |
| **Where Reported:** | [1978] 1 EGLR 128 |

**Date of Award:**        November 22, 1977

**Brief Facts of Case:**    Roots of lime tree planted by B in the vicinity of M's property undermined the foundations of the house. Builder had reported that front bay in danger of subsiding. Repair works consisted of demolishing and rebuilding bay and underpinning wall. On advice of solicitors M's father had transferred property to M to raise money for repair works by way of mortgage. M brought proceedings alleging continuous nuisance.

**Award:**            £1,133.33 damages in respect of cost of repair works. No award for distress or inconvenience.

(Special damages: £1,133.33.)

*Property – Nuisance – tree root damage*

*and*

*Tree root damage – nuisance*

# Solicitor's Negligence

| | |
|---|---|
| **Name of Case:** | *Aran Caterers Ltd v Stephen Lake Gilbert & Paling (a firm)* |
| **Cause/s of Action:** | Solicitor's negligence – failure to renew business tenancy |
| **Tribunal and Judge:** | Chancery Division, Judge Howarth |
| **Where Reported:** | [2002] 1 EGLR 69; CL (November) Digest 2002; [2002] 1 EG 76 |
| **Date of Award:** | June 26, 2001 |
| **Brief Facts of Case:** | A occupied premises on a four-year lease expiring in September 1997. The lease was protected under Part II of the Landlord and Tenant Act 1954 and the premises had Class A3 planning permission. A was unsuccessful in negotiating a renewal and instructed S who failed to advise an application for the grant of a new lease in time. Less favourable lease terms were agreed together with a redevelopment break clause. The lease expired in 2001. |
| | S admitted negligence and damages were assessed based on the type of lease the court would have granted in 1997 if A had applied in time i.e. a 4-year lease without a break clause (due to the landlord not intending to redevelop until 2006 because of other extant leases). The method for determining the value of the premises was the years purchase method with the goodwill of A's business as at 1997. Profit estimate of £95,000 multiplied by years purchase figure of 2.75. |
| **Award:** | £315,000 damages: £83,000 for loss of protection of the Act. |
| | No award for relocation expenses as A would have moved in any event in 2006. |

**General Damages:**        £315,000

**Value of Award as at April 2004: £335,410**

*Property – Solicitor's negligence – failure to renew business tenancy*

---

**Name of Case:**        *Faragher v Gerber*

**Cause/s of Action:**   Solicitor's negligence

**Tribunal and Judge:**  Queen's Bench Division – HHJ Lachs sitting as a judge of the High Court

**Where Reported:**      [1994] EGCS 122

**Date of Award:**       June 27, 1994

**Brief Facts of Case:** F worked for London Docklands Development Corporation who were engaged in plans for a new highway in the area in which she wished to purchase a flat. Solicitor did not inform F of reply to local search to make enquiries of LDDC in respect of any new road or improvement to road. F put to great inconvenience when works on road began and had to move out of premises.

(£32,000 damages for loss suffered in capital value of property; £1,800 special damages for cracks and making good.)

**Award:**               £6,000 damages for loss of amenity.

**General Damages:**     £6,000

**Value of Award of £6,000 as at April 2004: £7,700**

*Property - Solicitor's negligence*

---

| | |
|---|---|
| **Name of Case:** | *Griffiths v Last Cawthra Feather* |
| **Cause/s of Action:** | Solicitor's negligence |
| **Tribunal and Judge:** | Queen's Bench Division (T & CC) – Judge Grenfell |
| **Where Reported:** | [2002] PNLR 27; 2002 10 CL 100 |
| **Date of Award:** | 2002 |
| **Brief Facts of Case:** | L (solicitors) failed to advise G on purchasing the property that G had a duty to maintain a water culvert under it at common law and under s264 of the Public Health Act 1936. L admitted liability. |
| | Held that G would not have purchased the property if he had known about this duty. In 1988 the property was worth £95,000 without the culvert and only £25,000 with it. The loss was the liability to pay for maintenance and repair and the proper date for assessment of diminution in value was 1988. The rate of interest from 1988 to date was the short-term interest rate. |
| **Award:** | £70,000 plus interest from 1988. |
| **General Damages:** | £70,000 |

**Value of Award of £70,000 as at April 2004: £71,699**

*Property – Solicitor's negligence*

---

| | |
|---|---|
| **Name of Case:** | *Kennedy v Van Emden; Jordan v Gershon Young Finer & Green (A Firm); Burdge and Lavender v Jacobs Kane & Blok* |
| **Cause/s of Action:** | Solicitor's negligence |
| **Tribunal and Judge:** | Court of Appeal – Nourse, Ward and Schiemann LJJ |

**Where Reported:**      (1997) 74 P & CR 19

**Date of Award:**      March 27, 1996

**Brief Facts of Case:**      The appellants were underlessees of flats who had taken a transfer of their underleases between 1982-1987 at a premium between £29,000 and £165,000 and an annual rent between £320 and £350. In 1990 the rent was increased to between £4,368 and £5,681. Appellants brought actions for professional negligence against solicitors on grounds that they had failed to advise 1) that Rent Act 1977 provisions made premiums unlawful and prohibited further assignment 2) as to onerous rent review provisions in their leases.

                        HH Judge Maddocks held no loss in respect of premiums (the Housing Act 1988 had subsequently allowed such premiums) and awarded damages in respect of rent review provisions. Appeal dismissed.

**Award:**      Assessment of damages in respect of rent review provisions of between £4,500 and £10,000 upheld.

*Breach of contract – Solicitor's negligence – failure to advise on assignment*

*and*

*Solicitor's negligence – failure to advise*

---

**Name of Case:**      *Murray v Lloyd*

**Cause/s of Action:**      Solicitor's negligence

**Tribunal and Judge:**      Chancery Division – Mummery J

**Where Reported:** September 1989 LAB 24; (1989) *Times* 27 June; 139 NLJ 938, 21 HLR 525

**Date of Award:** June 22, 1989

**Brief Facts of Case:** T brought proceedings against a firm of solicitors for negligently advising her that her tenancy should be in the name of a company registered in the Virgin Islands for tax reasons. She claimed that the firm had wrongfully advised that in assigning the tenancy to herself she would be able to obtain a statutory tenancy as there was a covenant against assignment in the lease.

**Award:** Damages of £115,000 assessed at 25% of the freehold value of the property (£460,000) notwithstanding evidence that L would not have sold the freehold to her.

**General Damages:** £115,000

**Value of Award of £115,000 as at April 2004: £185,056**

*Solicitor's negligence – Negligent advice on assignment*

---

**Name of Case:** *Smith v Drumm and others*

**Cause/s of Action:** Solicitor's negligence – Vendor/Purchaser - Misrepresentation by vendor

**Tribunal and Judge:** Queen's Bench Division – Mr Bruce Mauleverer QC sitting as deputy judge of the division

**Where Reported:** [1996] EGCS 192

**Date of Award:** November 19, 1996

**Brief Facts of Case:** Ps bought flat sold by D1. They had viewed the property and saw that the boiler had not been connected. P's firm of solicitors (D2) sent enquiries before contract to D1 but these were not answered before completion. Ps moved in but moved out because central heating not connected and electricity had been disconnected due to illegal fuse box. D1 made arrangements for supply but unable to connect because P failed to allow access. P made no mortgage repayments and flat repossessed. P brought proceedings claiming that D1 had misrepresented in the particulars of sale that supplies would be connected on completion and property not fit for habitation under 1972 Act and D2 had failed to advise.

**Award:**                    £250 damages for discomfort only.

**General Damages:**          £250

**Value of Award of £250 as at April 2004: £302**

*Solicitor's negligence – Vendor/Purchaser – Misrepresentation –*
*Defective Premises – Failure to connect mains services*

---

**Name of Case:**             *Wapshott and another v Davis Donovan & Co and others*

**Cause/s of Action:**        Solicitors' negligence

**Tribunal and Judge:**       Court of Appeal – Beldam, Hobhouse and Aldous LJJ

**Where Reported:**           (1996) 71 P & CR D41

**Date of Award:**            December 14, 1995

**Brief Facts of Case:**      Two flats purchased in mid-1980s on long leases financed by 100% mortgage. Both flats rendered unsaleable by defect in title discovered in 1993. Leaseholders claimed damage for loss of value of their leases, conveyancing and other expenses and a claim for additional damages for inconvenience and distress. Compensation payable by solicitors assessed with W and another being awarded £76,202 and £74,890 respectively. £3,000 general damages awarded for the leaseholders inconvenience, discomfort and distress. Solicitors appealed against the awards.

**Award:**             £3,000 general damages for inconvenience and distress. Appeal dismissed.

(Special damages: £76,202 and £74,890.)

**General Damages:**    £3,000

**Value of Award of £3,000 as at April 2004: £3,697**

*Property – Solicitors' negligence – defective title*

# Surveyor's Negligence

**Name of Case:**          *Ezekiel and another v McDade and others*

**Cause/s of Action:**     Surveyor's negligence

**Tribunal and Judge:**    Court of Appeal – Nourse and Henry LJJ and Sir
                           John Megaw

**Where Reported:**        [1994] EGCS 194; [1995] 47 EG 150; [1995]
                           CLY 3707; March 1996 LAB 15

**Date of Award:**         November 24, 1994

**Brief Facts of Case:**   E purchased property relying on a building society
                           valuation carried out by M without a structural
                           survey. Surveyor had failed to notice a defect which
                           only came to light when E tried to sell on.
                           Subsequently E was evicted, the building society
                           repossessed and sold the property at auction. E
                           brought proceedings against surveyor and his firm.

                           Judge found firm liable in negligence and
                           awarded damages of £36,000 representing the
                           difference between the purchase price and
                           valuation at trial and £6,000 damages for
                           inconvenience and distress.

**Award:**                 Damages reduced to £27,000 on basis of
                           difference between value of house in 1986 and its
                           actual value at auction.

                           Damages for inconvenience and distress reduced
                           to £4,000.

                           (Special damages: £23,000.)

**General Damages:**       £4,000

**Value of Award of £4,000 as at April 2004: £5,112**

*Property –Professional negligence – Surveyor's negligence*

| | |
|---|---|
| **Name of Case:** | *Farley v Skinner (No. 2)* |
| **Cause/s of Action:** | Surveyor's negligence |
| **Tribunal and Judge:** | House of Lords – Lord Steyn, Lord Browne-Wilkinson, Lord Clyde, Lord Hutton and Lord Scott of Foscote |
| **Where Reported:** | [2001] UKHL 49; [2001] 3 WLR 899; [2001] 42 EG 139 (CS); [2002] PNLR 20 |
| **Date of Award:** | October 11, 2001 |
| **Brief Facts of Case:** | C instructed D, a chartered surveyor, to report on whether the property he wished to purchase would be affected by aircraft noise. D concluded it was unlikely. C purchased the property and found it badly affected by the noise. C claimed £70,000 damages for diminution in value of property. Judge rejected the claim but found D to be negligent and awarded non-pecuniary damages of £10,000 for the distress and inconvenience caused by the noise. |
| | D appealed on basis that non-pecuniary compensation was not recoverable for breach of contract. Appeal allowed. C appealed to the House of Lords. |
| **Award:** | £10,000 non-pecuniary damages award should not be interfered with. (Appeal allowed.) |
| | NB: Court indicated award at highest margin for non-pecuniary loss. |
| **General Damages:** | £10,000 |

**Value of Award of £10,000 as at April 2004: £10,654**

*Surveyor's negligence – Nuisance – Aircraft noise*

| | |
|---|---|
| **Name of Case:** | *Holder v Countrywide Surveyors Ltd* |
| **Cause/s of Action:** | Surveyor's negligence |
| **Tribunal and Judge:** | QBD (T & CC) – HH Judge Havery QC |
| **Where Reported:** | [2002] EWHC 856; [2003] PNLR 3; 2003 3 CL 390 |
| **Date of Award:** | March 11, 2002 |
| **Brief Facts of Case:** | H claimed that C had negligently overvalued the house which she bought in 1993 for £230,000. C had valued it at £215,000 but had not identified structural defects and major roof problems. C sought damages for the up to date cost of the repair works, with the cost of alternative accommodation while the works were carried out and damages for inconvenience, stress and overpaid stamp duty. |
| | Held C had been negligent and could have entered most of the roof space to find the defects and where this was not possible should have instructed a structural engineer. The measure of damages was the reduction in value in the property i.e. the difference between C's valuation and the actual value of the house on the valuation date taking into the cost of repairs in 1993. |
| **Award:** | £102,500 damages for the reduction in the property's value |
| | £2,000 damages for distress and inconvenience |
| | (Special damages for the overpaid stamp duty as a result of the overvaluation and £5,000 for the costs of alternative accommodation.) |
| **General Damages:** | £2,000 |

## Value of Award of £2,000 as at April 2004: £2,128

*Property – Surveyor's negligence*

---

| | |
|---|---|
| **Name of Case:** | *McKinnon v e.surv Ltd (formerly known as GA Valuation & Survey Ltd)* |
| **Cause/s of Action:** | Surveyor's negligence |
| **Tribunal and Judge:** | Chancery Division |
| **Where Reported:** | April 2003 LAB 22 |
| **Date of Award:** | January 14, 2003 |
| **Brief Facts of Case:** | M purchased a house in June 1999 at price of £185,000 relying on a valuation by the defendant surveyor stating that whilst minor structural movement had been suffered in the past it appeared to be long-standing and unlikely to be progressive. Subsequently, M received advice that further movement risk was greater than originally advised. |

Judgment was entered in April 2002 with damages to be assessed. Agreed that competent surveyor would have suggested that possibility of movement was to be assessed and monitored over time and that pending this the house would be unmortgageable and worth £90,000. A retrospective valuation of £148,000 had been made to June 1999. M argued that damages should be assessed on the difference between purchase price and £90,000 whereas the surveyor company maintained it should be based on £148,000.

Held that whilst the proper measure of damage should be the difference between the value in its assumed good condition and its value in bad condition, regard should be had to the principle that an injured party should only be compensated to the extent needed to put it in the same position as it would have been had it not sustained the wrong in question and therefore an award of £95,000 would overcompensate M.

**Award:**          £37,000

**Value of Award of £37,000 as at April 2004: £38,514**

*Property – Surveyor's negligence*

---

**Name of Case:**         *Merrett v Babb*

**Cause/s of Action:**    Surveyor's negligence

**Tribunal and Judge:**   Court of Appeal – Aldous and May LJJ and Wilson J

**Where Reported:**       [2001] EWCA Civ 214; [2001] PNLR 29; [2001] EGCS 24; [2001] CL Mar 565

**Date of Award:**        February 15, 2001

**Brief Facts of Case:**  B and her mother purchased property jointly subject to a mortgage following a mortgage valuation report by M, an employee of a valuation firm instructed by the mortgagee. Subsequently the interest in the property was transferred to B subject to her mother's right of occupation. The report had not mentioned settlement cracks between the building and the extension and the house was overvalued. B issued proceedings against M personally for negligence. M appealed the judge's award of damages for the overvaluation.

**Award:**                £14,500 damages for overvaluation. (Appeal dismissed.)

**General Damages:**      £14,500

**Value of Award as at April 2004: £15,655**

*Surveyor's negligence – negligent survey*

| | |
|---|---|
| **Name of Case:** | *Patel v Hooper & Jackson (a firm)* |
| **Cause/s of Action:** | Surveyor's negligence |
| **Tribunal and Judge:** | Court of Appeal – Nourse LJ |
| **Where Reported:** | *The Times* December 3, 1998; [1998] CLY 3958; April 1999 LAB 15 |
| **Date of Award:** | November 10, 1998 |
| **Brief Facts of Case:** | Ps were first-time buyer's who relied on a valuation from D's surveyors. The house was purchased in 1988 for £99,000 but its true value was £65,000. Ps could not move in because it was uninhabitable and had to rent alternative property because they did not have the finance to renovate or purchase another home. |
| **Award:** | £2,000 each in general damages for having lived in relative discomfort, £25,000 damages for diminution in value and additional damages for reasonable costs of extracting themselves from the purchase i.e. the costs of alternative accommodation until their house could be sold and another purchased. |
| **General Damages:** | £2,000 |

**Value of Award of £2,000 as at April 2004: £2,259**

*Property – Surveyor's negligence – overvaluation*

| | |
|---|---|
| **Name of Case:** | *Syrett v Carr and Neave* |
| **Cause/s of Action:** | Surveyor's negligence - Nuisance by infestation |
| **Tribunal and Judge:** | Queens Bench Division – Judge Peter Bowsher QC |
| **Where Reported:** | December 1990 LAB 17 |
| **Date of Award:** | July 1990 |
| **Brief Facts of Case:** | Home owner purchased property which suffered from a death watch beetle infestation in respect of which her surveyors had failed to report. |
| **Award:** | £8,000 general damages for inconvenience over a period of less that 2 years. |
| **General Damages:** | £8,000 |

**Value of Award of £8,000 as at April 2004: £11,716**

*Surveyor's negligence – Infestation by beetles*

# Vendor/Purchaser

**Name of Case:**            *Smith v Drumm and others*

**Cause/s of Action:**       Solicitor's negligence – Vendor/Purchaser - Misrepresentation by vendor

**Tribunal and Judge:**      Queen's Bench Division – Mr Bruce Mauleverer QC sitting as deputy judge of the division

**Where Reported:**          [1996] EGCS 192

**Date of Award:**           November 19, 1996

**Brief Facts of Case:**     Ps bought flat sold by D1. They had viewed the property and saw that the boiler had not been connected. P's firm of solicitors (D2) sent enquiries before contract to D1 but these were not answered before completion. Ps moved in but moved out because central heating not connected and electricity had been disconnected due to illegal fuse box. D1 made arrangements for supply but unable to connect because P failed to allow access. P made no mortgage repayments and flat repossessed. P brought proceedings claiming that D1 had misrepresented in the particulars of sale that supplies would be connected on completion and property not fit for habitation under 1972 Act and D2 had failed to advise.

**Award:**                   £250 damages for discomfort only.

**General Damages:**         £250

**Value of Award of £250 as at April 2004: £302**

*Solicitor's negligence – Vendor/Purchaser – Misrepresentation – Defective Premises – Failure to connect mains services*

# Misrepresentation

| | |
|---|---|
| **Name of Case:** | *Bridgegrove Ltd v Smith & another* |
| **Cause/s of Action:** | Misrepresentation |
| **Tribunal and Judge:** | Court of Appeal – Nourse, Potter and Mummery LJJ |
| **Where Reported:** | [1997] 2 EGLR 40 |
| **Date of Award:** | March 20, 1997 |
| **Brief Facts of Case:** | L (plaintiff) advertised premises as suitable for any storage workshop use and car repairs. Ds were partners in a garage business and took a 6 month lease of premises. Complaints were received and statutory notices served in respect of fumes and spraying associated with Ds' business. Ds continued in possession under monthly tenancy after expiry of the term. Enforcement notices were served alleging use without benefit of planning permission. L commenced proceedings for forfeiture and arrears of rent. D's counterclaim was for damages for misrepresentation. County Court Judge awarded Ds damages (after deducting rent arrears of £8,470). L appealed. |
| **Award:** | £17,230 award of damages for misrepresentation upheld. |
| | (Appeal dismissed.) |
| **General Damages:** | £17,230 |

**Value of Award as at April 2004: £20,590**

*Misrepresentation – vendor/purchaser*

**Name of Case:**  *Clements v Simmonds*

**Cause/s of Action:**  Misrepresentation - Compensation for loss of statutory tenancy

**Tribunal and Judge:**  Queen's Bench Division – Burton J

**Where Reported:**  [2002] EWHC 1652; [2002] 41 EG 178

**Date of Award:**  April 17, 2002

**Brief Facts of Case:**  C held a Rent Act 1977 statutory tenancy of a flat in a house owned by D. In the county court an order for possession was made in May 2000 for possession in D's favour on the basis that she required it for occupation as a residence on her return from America. C vacated in November 2000. D put the property on the market in November 2000 on the basis that it was in a very bad condition and her ill-health prevented her from improving it. She subsequently sold the house in 2001 for £1.25m. C brought a claim for damages under s102 of the 1977 Act arguing that the basis upon which possession had been obtained was false and D's intentions to reside there had been a misrepresentation.

Held claim allowed. There was no disastrous damage to the property in November 2000. D had not intended to live at the property and there was no change of mind between May 2000 (when possession was ordered) and November 2000. C had proved that D's representation of requiring the property for residence was false when made in May 2000. C had not been deprived of living permanently in the flat – she had been deprived of compensation for the loss of a statutory tenancy and the opportunity to negotiate the payment.

**Award:**  £60,000 compensation (less small admitted sum on counterclaim).

**General damages:** £60,000

**Value of Award of £60,000 as at April 2004: £63,415**

*Property – Landlord & Tenant - Compensation for loss of statutory tenancy*

---

| | |
|---|---|
| **Name of Case:** | *Smith v Drumm and others* |
| **Cause/s of Action:** | Solicitor's negligence – Vendor/Purchaser - Misrepresentation by vendor |
| **Tribunal and Judge:** | Queen's Bench Division – Mr Bruce Mauleverer QC sitting as deputy judge of the division |
| **Where Reported:** | [1996] EGCS 192 |
| **Date of Award:** | November 19, 1996 |
| **Brief Facts of Case:** | Ps bought flat sold by D1. They had viewed the property and saw that the boiler had not been connected. P's firm of solicitors (D2) sent enquiries before contract to D1 but these were not answered before completion. Ps moved in but moved out because central heating not connected and electricity had been disconnected due to illegal fuse box. D1 made arrangements for supply but unable to connect because P failed to allow access. P made no mortgage repayments and flat repossessed. P brought proceedings claiming that D1 had misrepresented in the particulars of sale that supplies would be connected on completion and property not fit for habitation under 1972 Act and D2 had failed to advise. |
| **Award:** | £250 damages for discomfort only. |
| **General Damages:** | £250 |

**Value of Award of £250 as at April 2004: £302**

*Solicitor's negligence – Vendor/Purchaser – Misrepresentation – Defective Premises – Failure to connect mains services*

---

| | |
|---|---|
| **Name of Case:** | *Neil v Kingsworth* |
| **Cause/s of Action:** | Misrepresentation under s102 of Rent Act 1977 |
| **Tribunal and Judge:** | Shoreditch County Court – Registrar Lipton |
| **Where Reported:** | December 1987 LAB 9; March 1988 LAB 21; September 1989 LAB 24 |
| **Date of Award:** | December 9, 1987 |

**Brief Facts of Case:** L brought possession proceedings on the basis that she intended to live in the premises. After the order was made she sold the property and it was converted into 4 flats. Evidence was given at the hearing that she was likely to have made £10,000 by obtaining vacant possession.

**Award:** £750 general damages for worry and inconvenience (she subsequently secured better accommodation)

£5,000 exemplary damages

(Special damages: £170.)

**General Damages:** £750

**Value of Award of £750 as at April 2004: £870**

**Value of Award of £5000 exemplary damages as at April 2004:**

*Property – Landlord & Tenant – Misrepresentation*

# Compulsory Purchase

**Name of Case:**          *Prielipp v Secretary of State for the Environment,*
                           *Transport and the Regions*

**Cause/s of Action:**     Compulsory Purchase – Compensation

**Tribunal and Judge:**    Lands Tribunal – PR Francis FRICS

**Where Reported:**        [2002] RVR 169; 2002 10 CL 346

**Date of Award:**         February 8, 2002

**Brief Facts of Case:**   P referred compensation for the compulsory
                           purchase of his riding stables business assessed at
                           £51,400 under the s5 of the Land Compensation
                           Act 1961 rule 2 on the basis of £51,400 for total
                           extinguishment and £49,000 for relocation.

                           P rented the premises on a 14-year lease and
                           sought: £286,475 for equivalent reinstatement (s5
                           rule 5); £358,942 for disturbance (on the basis
                           that although the business would have continued
                           but for the compulsory purchase, there was no
                           market for land for the purpose).

                           Held equivalent reinstatement did not apply as
                           there was evidence that there was a demand for
                           land used for that purpose and P had relocated
                           nearby with no loss to his client base.
                           Compensation was assessed on the relocation
                           basis with an allowance for consequent loss was
                           reasonable. No loss of goodwill was allowable
                           due to P's successful relocation.

**Award:**                 £119,438 compensation.

**Value of Award of £119,438 as at April 2004: £127,616**

*Property – Compulsory Purchase – Compensation*

| | |
|---|---|
| **Name of Case:** | *Richards v Somerset County Council (No 3)* |
| **Cause/s of Action:** | Compulsory Purchase – Compensation |
| **Tribunal and Judge:** | Lands Tribunal – PH Clarke, FRICS |
| **Where Reported:** | 2003 2 CL 413; [2002] RVR 328 |
| **Date of Award:** | September 2, 2002 |
| **Brief Facts of Case:** | S compulsorily purchased half an acre of land from R (the freeholder) for the construction of a road. R claimed 4.5 million pounds as a ransom value far higher than its actual use value on the basis that it could have been sold to a local business interests consortium for access to facilitate their applications for planning permission. S maintained that the access would have had no bearing on the hypothetical buyer and in risking the chance of a ransom value in the future the buyer would have paid £100,000. |
| | It was held that the local planning situation was unpredictable and therefore there was no suggestion that permission would have been dependent on the road construction. Local businesses would be more likely to compete on such a purchase and then pay for only the benefit they alone would derive from it. |
| **Award:** | £100,000 compensation. |

**Value of Award of £100,000 as at April 2004: £104,561**

*Property – Compulsory Purchase – Compensation*

---

| | |
|---|---|
| **Name of Case:** | *Roberts v South Gloucestershire District Council; Roberts v South Gloucestershire Council* |
| **Cause/s of Action:** | Compulsory Purchase – Compensation |

| | |
|---|---|
| **Tribunal and Judge:** | Court of Appeal – Carnwath LJ |
| **Where Reported:** | 2003 4 CL 387; [2002] EWCA Civ 1568; [2003] RVR 43; [2003]18 EG 114 |
| **Date of Award:** | November 7, 2002 |
| **Brief Facts of Case:** | R's agricultural land was compulsorily purchased for the construction of a section of ring road. R was awarded £17,000 by the Lands Tribunal on the basis of its agricultural value and appealed maintaining that as the excavation of materials had been required for the construction of the road, it should have been assessed on the basis of potential for mineral extraction. He argued that under the Land Compensation Act 1961 a hypothetical purchaser would have been granted permission for mineral extraction without an obligation to finish the road. |
| | Held that there was a distinction between the land's valuation and its planning status. The benefit or detriment of the Council's scheme was to be disregarded. The permission was for the construction of a section of a road and for valuation purposes regard had to be had to the landowner's right to build the same which was unlikely to give additional value. There was no expectation of realising the value of minerals in the foreseeable future. |
| **Award:** | Appeal dismissed. Award upheld. |

**Value of Award of £17,000 as at April 2004: £17,715**

*Property – Compulsory purchase – Compensation*

# Party Walls

| | |
|---|---|
| **Name of Case:** | *Rees v Skerrett* |
| **Cause/s of Action:** | Party wall - wrongful removal |
| **Tribunal and Judge:** | Court of Appeal – Waller LJ and Lloyd J |
| **Where Reported:** | [2001] EWCA Civ 760; (2001) 1 WLR 1541; February 2002 LAB 22 |
| **Date of Award:** | May 23, 2001 |
| **Brief Facts of Case:** | R acquired a terraced house sharing a common wall with his neighbour S. S pulled down his house leaving the common wall exposed without support causing disrepair. R sought damages for costs of remedial works, damp-proofing and professional fees. Judge held wind suction damage was not within the scope of a right to support. R appealed. |
| **Award:** | £40,000 damages claim allowed in full. There was a duty on S to take reasonable steps to weatherproof the dividing wall once exposed. |
| **General Damages:** | £40,000 |

**Value of Award of £40,000 as at April 2004: £42,641**

*Property – Party wall – Wrongful removal*

**Name of Case:**       *Saunders v Williams*

**Cause/s of Action:**   Party Wall - Negligent building works

**Tribunal and Judge:**  Court of Appeal – Pill, Chadwick and Clarke LLJ

**Where Reported:**      (2003) BLR 125; [2002] EWCA Civ 673

**Date of Award:**       April 25, 2002

**Brief Facts of Case:**  S appealed against a decision of Jacob J on 11
July 2001 sitting as a judge of the Technology
and Construction Court. The party wall to S's
property was damaged following building work
carried out to the adjoining semi-detached
property by the owner W in December 1992.
Liability was admitted. Damages for
reinstatement awarded at £24,572 for cost of
removing wall, re-instating it and repairing the
roof. Further sum of £1,000 per annum awarded
in respect of distress and inconvenience over a
period of 8 years.

S appealed on quantification of damages. Appeal
allowed in part. W could have foreseen upon
damaging the wall that S would suffer damage in
repair and diminution in the use of her property.
W had failed to establish the burden upon him
that S did not take reasonable measures to
mitigate her loss. Remission of the matter was
not justified on the ground of proportionality and
the Court assessed damages themselves.

**Award:**               £8,000 (8 years @£1,000 per year)

**Value of Award of £8,000 as at April 2004: £8,455**

*Property – Negligence – Party Wall*

# Breach of Contract

| | |
|---|---|
| **Name of Case:** | *Bayoumi v Protim Services Ltd* |
| **Cause/s of Action:** | Breach of contract to repair |
| **Tribunal and Judge:** | Court of Appeal – Leggatt, Swinton Thomas and Mummery LJJ |
| **Where Reported:** | [1996] EGCS 187 |
| **Date of Award:** | November 6, 1996 |
| **Brief Facts of Case:** | The owner of a pair of gatehouses converted one into a dwelling house. In 1978 P was engaged to carry out damp and waterproofing services. B thought damp problem solved when he purchased house but property still suffered from renewed water penetration and condensation. By 1989 attempts to stop damp were unsuccessful – P supplied dehumidifier but due to faulty switch overflow caused damage to B's furniture and possessions. P held liable for failure to carry out remedial damp proofing work in discharge of duty under Defective Premises Act 1972. |
| | County Court Judge awarded damages (to include sum for loss of use of premises in substitution for claim for loss of rent). P appealed. |
| **Award:** | £6,000 for loss of use of premises. Appeal dismissed. |
| | Special damages: £11,149. |
| **General Damages:** | £6,000 |

**Value of Award of General Damages as at April 2004: £7,240**

*Property –Breach of Contract to repair – damp proofing – loss of use of premises*

**Name of Case:**       *Jones & Jones v Derval Dampcoursing Co*

**Cause/s of Action:**       Breach of contract to repair

**Tribunal and Judge:**       Consett County Court – HH Judge RA Percy

**Where Reported:**       [1988] CLY 1048; December 1988 LAB 20

**Date of Award:**       March 11, 1988

**Brief Facts of Case:**       Defective damp course installed by defendant company in 1980. Between 1981 and 1983 plaintiffs repeatedly complained. Company's attempts to rectify in 1983 were unsuccessful. Plaintiffs whose baby was born in 1981suffered distress due to state of their home and were unable to decorate downstairs until 1984. Re-housed by Council in 1985.

**Award:**       £2,500 general damages (taking into account cost of £1,099 of Council accommodation as evidence of plaintiffs loss of enjoyment of their home and inconvenience).

**General Damages:**       £2,500

**Value of Award of £2,500 as at April 2004: £4,460**

*Breach of contract – defective damp course*

---

**Name of Case:**       *Makan v British Gas*

**Cause/s of Action:**       Breach of contract, defective repairs

**Tribunal and Judge:**       Epsom County Court – DJ Bradfield

**Where Reported:**       [1994] CLY 1466; March 1995 LAB 15

**Date of Award:**       July 27, 1994

**Brief Facts of Case:**       In July 1991 D replaced a faulty hot water cylinder in P's home. Water began to pour out of it an hour later causing a flood. Parts of the bathroom and living room ceilings collapsed, depositing plaster dust and debris on the carpets, decorations and furniture of the rooms below. A large hole was left until April 1992 making the living room unusable.

**Award:** £2,000 general damages for the inconvenience and loss of use of the living room for 9 months.

(Special damages: £2,663.)

**General Damages:** £2,000

**Value of Award of £2,000 as at April 2004: £2,579**

*Breach of contract – Defective repairs*

---

**Name of Case:** *Murray v Sturgis and others*

**Cause/s of Action:** Breach of contract of management by estate agent, (dilapidations caused by tenants' damage to decorations and furnishings)

**Tribunal and Judge:** Queen's Bench Division – Sir Douglas Frank QC sitting as deputy judge

**Where Reported:** [1981] 2 EGLR 22

**Date of Award:** April 10, 1981

**Brief Facts of Case:** M had instructed firm of S as managing agents to let his furnished flat whilst he took up an appointment abroad. M had put in new curtains, carpets and intended to return to live there. S breached the contract of management by its failure to take up references of prospective tenants, check inventories, obtain rent in advance and arrange for services to be put in the names of the tenants. Two tenants caused damage to furnishings and decorations.

**Award:**                    £100 general damages for anxiety and
                              inconvenience suffered by M.

                              (Special damages: £5,886 total for unpaid rent,
                              telephone bill, and dilapidations.)

**General Damages:**          £100

**Value of Award of £100 as at April 2004: £251**

*Breach of Contract –Managing Agent – dilapidations by tenant*

---

**Name of Case:**             *Ruxley Electronics and Construction Ltd v
                              Forsyth and another*

**Cause/s of Action:**        Breach of contract

**Tribunal and Judge:**       House of Lords – Lord Keith of Kinkel, Lord
                              Bridge of Harwich, Lord Jauncey of Tullichettle,
                              Lord Mustill and Lord Lloyd of Berwick

**Where Reported:**           [1995] 3 All ER 268 HL; [1995] EGCS 117;
                              April 1996 LAB 19

**Date of Award:**            June 29, 1995

**Brief Facts of Case:**      P was contracted to build a swimming pool and
                              enclosure. Diving area was 6ft not 7ft 6ins deep
                              as specified in the contract. This did not have any
                              adverse effect on the value of the property. The
                              estimated cost of rebuild was £21,560. P sued for
                              outstanding balance under contract. D
                              counterclaimed for damages equivalent to cost of
                              replacement.

                              Judgment for outstanding balance of contract
                              price. D awarded damages of £2,500 for loss of
                              amenity but counterclaim for breach of contract
                              dismissed. D appealed.

Court of Appeal allowed appeal. D's loss was the amount required to put him in the same position as he would have been if contract had been performed. P appealed to House of Lords.

**Award:**               £2,500 award of damages for loss of amenity reinstated. High Court judgment restored. D's loss did not extend to cost of re-instatement. Appeal allowed.

**General Damages:**    £2,500

**Value of Award of £2,500 as at April 2004: £3,099**

*Property – Breach of contract – Construction of swimming pool – Loss of amenity*

# Breach of Statutory Duty

**Name of Case:** *Ahmad v Cirant*

**Cause/s of Action:** Breach of covenant of repair under s11 Landlord and Tenant Act 1985 – Breach of duty under s4 Defective Premises Act 1972

**Tribunal and Judge:** Bristol County Court – Assistant Recorder Rutherford

**Where Reported:** March 1992 LAB 13

**Date of Award:** January 17, 1992

**Brief Facts of Case:** L sought possession for arrears of rent. T lodged a defence and counterclaim for damages. T had withheld rent after L refused to carry out works of repair contained in a 9-page schedule of works.

**Award:** General damages of £18 per week for 6 years

Total: £5,616 to be set off against unpaid rent.

Ts recovered balance of £2,700.

(Special damages: £500.)

**General Damages:** £5,616

**Value of Award of General Damages of £18 per week as at April 2004: £25 per week**

*Property – Landlord & Tenant – Breach of covenant to repair – Breach of statutory duty*

---

**Name of Case:** *R (Bernard) v Enfield LBC*

**Cause/s of Action:** Failure to house under National Assistance Act 1948 – Damages under Human Rights Act 1998

**Tribunal and Judge:** Sullivan J

**Where Reported:** [2002] EWHC 2282 Admin; December 2002 LAB 23

**Date of Award:**            October 25, 2002

**Brief Facts of Case:**      B was a couple with 6 children. Mr B was carer for Mrs B who was a stroke victim and had been confined to a wheelchair. Their home was unsuitable for a disabled person in that it was unmodified and not wheelchair accessible and the claimants were confined to one room. The Council's housing department failed to act on the social services assessment acknowledging a duty to secure suitable accommodation under s21 of the National Assistance Act 1948. The Council had previously found B to be intentionally homeless but was ordered on judicial review to secure suitable accommodation in 3 months which it failed to do for over 2 years. B sought damages for the unlawful infringement of their rights under the European Convention on Human Rights.

Held that B's living conditions had made it impossible for them to have any meaningful family life. There had been a lack of respect of the right to family life contrary to Article 8. The purpose of damages under the Convention was to make good the invasion of that right. Damages under the Human Rights Act 1998 should not be less than damages in tort and should not be minimal as this would undermine respect for the rights under the Convention.

**Award:**                    £10,000 total damages:

£8,000 for Mrs B

£2,000 for Mr B

**General Damages:**          £10,000

**Value of Award of £10,000 as at April 2004: £10,438**

*Property – Breach of statutory duty – Failure to house under National Assistance Act 1948 – Damages under Human Rights Act 1998*

| | |
|---|---|
| **Name of Case:** | *R (Bravo) v Haringey LBC* |
| **Cause/s of Action:** | Failure to provide interim accommodation under s188 Housing Act 1996 |
| **Tribunal and Judge:** | Unreported |
| **Where Reported:** | December 2002 LAB 23 |
| **Date of Award:** | September 27, 2002 |
| **Brief Facts of Case:** | B was suffering from depression and of no fixed abode. He applied to the council for accommodation as a homeless person giving evidence of his condition and medication on Friday 19 April. The council made an appointment to interview him the following Monday but provided no interim accommodation in breach of s188 Housing Act 1996. B slept rough over the weekend and was asked to provide a hospital report and letter from his wife that she had required him to leave but still failed to provide accommodation. A day later (23 April) an injunction was granted in judicial review proceedings requiring the Council to house B. His claim was amended to seek damages for the 4-night period during which he slept rough at underground and railway stations. The experience left him feeling vulnerable and exacerbated his mental condition. |
| **Award:** | £1,350 agreed. |
| **General Damages:** | £1,350 |

**Value of Award as at April 2004: £1,404**

*Property – Failure to provide interim accommodation under s188 Housing Act 1996*

---

| | |
|---|---|
| **Name of Case:** | *Conroy and others v Hire Token Ltd* |
| **Cause/s of Action:** | Breach of covenant to repair –Breach of duty of care under s4 Defective Premises Act 1972 |

**Tribunal and Judge:** Manchester County Court – HHJ Holman

**Where Reported:** February 2002 LAB 22

**Date of Award:** May 29, 2001

**Brief Facts of Case:** T occupied under an assured shorthold tenancy but vacated after 6 months due to L's failure to carry out repair to premises which were affected by dampness and mould growth. T claimed damages for personal injury for breach of duty of care under s4 Defective Premises Act 1972 in respect of her daughter aged 4 and son aged 3 for coughs and colds over a 6-month period.

**Award:** £650 damages for each child.

**General Damages:** £650

**Value of Award of £650 as at April 2004: £693**

*Property – Landlord & Tenant – Breach of covenant to repair – Breach of statutory duty*

---

**Name of Case:** *Flanagan and Suarez Alvarez v Maltby*

**Cause/s of Action:** Breach of Statutory Duty: (Housing Act and Defective Premises Act).

**Tribunal and Judge:** West London County Court – HHJ Compston

**Where Reported:** September 1993 LAB 16

**Date of Award:** April 30, 1993

**Brief Facts of Case:** Two women died in fire in house in multiple occupation. L had failed to provide fire escapes as required by a statutory notice. Personal representatives of the deceased brought proceedings for damages.

**Award:**          £39,036.32 and £30,701.14;

£500 aggravated damages as L had known of hazards and the existence of the statutory notice and if he had complied the women would have been likely to have survived.

**Value of Award of £500 aggravated damages as at April 2004: £660**

*Property – Landlord & Tenant – Failure to comply with statutory notice – aggravated damages*

---

**Name of Case:**          *Mirza v Bhandal*

**Cause/s of Action:**     Breach of statutory duty under s1 Defective Premises Act 1972

**Tribunal and Judge:**    Queen's Bench Division – Latham J

**Where Reported:**        August 1999 LAB 24

**Date of Award:**         April 27, 1999

**Brief Facts of Case:**   Ds were trading as building merchants. They pulled down an end of terrace house, rebuilt it and sold it to Ps in 1991. In 1995 cracks began to appear which worsened by 1995. A consulting engineer found that they were caused by subsidence due to inadequate foundations. The property would become too dangerous to occupy in 5 years' time and would eventually collapse unless it was underpinned.

**Award:**                 Agreed damages of £43,000.

**General Damages:**       £43,000

**Value of Award of £43,000 as at April 2004: £48,336**

*Property – Landlord & Tenant – Breach of statutory duty*

---

| | |
|---|---|
| **Name of Case:** | *Rushton and another v Worcester City Council* |
| **Cause/s of Action:** | Breach of statutory duty |
| **Tribunal and Judge:** | Court of Appeal – Potter and Jonathan Parker LJJ |
| **Where Reported:** | [2001] EGCS 41; [2001] EWCA Civ 367, CA; June 2001 LAB 23; [2000] *Inside Housing* 12 May; LAB January 2001 25; [2002] HLR 9; 2002 6 CL 375 |
| **Date of Award:** | March 16, 2001 |
| **Brief Facts of Case:** | R and her son were council tenants. R applied to purchase an Orlit-type council house under the right to buy scheme. Local authorities were aware at the time that such properties suffered from defects known as "PRC carbonation" and "conversion". The Council informed R of carbonation problem before the sale of the property to her under s126 of Housing Act 1985, but not the hazards of conversion. Owing to the defects the property had no resale value. R brought proceedings and was awarded damages for breach of statutory duty under s125 (4A) of 1985 Act and misrepresentation under the 1967 Act. |

£25,686 damages awarded comprising wasted purchase costs including total mortgage payments of £13,720; loss of discount on the value of the house in proper repair in 2000 (£22,800); costs of alternative accommodation whilst repairs carried out (£2,700); removal costs of £600 and general damages of £1,500 for disruption and inconvenience less £15,695.36 being the amount of rent which would have been paid had the claimants not purchased in 1991.

The Council appealed.

Judge's finding of liability for misrepresentation set aside. R's right to buy derived from Housing Act

1985 provisions rather than a contract and therefore there was no cause of action under the 1967 Act

**Award:** (Appeal allowed.) Award reduced to £20,886 on the basis that the claimants were not entitled to damages for cost of alternative accommodation, removal costs or the inconvenience they would have suffered whilst house under repair.

**General Damages:** £20,866 to include £1,500 for disruption and inconvenience

**Value of Award of £1,500 as at April 2004: £2,120**

*Property – Housing – Breach of statutory duty – Right to buy*

| | |
|---|---|
| **Name of Case:** | *Wallace v Manchester City Council* |
| **Cause/s of Action:** | Breach of covenant to repair under s11 Landlord and Tenant Act 1985 – Breach of duty of care under s4 Defective Premises Act 1972 |
| **Tribunal and Judge:** | Court of Appeal – Kennedy and Morritt LJJ |
| **Where Reported:** | (1998) 30 HLR 1111 |
| **Date of Award:** | July 7, 1998 |
| **Brief Facts of Case:** | From 1989 T was the secure tenant of a council house. In 1996 surveyors reported defects including a collapsed wall, rotten window, mould, defective plaster and skirting board and leaky rainwater pipe. T had complained of the coldness of the rooms and rats from 1994. |

In 1997 T issued proceedings. The Judge awarded damages to T's children and to T for her distress and inconvenience but declined to make a separate award reflecting the diminution in the value of the tenancy based on the amount of rent paid.

T appealed on the basis that the Judge should have made an award for diminution in value and that the award was too low.

The Court of Appeal held that the judge was not bound to assess damages under 2 separate heads and declined to interfere with the award.

**Award:** £2,000 to each of T's 2 children, £3,500 for distress, inconvenience & disruption to T's lifestyle. (Special damages: £780.)

**General Damages:** **£7,500**

**Value of Award of £7,500 as at April 2004: £8,544**

**Value of Award of £2,000 per annum as at April 2004: £2,279**

**Value of Award of £3,500 per annum as at April 2004: £3,987**

*Property – Housing – Breach of covenant to repair*

---

**Name of Case:** *Weller v London Borough of Lewisham*

**Cause/s of Action:** Breach of covenant to repair – Breach of duty of care under section 4 Defective Premises Act 1972

**Tribunal and Judge:** Bromley County Court

**Where Reported:** September 1988 LAB 15

**Date of Award:** January 18, 1988

**Brief Facts of Case:** T brought proceedings on the basis of an independent environmental health officer's report. The property was declared unfit for human habitation under the Housing Act 1985 before trial. Council agreed to waive county court limit for damages.

**Award:** £6,250 damages (to include special damages).

(Special damages: £1,107.60.)

**General Damages:** £5,142.40

**Value of Award of £5,142.40 as at April 2004: £9,244.37**

*Property – Housing – Breach of covenant to repair*

**Name of Case:**          *Welsh v MacBryde Homes plc*

**Cause/s of Action:**     Breach of statutory duty under s1 Defective
                           Premises Act 1974

**Tribunal and Judge:**    Liverpool County Court – Recorder Hernarez

**Where Reported:**        [1999] CLY 788; August 1999 LAB 26

**Date of Award:**         December 11, 1998

**Brief Facts of Case:**   Ps (a couple) and their 2 children moved into a
                           newly built house. The first floor was poorly
                           constructed and deflected when walked on.

**Award:**                 £30,049 total including £4,750 for discomfort
                           and inconvenience over 4 years and 8 months

                           Further damages awarded for costs of re-
                           decoration, new carpets, removal, storage and
                           alternative accommodation during remedial
                           works.

**General Damages:**       £4,750

**Value of Award of £4,750 as at April 2004: £5,365**

*Property – Breach of statutory duty – s1 Defective Premises Act 1974*

# Flying Freehold

| | |
|---|---|
| **Name of Case:** | *Abbahall Ltd v Smee* |
| **Cause/s of Action:** | Nuisance - Disrepair of roof in flying freehold – Breach of duty of care |
| **Tribunal and Judge:** | Court of Appeal – Chadwick LJ and Munby J |
| **Where Reported:** | [1994] 2 EGLR 181; [1994] 37 EG 151; [2002] EWCA Civ 1831; [2003] 28 EG 114; [2003] 1 All ER 465; [2003] 1 WLR 1472 |
| **Date of Award:** | December 19, 2002 |
| **Brief Facts of Case:** | A was the freehold owner of the ground floor of a 3-storey mews property let to a business tenant. S was the freehold owner of a flat on first and second floors plus the roof which she had acquired by way of adverse possession in 1988. S had allowed the roof to fall into disrepair whereby water leaked into ground floor with a danger of masonry falling *on* visitors. |

In 1994 following an injunction, A entered S's flat and carried out repair works (costing £7,255) and sought to recover the costs plus £23,617 to cover further necessary works on the basis that S owed a duty of care and A could recover costs incurred in abating a nuisance. Judge Cotran in West London County Court held that S was under a duty to contribute ¼ of the repair costs (£1,296) and made orders in respect of the further works. A appealed.

Held appeal allowed in part. A was entitled to ½ of repair costs. S owed a duty of care to A (her adjoining landowner) to do what was reasonable in the circumstances. A fair, just and reasonable approach had to be adopted. As a flying freehold the roof repair and future costs should be shared. It could not be adjusted according to the parties' respective financial resources.

**Award:**                     £2,592 damages for costs incurred. Special
                               damages: £11,808.50.

**General Damages:**           £2,592

**Value of Award of General Damages as at April 2004: £2,697**

*Property – Nuisance – Disrepair of roof in flying freehold - Breach of duty of care*

# Loss Of Statutory Tenancy

**Name of Case:**          *Clements v Simmonds*

**Cause/s of Action:**     Misrepresentation - Compensation for loss of statutory tenancy

**Tribunal and Judge:**    Queen's Bench Division – Burton J

**Where Reported:**        [2002] EWHC 1652; [2002] 41 EG 178

**Date of Award:**         April 17, 2002

**Brief Facts of Case:**   C held a Rent Act 1977 statutory tenancy of a flat in a house owned by D. In the county court an order for possession was made in May 2000 for possession in D's favour on the basis that she required it for occupation as a residence on her return from America. C vacated in November 2000. D put the property on the market in November 2000 on the basis that it was in a very bad condition and her ill-health prevented her from improving it. She subsequently sold the house in 2001 for £1.25m. C brought a claim for damages under s102 of the 1977 Act arguing that the basis upon which possession had been obtained was false and D's intentions to reside there had been a misrepresentation.

Held claim allowed. There was no disastrous damage to the property in November 2000. D had not intended to live at the property and there was no change of mind between May 2000 (when possession was ordered) and November 2000. C had proved that D's representation of requiring the property for residence was false when made in May 2000. C had not been deprived of living permanently in the flat – she had been deprived of compensation for the loss of a statutory tenancy and the opportunity to negotiate the payment.

**Award:**                 £60,000 compensation (less small admitted sum on counterclaim).

**General damages:**          £60,000

**Value of Award of £60,000 as at April 2004: £63,415**

*Property – Landlord & Tenant - Compensation for loss of statutory tenancy*

---

| | |
|---|---|
| **Name of Case:** | *Sutherland v Wall and Wall* |
| **Cause/s of Action:** | Breach of covenant for quiet enjoyment - loss of protected tenancy |
| **Tribunal and Judge:** | Dartford County Court – District Judge Weedon |
| **Where Reported:** | [1994] CLY 1448; June 1994 LAB 12 |
| **Date of Award:** | May 3, 1994 |
| **Brief Facts of Case:** | T (aged 75) protected tenant of flat – Ls took a mortgage on the property prior to start of tenancy and then defaulted. Lenders repossessed flat and T moved into sheltered accommodation provided by local authority at a similar rent |
| **Award:** | £2,500 general damages for loss of Rent Act protected tenancy |
| | (Special damages: £309.65 plus £50 interest for expenses incurred as a result of eviction.) |

**General Damages:**          £2,500

**Value of Award of £2,500 as at April 2004: £3,208**

*Property – Landlord & Tenant – Breach of covenant for quiet enjoyment - Loss of protected tenancy*

---

# Loss of Licence to Occupy

| | |
|---|---|
| **Name of Case:** | *Brookes v Iddon* |
| **Cause/s of Action:** | Breach of contractual licence to occupy static caravan site |
| **Tribunal and Judge:** | CC (Llangefni) – District Judge Gaskell |
| **Where Reported:** | [2000] CLY 3917 |
| **Date of Award:** | October 13, 1999 |
| **Brief Facts of Case:** | B occupied static caravan on I's site under a periodic annual licence. In May 1998 B complained when he was detained on site following road surface works and I demanded that he vacate within 14 days. B had already paid £800 to remain until October and store the caravan until February 1999. |
| **Award:** | £3,000 damages (by reference to cost of hiring holiday accommodation for remainder of season). |
| | Special damages: £378.84 for wasted expenditure and removal costs. |
| **General Damages:** | £3,000 |

**Value of Award of £3,000 as at April 2004: £3,346**

*Breach of Contract – caravans – licence to occupy and Caravans – licence to occupy static site*

## Caravans

| | |
|---|---|
| **Name of Case:** | *Brookes v Iddon* |
| **Cause/s of Action:** | Breach of contractual licence to occupy static caravan site |
| **Tribunal and Judge:** | CC (Llangefni) – District Judge Gaskell |
| **Where Reported:** | [2000] CLY 3917 |
| **Date of Award:** | October 13, 1999 |
| **Brief Facts of Case:** | B occupied static caravan on I's site under a periodic annual licence. In May 1998 B complained when he was detained on site following road surface works and I demanded that he vacate within 14 days. B had already paid £800 to remain until October and store the caravan until February 1999. |
| **Award:** | £3,000 damages (by reference to cost of hiring holiday accommodation for remainder of season). |
| | Special damages: £378.84 for wasted expenditure and removal costs. |
| **General Damages:** | £3,000 |

**Value of Award of £3,000 as at April 2004: £3,346**

*Breach of Contract – caravans – licence to occupy*

*and*

*Caravans – licence to occupy static site*

# Assault

| | |
|---|---|
| **Name of Case:** | *Andreou v Reid* |
| **Cause/s of Action:** | Unlawful eviction – Breach of covenant for quiet enjoyment – Assault |
| **Tribunal and Judge:** | Edmonton County Court – HHJ Tibber |
| **Where Reported:** | [1987] 9 CL 175; September 1987 LAB 14, |
| **Date of Award:** | February 14, 1986 |
| **Brief Facts of Case:** | L unlawfully evicted T twice, putting his possessions in dustbin bags and threatening him with a chisel. L also arranged for T to be attacked whilst he was in temporary accommodation. Two men threatened him with a gun and caused him head injuries requiring stitches after hitting him with iron piping. His chest wall was also bruised. |
| **Award:** | £3,000 aggravated and exemplary damages for breach of covenant for quiet enjoyment (£2,000 for assault). |
| **General Damages:** | £3,000 |

**Value of Award of general and exemplary damages of £1,000 as at April 2004: £1,922**

**Value of Award of general damages for assault of £2,000 as at April 2004: £3,845**

*Property – Landlord & Tenant – Unlawful eviction – Breach of covenant for quiet enjoyment -- Assault*

---

| | |
|---|---|
| **Name of Case:** | *Ariwodo v Comfort* |
| **Cause/s of Action:** | Harassment – Assault |
| **Tribunal and Judge:** | Wandsworth County Court – HHJ Sumner |

| | |
|---|---|
| **Where Reported:** | March 1992 LAB 15 |
| **Date of Award:** | December 19, 1991 |
| **Brief Facts of Case:** | T was denied access to a shared bathroom and was assaulted by L and his wife. T suffered from a small cut and abrasion to her face and ran to the police station in her nightclothes. |
| **Award:** | £600 general damages |
| | £1,750 aggravated damages |

**Value of Award of £600 general damages as at April 2004: £821**

**Value of Award of £1,750 aggravated damages as at April 2004: £2,395**

*Property – Landlord & Tenant – Harassment - Assault*

---

| | |
|---|---|
| **Name of Case:** | *Burke v Berioit* |
| **Cause/s of Action:** | Unlawful eviction – Breach of covenant for quiet enjoyment – Trespass to goods – Assault |
| **Tribunal and Judge:** | Central London County Court – Mr Recorder Hockman QC |
| **Where Reported:** | [1995] CLY 1572; March 1995 LAB 13 |
| **Date of Award:** | September 25, 1994 |
| **Brief Facts of Case:** | L liable for breach of covenant for quiet enjoyment and trespassing his goods and person. |
| **Award:** | £100 per day general damages for T's 2 months of homelessness – total £6,000 |
| | £1,500 exemplary damages for threats & violence |
| | £500 damages for trespass to goods |
| | £250 aggravated damages |
| | Total £8,250 exceeded statutory damages assessed at £5,000. |

**General Damages:**          £8,250

**Value of Award of general damages, £100 per day as at April 2004: £145**

**Value of Award of £1,500 exemplary damages as at April 2004: £1,921**

**Value of Award of £500 damages for trespass to goods as at April 2004: £640**

**Value of Award of £250 aggravated damages as at April 2004: £320**

*Property – Landlord and Tenant – Unlawful eviction – Breach of covenant for quiet enjoyment and Landlord and Tenant – trespass to goods – assault*

---

**Name of Case:**          *Miller and Wartnaby v Clarke*

**Cause/s of Action:**     Breach of covenant for quiet enjoyment - assault

**Tribunal and Judge:**    Lambeth County Court – HHJ James

**Where Reported:**        June 1994 LAB 11

**Date of Award:**         February 16, 1994

**Brief Facts of Case:**   Ts occupied a flat over a shop. Building works were carried out to the shop over a week during which time the gas supply to the flat was disconnected.

                           When Ts brought this to the tenancy relation officer's attention L was abusive and threatened to evict Ts. He cut the wires to the electricity meter and assaulted one of the Ts. Electricity was restored within 3 weeks of an injunction being obtained.

**Award:**                 £1,226 total damages (including interest) comprising:

                           £400 to each T general damages for breach of covenant for quiet enjoyment

                           £200 for assault

(Special damages: £226.)

**General Damages:**     £600

**Value of Award of £400 as at April 2004: £523**

**Value of Award of £200 as at April 2004: £261**

*Property – Landlord & Tenant – Breach of covenant for quiet enjoyment - Assault*

---

| | |
|---|---|
| **Name of Case:** | *Sam-Yorke v Ali Jawad* |
| **Cause/s of Action:** | Harassment– Breach of covenant for quiet enjoyment– Assault |
| **Tribunal and Judge:** | Wandsworth County Court – HHJ Winstanley |
| **Where Reported:** | March 2003 LAB 30 |
| **Date of Award:** | November 21, 2002 |
| **Brief Facts of Case:** | L was involved in three incidents. Firstly he said to T (an assured tenant) "I want to find you gone", then grabbed a key from T's wife who was alone with their young child and refused to leave until police arrived and finally slapped T in the face and kicked him in the waist causing bruising to the head, groin and shoulder. |
| | Held the last incident was a trespass to the person and also a breach of covenant for quiet enjoyment. |
| **Award:** | £900 in respect of all 3 incidents. |
| **General Damages:** | £900 |

**Value of Award of £900 as at April 2004: £938**

*Property – Landlord & Tenant – Harassment – Breach of covenant for quiet enjoyment – Assault*

---

| | |
|---|---|
| **Name of Case:** | *Sharma v Kirwan and Coppock* |
| **Cause/s of Action:** | Unlawful eviction – Assault |
| **Tribunal and Judge:** | Central London County Court – HHJ Quentin Edwards QC |
| **Where Reported:** | [1995] CLY 1850; June 1995 LAB 20 |
| **Date of Award:** | February 9, 1995 |
| **Brief Facts of Case:** | Ts were separate assured tenants of 2 rooms in a house and were threatened and harassed by L or his followers prior to return date for possession proceedings. L slapped and threatened Ts with violence, moved in men who disturbed Ts and damaged their property. Judge allowed Ts to remain until determination but they were forced to flee when 5 men visited property. Ts stayed with friends before finding accommodation. One T was unable to recover possessions. |
| **Award:** | For T1: |

Damages for 2 assaults: £400 for slap, £600 for being chased and grabbed;

£750 general damages for wrongful eviction;

£1,500 exemplary damages;

£2,650 statutory damages under ss.27 & 28 Housing Act 1988

For T2:

£850 damages for assault;

£750 general damages for wrongful eviction;

£1,500 exemplary damages;

£2,650 statutory damages under ss.27 & 28 Housing Act 1988;

(Special damages: £2,302.44.)

**General Damages:**    £750

**Value of Award of £750 as at April 2004: £948**

**Value of Awards of £400, £600 and £850 respectively as at April 2004: £506, £758 and £1,075**

**Value of Award of £1,500 exemplary damages as at April 2004: £1,896**

*Property – Landlord & Tenant – Unlawful eviction – Assault*
*Assault*

---

| | |
|---|---|
| **Name of Case:** | *Youziel v Andrews* |
| **Cause/s of Action:** | Harassment – Unlawful eviction – Assault – Breach of covenant for quiet enjoyment |
| **Tribunal and Judge:** | Lambeth County Court – DJ Jacey |
| **Where Reported:** | LAB March 2003 30 |
| **Date of Award:** | January 23, 2003 |
| **Brief Facts of Case:** | P was assured shorthold tenant of a flat. Initially was his landlord but he subsequently transferred his interest to a third party without giving notice of the transfer under s 3 Landlord and Tenant Act 1985. R continued to manage the property. P (an asylum-seeker) was in rent arrears due to his ineligibility for housing benefits. R harassed P on 10 occasions over a period of 6 weeks by threatening him (including shouting that he "would pay with his life"), telephoning, entering without permission. R and his 2 friends also assaulted P by slapping, kicking and throwing him to the ground in respect of which r was prosecuted. P sustained a knee injury found to be within the upper end of the scale of the moderate category (assessed at £7,750 to £14,000) by the JSB guidelines for general damages for personal injury). P suffered anxiety and stress causing him |

|              | to lose 12lbs in weight. He left the property 6 months later. |
|--------------|---|
| **Award:**   | £20,000 total damages comprising: |

£13,000 for personal injury

£4,300 aggravated damages for the assault

£2,700 damages for breach of covenant for quiet enjoyment in respect of other incidents

£200 interest

**General Damages:**  £2,700

 **Value of Award of £2,700 as at April 2004: £2,810**

**Value of Award of £4,000 aggravated damages as at April 2004: £4,164**

*Property – Landlord & Tenant – Harassment – Unlawful eviction – Assault – Breach of covenant for quiet enjoyment*

# Derogation From Grant

| | |
|---|---|
| **Name of Case:** | *Lawson v Hartley-Brown* |
| **Cause/s of Action:** | Breach of covenant for quiet enjoyment – Trespass - derogation from grant |
| **Tribunal and Judge:** | Court of Appeal – Hirst and Aldous LJJ and Forbes J |
| **Where Reported:** | (1996) 71 P&CR 242 |
| **Date of Award:** | November 8, 1995 |

**Brief Facts of Case:**

T was tenant of retail premises which L was to redevelop by adding 2 additional floors. T sought possession of roof and air space over unit by bringing proceedings in the County Court which were consolidated with proceedings in the High Court. In 1998 L served notice to terminate the tenancy under s25 Landlord and Tenant Act 1954. T applied for the grant of a new tenancy. This was subsequently withdrawn and T vacated in 1992. L brought proceedings for arrears of rent which were consolidated with the other proceedings.

T appealed against County Court Judge's award of £20 nominal damages for trespass by L of flat roof which had been demised to T.

**Award:**

£8,100 damages for trespass (equivalent to 1½ years rent) based on the bargain that may have been struck by a willing lessor & lessee taking into account the advantage to L, & disturbance & potential loss of profit to T. (Appeal allowed in part.)

**General Damages:**      £8,100

**Value of Award of £8,100 as at April 2004: £10,041**

*Property – Breach of Covenant for Quiet Enjoyment – Derogation from Grant – Trespass*

**Name of Case:**          *Saeed v Plustrade Ltd*

**Cause/s of Action:**     Derogation from grant, interference with right to
                           park

**Tribunal and Judge:**    Court of Appeal – Auld and Walker LJJ and Sir
                           Christopher Slade

**Where Reported:**        [2001] EWCA Civ 2011; January 2001 LAB 27;
                           [2002] 02 EGCS 102; [2002] 25 EG 154; March
                           2002 LAB 17

**Date of Award:**         December 20, 2001

**Brief Facts of Case:**   In 1985 S took assignment of a leasehold interest
                           in a flat which gave her the right to park in
                           common with others similarly entitled on such
                           part of the retained property reserved by the
                           lessor from time to time for parking when space
                           is available. At that time 10-13 informal spaces
                           were available on the forecourt of the block. The
                           lessor began refurbishment of the block and the
                           forecourt was unavailable. Thereafter the lessor
                           prohibited parking on the forecourt. From 1
                           August 2000 the lessor provided 4 marked spaces
                           on a first-come first-served basis, the rest were
                           offered for sale to new tenants.

                           Bernard Livesey QC sitting as a High Court
                           judge in the Chancery Division awarded S
                           damages for interference with the right to park
                           between May 1997 and November 2000. P
                           appealed.

                           Held that precluding S from parking was a clear
                           derogation from grant under the lease between
                           1997 and 2000. From 2000 the reduction in
                           parking spaces constituted a substantial
                           interference with her right to park. T's rights
                           were binding on L as an overriding interest under
                           s 70(1)(g) of Land Registration Act 1925.

**Award:**                     Appeal dismissed. Award of £6,300 upheld.

**General Damages:**      £6,300

**Value of Award of £6,300 as at April 2004: £6,747**

*Property – Landlord & Tenant – Derogation from grant –Interference with right to park*

# Nuisance by Disrepair or Waste

**Name of Case:**            *Abbahall Ltd v Smee*

**Cause/s of Action:**        Nuisance - Disrepair of roof in flying freehold – Breach of duty of care

**Tribunal and Judge:**     Court of Appeal – Chadwick LJ and Munby J

**Where Reported:**         [1994] 2 EGLR 181; [1994] 37 EG 151; [2002] EWCA Civ 1831; [2003] 28 EG 114; [2003] 1 All ER 465; [2003] 1 WLR 1472

**Date of Award:**           December 19, 2002

**Brief Facts of Case:**     A was the freehold owner of the ground floor of a 3-storey mews property let to a business tenant. S was the freehold owner of a flat on first and second floors plus the roof which she had acquired by way of adverse possession in 1988. S had allowed the roof to fall into disrepair whereby water leaked into ground floor with a danger of masonry falling *on* visitors.

In 1994 following an injunction, A entered S's flat and carried out repair works (costing £7,255) and sought to recover the costs plus £23,617 to cover further necessary works on the basis that S owed a duty of care and A could recover costs incurred in abating a nuisance. Judge Cotran in West London County Court held that S was under a duty to contribute ¼ of the repair costs (£1,296) and made orders in respect of the further works. A appealed.

Held appeal allowed in part. A was entitled to ½ of repair costs. S owed a duty of care to A (her adjoining landowner) to do what was reasonable in the circumstances. A fair, just and reasonable approach had to be adopted. As a flying freehold the roof repair and future costs should be shared. It could not be adjusted according to the parties' respective financial resources.

**Award:**               £2,592 damages for costs incurred. Special damages: £11,808.50.

**General Damages:**          £2,592

**Value of Award of General Damages as at April 2004:**

*Property – Nuisance – Disrepair of roof in flying freehold - Breach of duty of care*

---

**Name of Case:**          *Smith v Nixon*

**Cause/s of Action:**          Nuisance by disrepair of adjoining house

**Tribunal and Judge:**          Liverpool County Court – District Judge Knopf

**Where Reported:**          [1995] CLY 1642; December 1995 LAB 22

**Date of Award:**          August 17, 1995

**Brief Facts of Case:**          S owned semi-detached house. Adjoining owner N allowed his property to become derelict and insecure leading to use by vandals and drug addicts who disturbed S. Party wall of S's home left unexposed for 2 years – the house suffered from damp, vermin and draughts over a period of 3 years. Rubble affected the damp proof course, causing rising damp. Rear bedroom became unusable – S and 2 children had to share bedroom.

(Special damages: £1,330 and £363 interest.)

**Award:**          £8,000 general damages (£2,500 per year).

**General Damages:**          £8,000

**Value of Award of £8,000 as at April 2004: £9,911**

**Value of Award of £2,500 per annum as at April 2004: £3,097**

*Property – Nuisance – Waste of adjoining owner*

*Nuisance – disrepair of adjoining property*

---

# Malicious Suit

| | |
|---|---|
| **Name of Case:** | *Zaman v Kerr* |
| **Cause/s of Action:** | Malicious use of civil process |
| **Tribunal and Judge:** | Birmingham County Court – HHJ Durman |
| **Where Reported:** | May 1997 LAB 22 |
| **Date of Award:** | December 19, 1996 |
| **Brief Facts of Case:** | K and her partner rented a property from L on an assured tenancy. When arrears began to accrue L's agent Z sent a letter stating that unless the arrears were paid K would have to vacate. The letter did not comply with a s8 notice under HA 1988 but a possession order was made. A proper s8 notice had been served in the meantime and a second set of proceedings begun. Z applied for a warrant in the first set of proceedings and K was evicted. L died and K issued proceedings against Z for vexatious and malicious use of civil process. |
| **Award:** | £1,000 damages for four months in cramped conditions in a friend's spare room. |
| **General Damages:** | £1,000 |

**Value of Award as at April 2004: £1,203**

*Property – Malicious use of civil process*

# Failure to Give Consent

**Name of Case:** *S. Ayers v Long Acre Securities*

**Cause/s of Action:** Breach of covenant not unreasonably to withhold consent to assignment of lease

**Tribunal and Judge:** Uxbridge County Court –District Judge Freedman

**Where Reported:** [1994] CLY 1483

**Date of Award:** October 3, 1994

**Brief Facts of Case:** T granted declaration that consent to assign lease was unreasonably withheld for one month only and awarded damages, following L's withholding of consent to the assignment of a lease for a 7 month period. Damages considered for breach of statutory duty under s4 of Landlord and Tenant Act 1988.

**Award:** Total £537.26 representing loss of the benefit to T of the balance of the purchase money of £75,184 for 1 month at 12.25% per annum (the interest rate payable on T's overdraft) less the benefit to T of trading profits during the month at 30%.

**General Damages:** £537.26

**Value of Award of £537.26 as at April 2004: £687**

*Property – Landlord & Tenant – Assignment – consent unreasonably withheld*

| | |
|---|---|
| **Name of Case:** | *Smith v Nixon* |
| **Cause/s of Action:** | Nuisance by disrepair of adjoining house |
| **Tribunal and Judge:** | Liverpool County Court – District Judge Knopf |
| **Where Reported:** | [1995] CLY 1642; December 1995 LAB 22 |
| **Date of Award:** | August 17, 1995 |

**Brief Facts of Case:** S owned semi-detached house. Adjoining owner N allowed his property to become derelict and insecure leading to use by vandals and drug addicts who disturbed S. Party wall of S's home left unexposed for 2 years – the house suffered from damp, vermin and draughts over a period of 3 years. Rubble affected the damp proof course, causing rising damp. Rear bedroom became unusable – S and 2 children had to share bedroom.

(Special damages: £1,330 and £363 interest.)

**Award:** £8,000 general damages (£2,500 per year).

**General Damages:** £8,000

**Value of Award of £8,000 as at April 2004: £9,911**

**Value of Award of £2,500 per annum as at April 2004: £3,097**

*Property – Nuisance – Waste of adjoining owner*

*Nuisance – disrepair of adjoining property*

# Breach of Service Covenant

**Name of Case:**          *Joyce v Southwark LBC*

**Cause/s of Action:**     Breach of covenant to collect refuse

**Tribunal and Judge:**    Lambeth County Court – DJ Lacey

**Where Reported:**        May 1997 LAB 20

**Date of Award:**         February 20, 1996

**Brief Facts of Case:**   Ts were joint council tenants claiming damages for breach of express and implied terms of their tenancy agreement for the collection and removal of refuse. Between 1979-81 refuse from 16 flats had been collected infrequently from only 8 dustbins. For 11 years refuse was stored and infrequently removed from a converted washroom also used by schoolchildren for smoking and urinating. Fires had been started in the refuse including a serious fire one night under Ts' flat. For the last 2 years the wheelie bins had been infrequently emptied. For over 16 years the refuse had smelled and attracted pests. Ts were unable to open their windows or use the garden.

**Award:**                 £12,250 total damages including:

                           £600 per year general damages for 16 years

                           £1,000 for fear and sleeping difficulties in connection with the serious fire

                           (Special damages were awarded.)

**General Damages:**       £1,600

**Value of Award of £600 per annum as at April 2004: £738**

*Property – Housing – Breach of covenant*

# Index

**Adjoining owner**
    failure to give consent, 334
    nuisance by disrepair, 332
**Advice**
    solicitor's negligence, 278, 279,
    279—280
**Agricultural occupancy/tenancy**
    breach of covenant to repair, 133
    trespass, 46—47, 228—230
    unlawful eviction, 46—47
**Aircraft noise**
    surveyor's negligence, 285
**Amenity, loss of**
    breach of contract, 305
**Ants**
    infestation, 263—264
**Asbestos**
    breach of covenant to repair, 172
**Assault**
    breach of covenant for quiet
    enjoyment, 7, 17—18, 20, 68—69,
    94—95, 110—111, 321, 321—322,
    322—323, 324, 326—327
    harassment, 8 , 321—322, 324,
    326—327
    landlord and tenant, 321—327
    trespass to goods, 235, 322-323
    unlawful conviction, 96—97, 321,
    322—323, 325—326, 326—327
**Assignment of lease**
    failure to give consent, 334
**Assured shorthold tenants**
    assault, 110—111
    breach of covenant for quiet
    enjoyment, 34, 49, 58, 85, 105,
    110—111
    breach of covenant to repair, 119—
    120, 131—132, 147—148, 174—
    175, 205—206
    harassment, 4, 58, 110—111
    trespass to goods, 30, 85, 238—
    239, 242
    trespass to land, 85
    unlawful eviction, 4, 12—13, 25,
    30, 34, 49, 88—89, 89—90, 105,
    110—111
**Assured tenants**
    assault, 94—95, 96—97

    breach of covenant for quiet
    enjoyment, 1, 23, 27—28, 34—35,
    35—36, 41, 51—52, 94—95, 95—
    96, 97—98
    breach of covenant to repair, 165,
    173, 197—198
    harassment, 94—95
    trespass to goods, 23, 35—36, 82—
    83, 97—98, 239—240, 241, 243,
    unlawful eviction, 5—6, 11, 23,
    27—28, 31, 32, 34—35, 35—36,
    39, 76—77, 82—83, 96—97, 97—
    98, 104

**Bed and breakfast accommodation**
    breach of covenant for quiet
    enjoyment, 2—3
    harassment, 2—3
    trespass to goods, 2—3 , 233
**Bedsits**
    breach of covenant for quiet
    enjoyment, 36—37, 41, 56—57,
    64—65, 72
    breach of covenant to repair, 147—
    148, 148, 190, 191
    infestation, 265
    unlawful eviction, 24—25, 36—37,
    40, 43, 56, 56—57, 64—65, 72
**Beetle infestation**
    nuisance, 267
    surveyor's negligence, 290
**Boundary dispute**
    trespass to land, 225
**Breach of contract**
    construction works, 305
    damp proofing, 301, 302
    defective repairs, 302—303
    loss of amenity, 304
    loss of licence to occupy, 320
    loss of use of premises, 301
    managing agent, by, 303—304
    repairs, 301
**Breach of covenant for quiet enjoyment**
    assault, 7, 17—18, 20, 68—69,
    94—95, 110—111, 321, 322—323,
    323—324, 324 326—327
    breach of covenant to repair, 53,
    158—159
    derogation from grant, 54—55,
    54—55, 328
    disrepair, 16, 53, 158—159
    disturbance, 14—15

---